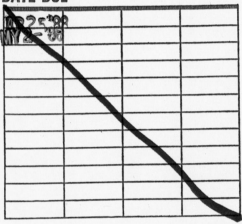

Mr. Justice Frankfurter and
the Constitution

Philip B. Kurland

Mr. Justice
Frankfurter and the
Constitution

The University of Chicago Press
Chicago and London

International Standard Book Number: 0-226-46405-9
Library of Congress Catalog Card Number: 77-133259

The University of Chicago Press, Chicago 60637
The University of Chicago Press, Ltd., London

To E. P. K. and A. H. K.
for fifty years

Contents

We do not sit like a kadi under a tree dispensing justice according to considerations of individual expediency.

Terminiello v. Chicago, 337 U.S. 1, 11 (1949)

Preface

On the day after he nominated Warren E. Burger to be Chief Justice of the United States, President Nixon asserted that in filling vacancies on the high court he would look for those who could follow in the judicial tradition of the late Mr. Justice Felix Frankfurter.

At the simple services held for Justice Frankfurter, Paul Freund's elegy appropriately quoted the words of Mr. Valiant-for-Truth in Bunyan's *Pilgrim's Progress*, just as Frankfurter had uttered these same words at a similar ceremony for Mr. Justice Brandeis. The quotation included the following: "My sword I give to him that shall succeed me in my pilgrimage, and my courage and skill to him that can get it." The pilgrimage is not only long and weary but exceedingly difficult. It will take one of extraordinary skill and courage to wield the sword that was Mr. Justice Frankfurter's. None should be bemused by the notion that it can be done as an act of mimicry. It requires a talent of great intelligence and inventiveness and an understanding of the complexities of law and life that are denied to all but a very few.

Whether one likes what Frankfurter did as a Justice of the Supreme Court or not — and there are many on both sides of that question — the fact remains that he was the latest of the great keepers of the legend: a legend of a nonpartisan Supreme Court dedicated to the maintenance of a government of laws founded on reason and based on a faith in democracy. One hopes he was not the last. For as Hal Borland tells us: "When the legends die, the dreams end. When the dreams end, there is no more greatness."

Really to understand what Justice Frankfurter was doing, it would be necessary to examine all the opinions he produced and the positions that he took in the context of particular cases. Some of my non-lawyer colleagues in the academic community in which I try to work have asked me to provide them with materials from the Justice's opinions shorter than a comprehensive compilation. This is essentially what is represented by the pages that follow: excerpts from the Justice's opinions on the Court and the Constitution, together with some of my own marginalia. (Because many of the citations in the opinions interfere with the flow of the writing, I have taken the liberty of emending them from the text and dropping them into footnotes without using ellipses.) I hope the collection proves informative to those who have asked for it and perhaps even to some who did not.

I am grateful to my colleague Professor Gerhard Casper for reading the manuscript, to my student Mr. Samuel Clapper for correcting the manuscript, and once again to my secretary, Mrs. Artie Scott, for translating the manuscript into publishable form.

1   Law and Reason

Felix Frankfurter's may be only a voice from the past. With any luck, it could be a voice for the future. Today, however, a spokesman for the fundamentals of democracy, in which Frankfurter had such a pervasive faith, and for the utilization of reason, which he saw as the essence of law, can find comparatively few to listen. In these times of domestic and foreign turbulence, "law and order" is a phrase taken to mean police oppression and "reason" is considered merely a device for the protection of "the establishment." In Yeats's words:[1]

> Turning and turning in the widening gyre
> The falcon cannot hear the falconer;
> Things fall apart; the centre cannot hold;
> Mere anarchy is loosed upon the world,
> The blood-dimmed tide is loosed, and everywhere
> The ceremony of innocence is drowned;
> The best lack all conviction, while the worst
> Are full of passionate intensity.

No man was so perennially young as Felix Frankfurter. But the "youth" of today would find him a totally alien figure. There was none whose emotions were more strongly committed than his to the social and economic betterment of the oppressed and depressed members of our society. And yet much of the force for change abroad today would find his views anathema. For he was as much concerned about proper means as about worthy ends. He abhorred those who would bring about good by doing evil. Felix Frankfurter was committed to constructive action. Mere talk or exhortation of others to act was an insufficient commitment. He felt only disdain and sorrow for those who would destroy rather than build. For him: "There is no inevitability in history except as men make it."[2] But men would accomplish little if quality were to be totally sacrificed to equality. When "elite" became a word of opprobrium, we entered a world totally foreign to Frankfurter's ethos.

---

1. THE COLLECTED POEMS OF W. B. YEATS 184 (1956 ed.).

2. See KURLAND, ed., FELIX FRANKFURTER ON THE SUPREME COURT 538 (1970).

1

For Frankfurter, law was indispensable to a democratic society and an independent judiciary was indispensable to law:[3]

. . . Law alone saves a society from being rent by internecine strife or ruled by mere brute power however disguised. . . . The conception of a government by laws dominated the thoughts of those who founded the Nation and designed its Constitution, although they knew as well as the belittlers of the conception that laws have to be made, interpreted and enforced by men. To that end, they set apart a body of men, who were to be depositories of law, who by their disciplined training and character and by withdrawal from the usual temptations of private interest may reasonably be expected to be "as free, impartial, and independent as the lot of humanity will admit."

The obligation to obey the law falls no less on the mighty than on the weak. There is an essential inconsistency between law and force so that the use of force even to sustain law strains the moral foundations of a lawful society. Force in opposition to law is totally destructive of that society. Frankfurter spoke out boldly in these terms when the state of Arkansas invoked its military power to attempt to frustrate the desegregation of the public schools in Little Rock. "The use of force to further obedience to the law is in any event a last resort and one not congenial to the spirit of the Nation. But the tragic aspect of this disruptive tactic was that the power of the State was used not to sustain law but as an instrument for thwarting law."[4] The Court was asked to stay enforcement of the order of desegregation because its enforcement would result in disorder. Frankfurter's response was clear:[5]

To yield to such a claim would be to enthrone official lawlessness, and lawlessness if not checked is the precursor of anarchy. On the few tragic occasions in the history of the Nation, North and South, when law was forcibly resisted or systematically evaded, it has signalled the breakdown of constitutional processes of government on which ultimately rest the liberties of all. Violent resistance to law cannot be made a legal reason for its suspension without loosening the fabric of our society. What could this mean but to acknowledge that disorder under the aegis of a State has moral superiority over the law of the Constitution? For those in authority thus to defy the

3. United States v. United Mine Workers, 330 U.S. 258, 308 (1947).
4. Cooper v. Aaron, 358 U.S. 1, 21 (1958).
5. *Id.* at 22.

law of the land is profoundly subversive not only of our constitutional system but of the presuppositions of a democratic society.

It may come as a surprise to some that Frankfurter acknowledged that the Supreme Court was the ultimate — or rather penultimate — arbiter of the meaning of the Constitution. But, as will later be shown, it was exactly because he thought the Court played so important a role that he believed the awesome power of judicial review should be exercised with great restraint. And, if he recognized the supremacy of the Supreme Court, he was also cognizant of its reliance on others for the maintenance of that supremacy. The distinction between criticism of the Court and defiance of it, which so many have blurred, was for him quite real:[6]

The duty to abstain from resistance to "the Supreme Law of the Land,"[7] as declared by the organ of our Government for ascertaining it, does not require immediate approval of it nor does it deny the right of dissent. Criticism need not be stilled. Active obstruction or defiance is barred. Our kind of society cannot endure if the controlling authority of the Law as derived from the Constitution is not to be the tribunal specially charged with the duty of ascertaining and declaring what is "the supreme Law of the Land." . . . Compliance with decisions of this Court, as the constitutional organ of the supreme Law of the Land, has often, throughout our history, depended on active support by state and local authorities. It presupposes such support. To withhold it, and indeed to use political power to try to paralyze the supreme Law, precludes the maintenance of our federal system as we have known and cherished it for one hundred and seventy years.

This was not a claim of infallibility for the Court or a rejection of the very real possibilities of change:[8]

Even this Court has the last say only for a time. Being composed of fallible men, it may err. But revision of its errors must be by orderly process of law. The Court may be asked to reconsider its decisions, and this has been done successfully again and again throughout our history. Or, what this Court has deemed its duty to decide may be changed by legislation, as it often has been, and, on occasion, by constitutional amendment.

6. *Id.* at 24, 26.
7. U.S. Const., Art. VI, ¶ 2. [F.F.]
8. 330 U.S. at 308.

In short, Frankfurter's position here may be summed up in the sentence that he was fond of quoting from the writings of Dean Roscoe Pound: "Civilization involves subjection of force to reason, and the agency of this subjection is law."[9] And, Frankfurter would add, in this country the highest expounder of the fundamental law is the Supreme Court of the United States.

9. Pound, *The Future of the Law*, 47 YALE L.J. 1, 13 (1937).

2   Judicial Restraint

The hallmark of that lonely crowd of jurists dedicated to "self-restraint," led by Holmes, Learned Hand, Brandeis, and Frankfurter, was their reluctance to exercise the judicial power to invalidate legislation. There are many aspects underlying this doctrine of self-abnegation as witnessed by these great judges. One is history and the obligation that constitutionalism imposes to adhere to the essential meaning put in the document by its framers. A second is the intrinsically undemocratic nature of the Supreme Court. A third is a corollary to the second, an abiding respect for the judgments of those branches of the government that are elected representatives of their constituents. A fourth is the recognition that judicial error at this level is more difficult of correction than other forms of judicial action. A fifth is respect for the judgments of earlier courts. But the essential feature of judicial restraint that has gained most attention and aroused the greatest doubts — probably because few men are themselves big enough to abide by its command — is the notion of rejection of personal preference. Over time, Frankfurter turned his judicial pen again and again to a treatment of each of these factors and others that go to make up the standards of judicial restraint.

Perhaps the deepest *cri de coeur* he uttered from the bench concerned the obligation to sublimate personal attitudes in rendering judgment on the validity of legislation. It came in his dissenting opinion in *Board of Education v. Barnette*.[1] The question presented in that case was whether a state could command students, required to attend school by the compulsory education law, to salute the American flag, even if such salute were inconsistent with their parents' religious instructions. The Court had, at first, sustained such legislation in *Minersville School District v. Gobitis*.[2] A bare three years later, after some change in the Court's personnel and some changes of minds among those who had

---

1. 319 U.S. 624 (1943). See COMMAGER, MAJORITY RULE AND MINORITY RIGHTS (1943); MANWARING, RENDER UNTO CAESAR: THE FLAG SALUTE CONTROVERSY (1962).

2. 310 U.S. 586 (1940).

sat on the earlier case, the Court reversed itself. Frankfurter's dissent opened in this way: [3]

One who belongs to the most vilified and persecuted minority in history is not likely to be insensible to the freedoms guaranteed by our Constitution. Were my purely personal attitude relevant I should wholeheartedly associate myself with the general libertarian views in the Court's opinion, representing as they do the thought and action of a lifetime. But as judges we are neither Jew nor Gentile, neither Catholic nor agnostic. We owe equal attachment to the Constitution and are equally bound by our judicial obligations whether we derive our citizenship from the earliest or latest immigrants to these shores. As a member of this Court I am not justified in writing my private notions of policy into the Constitution, no matter how deeply I may cherish them or how mischievous I may deem their disregard.

Frankfurter went on in this opinion to some of the other reasons underlying the concept of judicial restraint, including the "democratic conception" of American society, the intent of the authors of the Constitution, and the limited but long-lasting effect of such judicial action: [4]

When Mr. Justice Holmes, speaking for this Court, wrote that "it must be remembered that legislatures are ultimate guardians of the liberties and welfare of the people in quite as great a degree as the courts," [5] he went to the very essence of our constitutional system and the democratic conception of our society. He did not mean that for only some phases of our civil government this Court was not to supplant legislatures and sit in judgment upon the right or wrong of a challenged measure. He was stating the comprehensive judicial duty and role of this Court in our constitutional scheme whenever legislation is sought to be nullified on any ground, namely, that responsibility for legislation lies with legislatures, answerable as they are directly to the people, and this Court's only and very narrow function is to determine whether within the broad grant of authority vested in legislatures they have exercised a judgment for which reasonable justification can be offered.

The framers of the federal Constitution might have chosen to assign an active share in the process of legislation to this Court. They had before them the well-known example of New York's Council of Revision, which had been functioning since 1777. After stating that "laws inconsistent with the spirit of this constitution, or with the public

---

3. 319 U.S. at 646–47.

4. *Id.* at 649–50, 651–52.

5. Missouri, K. & T. Ry. v. May, 194 U.S. 267, 370 (1904). [F.F.]

good, may be hastily and unadvisedly passed," the state constitution
made the judges of New York part of the legislative process by providing that "all bills which have passed the senate and the assembly
shall, before they become laws," be presented to a Council of which
the judges constitute a majority, "for their revisal and consideration." [6]
Judges exercised this legislative function in New York for nearly
fifty years.[7] But the framers of the Constitution denied such legislative
powers to the federal judiciary. They chose instead to insulate the
judiciary from the legislative function. They did not grant to this
Court supervision over legislation.

The reason why from the beginning even the narrow judicial authority to nullify legislation has been viewed with a jealous eye is that
it serves to prevent the full play of the democratic process. The fact
that it may be an undemocratic aspect of our scheme of government
does not call for its rejection or disuse. But it is the best of reasons,
as this Court has frequently recognized, for the greatest caution in
its use. . . .

This is no dry, technical matter. It cuts deep into one's conception
of the democratic process — it concerns no less the practical differences between the means for making these accommodations that are
open to courts and to legislatures. A court can only strike down. It
can only say "This or that law is void." It cannot modify or qualify,
it cannot make exceptions to a general requirement. And it strikes
down not merely for a day. At least the finding of unconstitutionality
ought not to have ephemeral significance unless the Constitution is to
be reduced to the fugitive importance of mere legislation. When we
are dealing with the Constitution of the United States, and more
particularly with the great safeguards of the Bill of Rights, we are
dealing with principles of liberty and justice "so rooted in the traditions and conscience of our people as to be ranked as fundamental" —
something without which "a fair and enlightened system of justice
would be impossible." [8] If the function of this Court is to be essentially
no different from that of a legislature, if the considerations governing
constitutional construction are to be substantially those that underlie
legislation, then indeed judges should not have life tenure and they
should be made directly responsible to the electorate. There have been
many but unsuccessful proposals in the last sixty years to amend the
Constitution to that end.[9]

6. Art. III, N.Y. Const. of 1777. [F.F.]

7. See Art. I, § 12, N.Y. Const. of 1821. [F.F.]

8. Palko v. Connecticut, 302 U.S. 319, 325 (1937); Hurtado v. California,
110 U.S. 516, 530, 531 (1884). [F.F.]

9. See Sen. Doc. No. 91, 75th Cong., 1st Sess. 248–51 (1937). [F.F.]

The restraint expected in review of state legislation, as indicated in *Barnette*, was at least as important in the oversight of national legislation. Thus, in *Trop v. Dulles*,[10] Frankfurter took exception to a declaration of unconstitutionality of federal legislation declaring the forfeiture of American citizenship by any person in the armed forces who deserted in time of war:[11]

This legislation is the result of an exercise by Congress of the legislative power vested in it by the Constitution and of an exercise by the President of his constitutional power in approving a bill and thereby making it "a law." To sustain it is to respect the actions of the two branches of our Government directly responsive to the will of the people and empowered under the Constitution to determine the wisdom of legislation. The awesome power of this Court to invalidate such legislation, because in practice it is bounded only by our own prudence in discerning the limits of the Court's constitutional function, must be exercised with the utmost restraint.

Just as some members of the Court in *Trop* would have given new meaning to the Eighth Amendment's ban on "cruel and unusual punishment" to secure their objectives, so in *United States v. Lovett*,[12] a majority of the Court had reconstructed the bill of attainder provision. Again Frankfurter, this time in a concurring opinion, rehearsed the reasons for judicial restraint. In addition to the themes already noted, Frankfurter reiterated principles that were dear to him but somewhat elusive for many others. One was the duty to avoid constitutional decisions if possible. The other was even more sophisticated. For, as he so frequently said, the Constitution contains two different kinds of provisions that must be treated differently. Some are so specific, either by reason of the language or because of historical derivation, as to require "strict interpretation." Included in these, he contended, was the bill of attainder clause. Others, like "due process of law" and "equal protection of the laws," were so amorphous as to require the Court to give them meaning in keeping with the fundamental values of a changing society. Strict construction of ambiguous constitutional phrases was beyond the capacity of even a Felix Frankfurter. His opinion in *Lovett* included the following:[13]

---

10. 356 U.S. 86 (1958). See Roche, *The Expatriation Cases*, 1963 SUPREME COURT REVIEW 325.

11. 356 U.S. at 128.

12. 328 U.S. 303 (1946).

13. *Id.* at 320–25.

The inclusion of § 304 in the Appropriation Bill undoubtedly raises serious constitutional questions. But the most fundamental principle of constitutional adjudication is not to face constitutional questions but to avoid them, if at all possible. And so the "Court developed, for its own governance in the cases confessedly within its jurisdiction, a series of rules under which it has avoided passing upon a large part of all the constitutional questions pressed upon it for decision." [14] That a piece of legislation under scrutiny may be widely unpopular is as irrelevant to the observance of these rules for abstention from avoidable adjudications as that it is widely popular. Some of these rules may well appear over-refined or evasive to the laity. But they have the support not only of the profoundest wisdom. They have been vindicated, in conspicuous instances of disregard, by the most painful lessons of our constitutional history. . . .

Broadly speaking, two types of constitutional claims come before this Court. Most constitutional issues derive from the broad standards of fairness written into the Constitution (*e.g.* "due process," "equal protection of the laws," "just compensation"), and the division of power as between States and Nation. Such questions, by their very nature, allow a relatively wide play for individual legal judgment. The other class gives no such scope. For this second class of constitutional issues derives from very specific provisions of the Constitution. These had their source in definite grievances and led the Fathers to proscribe against recurrence of their experience. These specific grievances and the safeguards against their recurrence were not defined by the Constitution. They were defined by history. Their meaning was so settled by history that definition was superfluous. Judicial enforcement of the Constitution must respect these historic limits.

The prohibition of bills of attainder falls of course among these very specific constitutional provisions. The distinguishing characteristic of a bill of attainder is the substitution of legislative determination of guilt and legislative imposition of punishment for judicial finding and sentence. . . . It was this very special, narrowly restricted, intervention by the legislature, in matters for which a decent regard for men's interests indicated a judicial trial, that the Constitution prohibited. It must be recalled that the Constitution was framed in an era when dispensing justice was a well-established function of the legislature. The prohibition against bills of attainder must be viewed in the background of the historic situation when moves in specific litigation that are now the conventional and, for the most part, the exclusive concern of courts were commonplace legislative practices. . . .

14. Ashwander v. T.V.A., 297 U.S. 288, 346 (1936) (Brandeis, J., concurring). [F.F.]

All bills of attainder specify the offense for which the attainted person was deemed guilty and for which the punishment was imposed. There was always a declaration of guilt either of the individual or the class to which he belonged. The offense might be a pre-existing crime or an act made punishable *ex post facto*. Frequently a bill of attainder was thus doubly objectionable because of its *ex post facto* features. This is the historic explanation for uniting the two mischiefs in one clause — "No Bill of Attainder or ex post facto Law shall be passed." . . . When the framers of the Constitution proscribed bills of attainder, they referred to a form of law which had been prevalent in monarchical England and was employed in the colonies. They were familiar with its nature; they had experienced its use; they knew what they wanted to prevent. It was not a law unfair in general, even unfair because affecting merely particular individuals, that they outlawed by the explicitness of their prohibition of bills of attainder. "Upon this point a page of history is worth a volume of logic." [15] Nor should resentment against an injustice displace controlling history in judicial construction of the Constitution.

Not only does § 304 lack the essential declaration of guilt. It likewise lacks the imposition of punishment in the sense appropriate for bills of attainder. . . .

Punishment presupposes an offense, not necessarily an act previously declared criminal, but an act for which retribution is exacted. The fact that harm is inflicted by governmental authority does not make it punishment. Figuratively speaking all discomforting action may be deemed punishment because it deprives of what otherwise would be enjoyed. But there may be reasons other than punitive for such deprivation. . . .

Section 304 became law by the President's signature. His motive allowing it to become law is free from doubt. He rejected the notion that the respondents were "subversive," and explicitly stated that he wished to retain them in the service of the Government.[16] Historically, Parliament passed bills of attainder at the behest of the monarch.[17] The Constitution, of course, provides for the enactment of legislation even against disapproval by the Executive. But to hold that a measure which did not express a judgment of condemnation by the Senate and carried an affirmative disavowal of such condemnation by the President constitutes a bill of attainder, disregards the historic tests for

15. New York Trust Co. v. Eisner, 256 U.S. 345, 349 (1921). [F.F.]

16. H. Doc. No. 264, 78th Cong., 1st Sess. (1943). [F.F.]

17. See ADAMS, CONSTITUTIONAL HISTORY OF ENGLAND 228–29 (rev. ed. 1935). [F.F.]

determining what is a bill of attainder. At the least, there are such serious objections to find § 304 a bill of attainder that it can be declared unconstitutional only by a failure to observe that this Court reaches constitutional invalidation only through inescapable necessity. "It must be evident to anyone that the power to declare a legislative enactment void is one which the judge, conscious of the fallibility of the human judgment, will shrink from exercising in any case where he can conscientiously and with due regard to duty and official oath decline the responsibility." [18]

It is not that Frankfurter would never find that Congress had exceeded its authority by failing to remain within the confines that the Constitution placed on it. In *National Ins. Co. v. Tidewater Transfer Co.*,[19] for example, he would have rejected the legislative expansion of Article III that made citizens of the District of Columbia citizens of a "state" for purposes of adding to federal courts' diversity jurisdiction. And again, history played a part: [20]

No provisions of the Constitution, barring only those that draw on arithmetic, as in prescribing the qualifying age for a President and members of a Congress or the length of their tenure of office, are more explicit and specific than those pertaining to courts established under Article III. "The judicial power" which is "vested" in these tribunals and the safeguards under which their judges function are enumerated with particularity. Their tenure and compensation, the controversies which may be brought before them, and the distribution of original and appellate jurisdiction among these tribunals are defined and circumscribed, not left at large by vague and elastic phrasing. The precision which characterizes these portions of Article III is in striking contrast to the imprecision of so many other provisions of the Constitution dealing with other very vital aspects of government. This was not due to chance or ineptitude on the part of the Framers. The differences in subject-matter account for the drastic differences in treatment. Great concepts like "Commerce . . . among the several States," "due process of law," "liberty," "property" were purposely left to gather meaning from experience. For they relate to the whole domain of social and economic fact, and the statesmen who founded this Nation knew too well that only a stagnant society remains unchanged. But when the Constitution in turn gives strict definition of power or specific limitations upon it we cannot extend the definition

18. 1 Cooley, Constitutional Limitations 332 (8th ed. 1927). [F.F.]

19. 337 U.S. 582 (1949).

20. *Id.* at 646–47, 655.

or remove the translation. Precisely because "it is a *constitution* we are expounding it," [21] we ought not to take liberties with it.

There was deep distrust of a federal judicial system, as against the State judiciaries, in the Constitutional Convention. This distrust was reflected in the evolution of Article III. Moreover, when they dealt with the distribution of judicial power as between the courts of the States and the courts of the United States, the Framers were dealing with a technical subject in a professional way. More than that, since the judges of the courts for which Article III made provisions not only had the last word (apart from amending the Constitution) but also enjoyed life tenure, it was an essential safeguard against control by the judiciary of its own jurisdiction, to define the jurisdiction of those courts with particularity. The Framers guarded against the self-will of the courts as well as against the will of Congress by marking with exactitude the outer limits of federal judicial power. . . .

Of course every indulgence must be entertained in favor of constitutionality when legislation of Congress can fairly be deemed an exercise of the discretion, in the formulation of policy, given to Congress by the Constitution. But the cases to which jurisdiction may be extended under Article III to the courts established under it preclude any claim of discretionary authority to add to the cases listed by Article III or to change the distribution as between original and appellate jurisdiction made by that Article. Congress need not establish inferior courts; Congress need not grant the full scope of jurisdiction which it is empowered to vest in them; Congress need not give this Court any appellate power; it may withdraw appellate jurisdiction once conferred and it may do so even while a case is *sub judice*.[22] But when the Constitution defined the ultimate limits of judicial power exercisable by courts which derive their sole authority from Article III, it is beyond the power of Congress to extend those limits. If there is one subject as to which this Court ought not to feel inhibited in passing on the validity of legislation by doubts of its own competence to judge what Congress has done, it is legislation affecting the jurisdiction of the federal courts. When Congress on a rare occasion through inadvertence or generosity exceeds those limitations, this Court should not good-naturedly ignore such a transgression of congressional powers.

A substantial majority of the Court agrees that each of the two grounds urged in support of the attempt by Congress to extend diversity jurisdiction to cases involving citizens of the District of Columbia must be rejected — but not the same majority. And so, conflicting

21. M'Culloch v. Maryland, 4 Wheat. 316, 407 (1819). [F.F.]
22. *Ex parte* McCardle, 7 Wall. 506 (1869). [F.F.]

minorities in combination bring to pass a result — paradoxical as it may appear — which differing majorities of the Court find insupportable.

Such issues as these were never to be covered over by labels. A tax measure that was not a tax measure, but rather an attempt at regulation of matters then held to be beyond the competence of Congress, should be considered in its true light. Frankfurter would have invalidated the gambling tax that came under scrutiny in *United States v. Kahriger*:[23]

The Court's opinion manifests a natural difficulty in reaching its conclusion. Constitutional issues are likely to arise whenever Congress draws on the taxing power not to raise revenue but to regulate conduct. This is so, of course, because of the distribution of legislative power as between the Congress and the State Legislatures in the regulation of conduct.

To review in detail the decisions of this Court, beginning with *Veazie Bank* v. *Fenno*,[24] dealing with this ambivalent type of revenue enactment, would be to rehash the familiar. Two generalizations may, however, safely be drawn from this series of cases. Congress may make an oblique use of the taxing power in relation to activities with which Congress may deal directly, as for instance, commerce between the States. . . . However, when oblique use is made of the taxing power as to matters which substantively are not within the powers delegated to Congress, the Court cannot shut its eyes to what is obviously, because designedly, an attempt to control conduct which the Constitution left to the responsibility of the States, merely because Congress wrapped the legislation in the verbal cellophane of a revenue measure.

Concededly the constitutional questions presented by such legislation are difficult. On the one hand, courts should scrupulously abstain from hobbling congressional choice of policies, particularly when the vast reach of the taxing power is concerned. On the other hand, to allow what otherwise is excluded from congressional authority to be brought within it by casting legislation in the form of a revenue measure could . . . offer an easy way for the legislative imagination to control "any one of the great number of subjects of public interest, jurisdiction of which the States have never parted with. . . ."[25] Issues of such gravity affecting the balance of powers within our federal

---

23. 345 U.S. 22, 37–39, 40 (1953). *Kahriger* was, indeed, later reversed, but on the ground that the statute violated the self-crimination provision of the Fifth Amendment. Marchetti v. United States, 390 U.S. 39 (1968); Grosso v. United States, 390 U.S. 62 (1968).

24. 8 Wall. 533 (1869). [F.F.]

25. Child Labor Tax Case, 259 U.S. 20, 38 (1922). [F.F.]

system are not susceptible of comprehensive statement by smooth formulas such as that a tax is nonetheless a tax although it discourages the activities taxed, or that a tax may be imposed although it may effect ulterior ends. No such phrase, however fine and well-worn, enables one to decide the concrete case.

What is relevant to judgment here is that, even if the history of this legislation as it went through Congress did not give one the libretto to the song, the context of the circumstances which brought forth this enactment — sensationally exploited disclosures regarding gambling in big cities and small, the relation of this gambling to corrupt politics, the impatient public response to these disclosures, the feeling of ineptitude or paralysis on the part of local law-enforcing agencies — emphatically supports what was revealed on the floor of Congress, namely, that what was formally a means of raising revenue for the Federal Government was essentially an effort to check if not to stamp out professional gambling. . . .

. . . The motive of congressional legislation is not for our scrutiny, provided only that the ulterior purpose is not expressed in ways which negative what the revenue words on their face express and which do not seek enforcement of the formal revenue purpose through means that offend those standards of decency in our civilization against which due process is a barrier.

Frankfurter was equally a realist in his disposition of constitutional questions raised by state legislation. He was not to be put off by conformity with formal requirements if, in fact, the constitutional abuse obviously existed. It did not matter whether the case involved economic issues or those that have come to be considered more basic rights of citizenship and residence. Thus, in his very first opinion for the Court, in *Hale v. Bimco Trading, Inc.*[26] he rejected a claim of regulation based on state police power because he saw, in fact, an effort to discriminate against interstate commerce. And Oklahoma's persistent efforts to avoid the requirements of the Fifteenth Amendment by subterfuge received comparably short shrift in Frankfurter's opinion for the Court in *Lane v. Wilson.*[27]

The reach of the Fifteenth Amendment against contrivances by a state to thwart equality in the enjoyment of the right to vote by citizens of the United States regardless of race or color, has been amply expounded by prior decisions. . . . The Amendment nullifies sophisticated as well as simple-minded modes of discrimination. It

26. 306 U.S. 375 (1939).
27. 307 U.S. 268, 275 (1939).

hits onerous procedural requirements which effectively handicap exercise of the franchise by the colored race although the abstract right to vote may remain unrestricted as to race. When in *Guinn* v. *United States*,[28] the Oklahoma "grandfather clause" was found violative of the Fifteenth Amendment, Oklahoma was confronted with the serious task of devising a new registration system consonant with her own political ideas but also consistent with the Federal Constitution. We are compelled to conclude, however reluctantly, that the legislation of 1916 partakes too much of the infirmity of the "grandfather clause" to be able to survive.

Such realism would be utilized to sustain as well as condemn state law. In *Nashville, C. & St. L. Ry.* v. *Browning*[29] the Court sustained a Tennessee tax on railroad property over the objection that it violated the Equal Protection Clause. The Court, through Frankfurter, insisted on making its own judgment about uniformity and classification:[30]

The Equal Protection Clause did not write an empty formalism into the Constitution. Deeply imbedded traditional ways of carrying out state policy, such as those of which petitioner complains, are often tougher and truer law than the dead words of the written text. . . . And if the state supreme court chooses to cover up under a formal veneer of uniformity the established system of differentiation between two classes of property, an exposure of the fiction is not enough to establish its unconstitutionality. Fictions have played an important and sometimes fruitful part in the development of law; and the Equal Protection Clause is not a command of candor. So we are of opinion that such a discrimination, not invidious but long-sanctioned and indeed conventional, would not be offensive to the Fourteenth Amendment simply because Tennessee had reached its by a circuitous road. It is not the Fourteenth Amendment's function to uproot systems of taxation inseparable from the state's tradition of fiscal administration and ingrained in the habits of its people.

The concept of judicial restraint here adumbrated should take on more meaning as it is seen in its application to some of the constitutional issues that the Court reviewed during Frankfurter's tenure.

28. 238 U.S. 347 (1915).
29. 310 U.S. 362 (1940).
30. *Id*. at 369–70.

3

Scarcity of Judicial Time and Its Proper Use

One of the attributes of the Frankfurter school was the objective of confining the business of the highest judicial tribunal to the kind of case appropriate to its jurisdiction. Professor Paul Freund in describing Brandeis's attitude used words applicable to Frankfurter as well: [1]

. . . [T]he sense of self-discipline marked Brandeis' view of the judicial function itself. No one was more alert than he to the procedural and jurisdictional limitations of the business of the Court. To some observers for whom liberalism and conservatism are each a monochrome of preferences, the concern of Brandeis for apparently technical procedural niceties seemed incompatible with his largeness of outlook in deciding questions of public law. In fact there was no real inconsistency. If the Court was to exercise its grave function of reviewing the validity of acts of co-ordinate branches of government, the Court must be careful to keep within its appointed bounds as a condition of judging whether others had kept within theirs. Moreover, to one who, like Brandeis, regarded the Supreme Court as an educational institution that ought to set the highest standard of quality and power in its work, it was important that the Court decide no more than was necessary. . . . Individual injustices that may have survived review in the lower courts did not press on Brandeis with sufficient force to divert him from the principle that the energies of the Court must be conserved for their broader and essential tasks. Sentimentality can be an enemy of greatness of spirit; firmness and even hardness can be its friend.

Mr. Justice Frankfurter was capable of reading at a rate that even today's speed-reading courses do not pretend to achieve. He dictated his opinions directly to the typewriter, although they would go through several revisions before completion. He slept less than most mortals. His speed of thought can be attested, sometimes with grim remembrance, by his law clerks among others. And yet he was worried lest the press of business on the Supreme Court make it impossible for it to perform its functions well. In part, this was because he saw the

---

1. Freund, *Mr. Justice Brandeis*, in DUNHAM & KURLAND, eds., MR. JUSTICE 188–89 (2d ed. 1964).

Supreme Court as a collegial body, not a group of individuals who did their work in the isolation of their chambers without need for testing and exchanging ideas with their brethren in the course of formulating an opinion. It was with grim foreboding that he saw the numbers of petitions for certiorari rising to astronomical figures. And he was equally distressed that his brethren did not adequately appreciate the importance of their lapses in undertaking to decide cases that did not belong in the high tribunal, either because of inherent unworthiness or jurisdictional defect.

In *Ex parte Peru*,[2] Frankfurter complained that the Court utilized an extraordinary writ to bypass the jurisdictional limitations imposed by Congress.[3]

The Judiciary Act of 1925 was aimed to extend the Court's control over its business by curtailing its appellate jurisdiction drastically. Relief was given by Congress to enable this Court to discharge its indispensable functions of interpreting the Constitution and preserving uniformity of decision among the eleven intermediate courts of appeals. Periodically since the Civil War — to speak only of recent times — the prodigal scope of the appellate jurisdiction of this Court brought more cases here than even the most competent tribunal could wisely and promptly adjudicate. Arrears became inevitable until, after a long legislative travail, the establishment in 1891 of intermediate appellate tribunals freed this Court of a large volume of business. By 1916, Congress had to erect a further dam against access to this Court of litigation that already had been through two lower courts and was not of a nature calling for the judgment of the Supreme Court. . . . But the increase of business — the inevitable aftermath of the Great War and of renewed legislative activity — soon caught up with the meager relief afforded by the Act of 1916. The old evils of an overburdened docket reappeared. . . .

In deciding whether to give a latitudinarian or a restricted scope to the appellate jurisdiction of this Court, the important factor is the number of instances in which applications for the exercise of the Court's jurisdiction has been or may be made, not the number of instances in which the jurisdiction has been exercised. And so it tells little that less than ten applications for mandamus have been granted since the Act of 1925. What is far more important is that merely for the first seven Terms after that Act not less than seventy-two applications for such writs were made. Every application consumes time in consideration, whether eventually granted or denied. . . .

2. 318 U.S. 578 (1943).

3. *Id.* at 592–93, 600, 602–04.

. . . The tremendous and delicate problems which call for the judgment of the nation's ultimate tribunal require the utmost conservation of time and energy even for the ablest judges. Listening to arguments and studying records and briefs constitute only a fraction of what goes into the judicial process. For one thing, as the present law reports compared with those of even a generation ago bear ample testimony, the types of cases that now come before the Court to a considerable extent require study of materials outside the technical law books. But more important, the judgments of this Court are collective judgments. Such judgments presuppose ample time and freshness of mind for private study and reflection in preparation for discussions in Conference. Without adequate study there cannot be adequate reflection; without adequate reflection there cannot be adequate discussion; without adequate discussion there cannot be that mature and fruitful interchange of minds which is indispensable to wise decisions and luminous opinions.

It is therefore imperative that the docket of the Court be kept down, that no case be taken which does not rise to the significance of inescapability for the responsibility entrusted to this Court. Every case that is allowed to come here which, judged by these standards, may well be left either to the state courts or to the circuit courts of appeals, makes inroads upon thought and energy which properly belong to the limited number of cases which only this Court can adjudicate. Even a judge of such unique gifts and experience as Mr. Justice Holmes felt at the very height of his powers, as we now know, the whip of undue pressure in his work. One case is not just one case more, and does not stop with being just one more case. Chief Justice Taft was not the last judge who, as he said to himself, "having a kind heart, I am inclined to grant probably more [discretionary reviews] than is wise." [4]

In a case like this, we should deny our power to exercise jurisdiction. But, in any event, we should refuse to exercise it. By such refusal we would discourage future applications of a similar kind, and thereby enforce those rigorous standards in this Court's judicial administration which alone will give us the freshness and vigor of thought and spirit that are indispensable for wise decisions in the causes committed to us.

In *Kinsella v. Krueger*,[5] Frankfurter pointed to one of the continuing problems faced by the Court, one of its own creation. Ever since

4. Hearings before the Committee on the Judiciary, House of Representatives, 68th Cong., 2d Sess., on H.R. 8206 27 (1924). [F.F.] See Hart, *The Time Chart of the Justices*, 73 HARV. L. REV. 84 (1959); Griswold, *Of Time and Attitudes — Professor Hart and Judge Arnold*, 74 HARV. L. REV. 81 (1960).

5. 351 U.S. 470 (1956).

the Roosevelt Court-packing plan, the Court has seemed anxious to assure the world that it is current in its business. The result, in part, has been the mad rush at the end of each Term to complete opinions in the most important cases so that the Court can clear its calendar before its unduly long summer recess. This "decision by deadline," as it has been called by one of the Court's more astute critics, several times caused Frankfurter and other Justices to postpone their own opinions until the following Term, even where the majority opinion came down in June. *Kinsella v. Krueger*, one of the cases of the "self-made widows," involved the question of court-martial jurisdiction over wives of military personnel at overseas bases. Perhaps the point of Frankfurter's complaint about rush to judgment is emphasized by the fact that rehearing was later granted and the judgment was reversed.[6] In *Kinsella*, Frankfurter wrote:[7]

Grave issues affecting the status of American civilians throughout the world are raised by these cases; they are made graver by the arguments on which the Court finds it necessary to rely in reaching its result. Doubtless because of the pressure under which the Court works during its closing weeks, these arguments have been merely adumbrated in its opinion. To deal adequately with them, however, demands of those to whom they are not persuasive more time than has been available to examine and to analyze in detail the historical underpinning and implication of the cases relied upon the Court, as a preliminary to a searching critique of their relevance to the problems now before the Court. . . .

Time is required not only for the primary task of analyzing in detail the materials on which the Court relies. It is equally required for adequate reflection upon the meaning of these materials and their bearing on the issues now before the Court. Reflection is a slow process. Wisdom, like good wine, requires maturing.

Moreover, the judgments of this Court are collective judgments. They are neither solo performances nor debates between two sides, each of which has its mind quickly made up and then closed. The judgments of this Court presuppose full consideration and reconsideration by all of the reasoned views of each. Without adequate study there cannot be adequate reflection. Without adequate reflection there cannot be adequate deliberation and discussion. And without these, there cannot be that full interchange of minds which is indispensable to wise decision and its persuasive formulation.

6. Reid v. Covert, 354 U.S. 1 (1957).
7. 351 U.S. at 483–85.

From the beginning of his tenure, Frankfurter was concerned that the Court confine itself to business appropriate to its function. Among his very early opinions was one in which he objected to jurisdiction over an alleged controversy between states that rested on an obviously fictitious basis. The state of Texas had been persuaded to file an interpleader action within the Court's original jurisdiction on the ground that four separate states claimed the right to inheritance duties from a single estate on the theory that the deceased was domiciled in each. The gossamer quality of the substantive claim itself vexed the new Justice. He was also prone to point out the adverse effects of accepting jurisdiction in a cause such as this. In *Texas v. Florida*,[8] he wrote:[9]

The authority which the Constitution has committed to this Court over "Controversies between two or more States," serves important ends in the working of our federalism. But there are practical limits to the efficacy of the adjudicatory process in the adjustment of interstate controversies. The limitations of litigation — its episodic character, its necessarily restricted scope of inquiry, its confined regard for considerations of policy, its dependence on the contingencies of a particular record, and other circumscribing factors — often denature and even mutilate the actualities of a problem and thereby render the litigatious process unsuited for its solution. Considerations such as these have from time to time led this Court or some of its most distinguished members either to deprecate resort to this Court by states for settlement of their controversies . . . , or to oppose assumption of jurisdiction. . . .

At this point, Mr. Justice Frankfurter dropped a footnote undoubtedly expressing his own views in the words of another:[10]

The spirit in which interstate litigation should be approached has been thus expressed by Mr. Chief Justice Fuller in *Louisiana* v. *Texas*:[11] "But it is apparent that the jurisdiction is of so deliberate and grave a character that it was not contemplated that it would be exercised save when the necessity was absolute and the matter in itself properly justiciable."

It was in this early opinion that Frankfurter made it clear that he

8. 306 U.S. 398 (1939).

9. *Id.* at 428.

10. *Id.* at 428, n. 1.

11. 176 U.S. 1, 15 (1900). [F.F.]

thought it appropriate to speak out on jurisdictional questions in hope of avoiding repetitious impositions on the Court: [12]
Jurisdictional doubts inevitably lose force once leave has been given to file a bill, a master has been appointed, long hearings have been held, and a weighty report has been submitted. And so, were this the last as well as the first assumption of jurisdiction by this Court of a controversy like the present, even serious doubts about it might well go unexpressed. But if experience is any guide, the present decision will give momentum to kindred litigation and reliance upon it beyond the scope of the special facts of this case. To be sure, the Court's opinion endeavors to circumscribe carefully the bounds of jurisdiction now exercised. But legal doctrines have, in an odd kind of way, the faculty of self-generating extension. . . .

Frankfurter's expressions of jurisdictional doubts were intended to serve the function opposite to that of a self-fulfilling prophecy. By prognosticating threats of an increase in business, he hoped to ward off the increase he prophesied. Sometimes it worked. More often, it didn't.

Frankfurter, like Brandeis before him, was particularly concerned that the Court heed the explicit and implicit limits on the exercise of its own authority. These procedural inhibitions were not for him — as they may have been for some of his colleagues — tactical methods of assuring the substantive results that he sought. He recognized and believed in their institutional importance.

In reviewing state courts, he had to be assured that the record demonstrated that the decision below rested on an actual resolution of a federal question. For, if it did not, the Court was engaged in either an act of supererogation or one of usurpation of power. He spoke of the problem in his dissent in *Irvin v. Dowd*: [13]

The problem represented by this case is as old as the Union and will persist as long as our society remains a constitutional federalism. It concerns the relation of the United States and the courts of the United States to the States and the courts of the States. The federal judiciary has no power to sit in judgment upon a determination of a state court unless it is found that it must rest on disposition of a claim under federal law. This is so whether a state adjudication comes directly under review in this Court or reaches us by way of the limited scope of habeas corpus jurisdiction originating in a District Court. (Judicial power is not so restrictively distributed in other federalisms

12. 306 U.S. at 434.
13. 359 U.S. 394, 407–08 (1959).

comparable to ours. Neither the Canadian Supreme Court nor the Australian High Court is restricted to reviewing Dominion and Commonwealth issues respectively. The former reviews decisions of provincial law and the latter may review state decisions resting exclusively on state law.) To such an extent is it beyond our power to review state adjudications turning on state law that even in the high tide of nationalism following the Civil War, this Court felt compelled to restrict itself to review of federal questions, in cases coming from state courts, by limiting broadly phrased legislation that seemingly gave this Court power to review all questions, state and federal, in cases jurisdictionally before it. It refused to impute to Congress such a "radical and hazardous change of a policy vital in its essential nature to the independence of the State courts. . . ." [14] This decision has not unjustifiably been called one of "the twin pillars" (the other is *Martin* v. *Hunter's Lessee*)[15] on which have been built "the main lines of demarcation between the authority of the state legal systems and that of the federal system." [16]

Something that thus goes to the very structure of our federal system in its distribution of power between the United States and the States is not a mere bit of red tape to be cut, on the assumption that this Court has general discretion to see justice done. Nor is it one of those "technical" matters that laymen, with more confidence than understanding of our constitutional system, so often disdain.

The "final judgment rule" that precludes premature interference with lower court jurisdiction was, to Frankfurter, also an important limitation, and all the more important in cases coming from state courts. In *Burns* v. *Ohio* [17] he was again in dissent in stating the relevance of the rule: [18]

It is the special obligation of this Court strictly to observe the limits of its jurisdiction. No matter how tempting the appeal of a particular situation, we should not indulge in disregard of the bounds by which Congress has defined our power of appellate review. There will be time enough to enforce the constitutional right, if right it be, which the Court now finds the petitioner to possess when it is duly presented for judicial determination here, and there are ample modes open to

14. Murdock v. Memphis, 20 Wall. 590, 630 (1875). [F.F.]

15. 1 Wheat. 304 (1816). [F.F.]

16. Hart, *The Relations between State and Federal Law*, 54 Colum. L. Rev. 489, 503–04 (1954). [F.F.]

17. 360 U.S. 252 (1959).

18. *Id.* at 259–60, 262–63.

the petitioner for assertion of such a claim in a way to require our adjudication.

The appellate power of this Court to review litigation originating in a state court can come into operation only if the judgment to be reviewed is the final judgment of the highest court of the State. That a judgment is the prerequisite for the appellate review of this Court is an ingredient of the constitutional requirement of the "Cases" or "Controversies" to which alone "The judicial Power shall extend." U.S. Const., Art. III, § 2. That it be a "final judgment" was made a prerequisite by the very Act which established this Court in 1789.[19] "Close observance of this limitation upon the Court is not regard for a strangling technicality."[20] Such has been the undeviating constitutional, legislative and judicial command binding on this Court and respected by it without exception or qualification to this very day.

The requisites of such a final judgment are not met by what a state court may deem to be a case or judgment in the exercise of the state court's jurisdiction.[21] Nor can consent of the parties to the determination of a cause by this Court overleap the jurisdictional limitations which are part of this Court's being. Litigants cannot give this Court power which the Constitution and Congress have withheld.[22] The President of the United States himself cannot secure from this Court determination of a legal question except when such a question duly arises in the course of adjudication of a case or controversy, even though he asks for needed help in a great national emergency.[23]

As the importance of the interrogator and the significance of the question confer no power upon this Court to render advisory opinions, a compassionate appeal cannot endow it with jurisdiction to review a judgment which is not final. One's sympathy, however deep, with petitioner's claim cannot dispense with the precondition of a final judgment for exercising our judicial power. If the history of this Court teaches one lesson as important as any, it is the regretful consequences of straying off the clear path of its jurisdiction to reach a desired result. This Court cannot justify a yielding to the temptation to cut corners in disregard of what the Constitution and Congress demand. . . .

19. Act of 24 September 1789, § 25, 1 Stat. 85, now 28 U.S.C. § 1257. [F.F.]

20. Republic Natural Gas Co. v. Oklahoma, 334 U.S. 62, 67 (1948). [F.F.]

21. See Tyler v. The Judges, 179 U.S. 405 (1900); Doremus v. Bd. of Educ., 342 U.S. 429 (1952). [F.F.]

22. Mansfield, C. & L. M. Ry. v. Swan, 111 U.S. 379, 382 (1884). [F.F.]

23. See President Washington's questions, in 33 WRITINGS OF WASHINGTON, 15–19, 28 (Fitzpatrick ed. 1940), and the correspondence between Secretary of State Thomas Jefferson and Chief Justice Jay, in 3 CORRESPONDENCE AND PUBLIC PAPERS OF JOHN JAY 486–89 (Johnston ed. 1891). [F.F.]

. . . It cannot be urged that necessity compels what the Constitution and statutes forbid — adjudication here of a claim which has not been rejected in a final judgment of a state court. Adherence to the dictates of the laws which govern our jurisdiction, though it may result in postponement of our determination of petitioner's rights, is the best assurance of the vindication of justice under law through the power of the courts. We should dismiss the writ of certiorari inasmuch as there has been no final judgment over which we have appellate power.

Even more important and certainly more amorphous is the rule requiring the case to involve a real and not merely a feigned controversy. The second attempt to have the Connecticut laws against dissemination of birth control advice held unconstitutional presented such an issue of a legitimate case or controversy. Frankfurter's opinion announcing the judgment of the Court in *Poe v. Ullman*[24] held the case not ripe for adjudication. It showed greater prescience than he knew, for when the case was finally resolved on the merits, the third time around, it resulted in some of the most horrendous opinions yet bestowed by the Supreme Court on its constituents.[25] Frankfurter wrote:[26]

Appellants' complaints in these declaratory judgment proceedings do not clearly, and certainly do not in terms, allege that appellee Ullman threatens to prosecute them for use of, or for giving advice concerning, contraceptive devices. The allegations are merely that, in the course of his public duty, he intends to prosecute any offenses against Connecticut law, and that he claims that use of and advice concerning contraceptives would constitute offenses. The lack of immediacy of the threat described by these allegations might alone raise serious questions of non-justiciability of appellants' claims.[27] But even were we to read the allegations to convey a clear threat of imminent prosecutions, we are not bound to accept as true all that is alleged on the face of the complaint and admitted, technically, by demurrer, any more than the Court is bound by stipulation of the parties.[28] Formal agreement between parties that collides with plausibility is too fragile a foundation for indulging in constitutional adjudication.

The Connecticut law prohibiting the use of contraceptives has been on the State's books since 1879.[29] During the more than three-quarters

24. 367 U.S. 497 (1961).

25. Griswold v. Connecticut, 381 U.S. 479 (1965).

26. 367 U.S. at 501–05, 507–09.

27. See United Public Workers v. Mitchell, 330 U.S. 75, 88 (1947). [F.F.]

28. Swift & Co. v. Hocking Valley Ry. Co., 243 U.S. 281, 289 (1916). [F.F.]

of a century since its enactment, a prosecution for its violation seems
never to have been initiated, save in *State* v. *Nelson.*[30] The circumstances of that case, decided in 1940, only prove the abstract character of what is before us. There, a test case was brought to determine
the constitutionality of the Act as applied against two doctors and
a nurse who had allegedly disseminated contraceptive information.
After the Supreme Court of Errors sustained the legislation on appeal
from a demurrer to the information, the State moved to dismiss the
information. Neither counsel nor our own researches have discovered
any attempt to enforce the prohibition of distribution or use of contraceptive devices by criminal process. The unreality of these law
suits is illumined by another circumstance. We were advised by counsel
for appellants that contraceptives are commonly and notoriously
sold in Connecticut drug stores. Yet no prosecutions are recorded;
and certainly such ubiquitous, open, public sales would more quickly
invite the attention of enforcement officials than the conduct in which
the present appellants wish to engage — the giving of private medi-
cal advice by a doctor to his individual patients, and their private
use of the devices prescribed. The undeviating policy of nullification
by Connecticut of its anti-contraceptive laws throughout all the long
years that they have been on the statute books bespeaks more than
prosecutorial paralysis. What was said in another context is relevant
here. "Deeply embedded traditional ways of carrying out state
policy . . ." — or not carrying it out — "are often tougher and truer
law than the dead words of the written text." [31]

The restriction of our jurisdiction to cases and controversies within
the meaning of Article III of the Constitution [32] is not the sole limitation on the exercise of our appellate powers, especially in cases
raising constitutional questions. The policy reflected in numerous cases
and over a long period was thus summarized in the oft-quoted statement of Mr. Justice Brandeis: "The Court [has] developed, for its
own governance in the cases confessedly within its jurisdiction, a series
of rules under which it has avoided passing upon a large part of all
the constitutional questions pressed upon it for decision." [33] In part
the rules summarized in the *Ashwander* opinion have derived from the
historically defined, limited nature and function of courts and from
the recognition that, within the framework of our adversary system,

29. Conn. Acts 1879, c. 78. [F.F.]

30. 126 Conn. 412, 11 A. 2d 856 (1940). [F.F.]

31. Nashville, C. & St. L. R. Co. v. Browning, 310 U.S. 362, 369 (1940). [F.F.]

32. See Muskrat v. United States, 219 U.S. 346 (1911). [F.F.]

33. Ashwander v. T.V.A., 297 U.S. 288, 341, 346 (1936) (concurring opinion).
[F.F.]

the adjudicatory process is most securely founded when it is exercised under the impact of a lively conflict between antagonistic demands, actively pressed, which make resolution of the controverted issue a practical necessity.[34] In part they derive from the fundamental federal and tripartite character of our National Government and from the role — restricted by its very responsibility — of the federal courts, and particularly this Court, within that structure.[35]

These considerations press with special urgency in cases challenging legislative action or state judicial action as repugnant to the Constitution. "The best teaching of this Court's experience admonishes us not to entertain constitutional questions in advance of the strictest necessity." [36] The various doctrines of "standing," "ripeness," and "mootness," which this Court has evolved with particular, though not exclusive, reference to such cases are but several manifestations — each having its own "varied application" — of the primary conception that federal judicial power is to be exercised to strike down legislation, whether state or federal, only at the instance of one who is himself immediately harmed, or immediately threatened with harm, by the challenged action.[37] "This court can have no right to pronounce an abstract opinion upon the constitutionality of a State law. Such law must be brought into actual, or threatened operation upon rights properly falling under judicial cognizance, or a remedy is not to be had here." [38] "The party who invokes the power [to annul legislation on grounds of its unconstitutionality] must be able to show not only that the statute is invalid but that he has sustained or is immediately in danger of sustaining some direct injury as the result of its enforcement. . . ." [39]

Insofar as appellants seek to justify the exercise of our declaratory

34. See Little v. Bowers, 134 U.S. 547, 558 (1890); California v. San Pablo & Tulare R.R., 149 U.S. 308, 314 (1892); United States v. Fruehauf, 365 U.S. 146, 157 (1961). [F.F.]

35. See the Note to Hayburn's Case, 2 Dall. 409 (1792); Massachusetts v. Mellon, 262 U.S. 447, 448–49 (1923); Watson v. Buck, 313 U.S. 387, 400–03 (1941); Alabama State Federation of Labor v. McAdory, 325 U.S. 450, 471 (1945). [F.F.]

36. Parker v. County of Los Angeles, 338 U.S. 327, 333 (1949); see also Liverpool, N.Y. & P. S. S.S. Co. v. Commissioners, 113 U.S. 33, 39 (1885). [F.F.]

37. Stearns v. Wood, 236 U.S. 75 (1915); Texas v. Interstate Commerce Commission, 258 U.S. 158 (1922); United Public Workers v. Mitchell, 330 U.S. 75, 89–90 (1947). [F.F.]

38. Georgia v. Stanton, 6 Wall. 50, 75 (1867), approvingly quoting Mr. Justice Thompson, dissenting, in Cherokee Nation v. Georgia, 5 Pet. 1, 75 (1831); also quoted in New Jersey v. Sargent, 269 U.S. 328, 331 (1926). [F.F.]

39. Massachusetts v. Mellon, 262 U.S. 447, 488 (1923). [F.F.]

power by the threat of prosecution, facts which they can no more
negative by complaint and demurrer than they could by stipulation
preclude our determining their appeals on the merits.[40] It is clear that
the mere existence of a state penal statute would constitute insufficient
grounds to support a federal court's adjudication of its constitutionality in proceedings brought against the State's prosecuting officials
if real threat of enforcement is wanting.[41] If the prosecutor expressly
agrees not to prosecute, a suit against him for declaratory and injunctive relief is not such an adversary case as will be reviewed here.[42]
Eighty years of Connecticut history demonstrate a similar, albeit
tacit agreement. The fact that Connecticut has not chosen to press the
enforcement of this statute deprives these controversies of the immediacy which is an indispensable condition of constitutional adjudication. This Court cannot be umpire to debates concerning harmless,
empty shadows. To find it necessary to pass on these statutes now,
in order to protect appellants from the hazards of prosecution, would
be to close our eyes to reality.

Nor does the allegation by the Poes and Doe that they are unable to
obtain information concerning contraceptive devices from Dr. Buxton, "for the sole reason that the delivery and use of such information
and advice may or will be claimed by the defendant State's Attorney
to constitute offenses," disclose a necessity for present constitutional
decision. It is true that this Court has several times passed upon
criminal statutes challenged by persons who claimed that the effects
of the statutes were to deter others from maintaining profitable or
advantageous relations with the complainants.[43] But in these cases the
deterrent effect complained of was one which was grounded in a
realistic fear of prosecution. We cannot agree that if Dr. Buxton's
compliance with these statutes is uncoerced by the risk of their enforcement, his patients are entitled to a declaratory judgment concerning the statute's validity. And, with due regard to Dr. Buxton's
standing as a physician and to his personal sensitiveness, we cannot
accept, as the basis of constitutional adjudication, other than as
chimerical the fear of enforcement of provisions that have during so
many years gone uniformly and without exception unenforced.

Justiciability is of course not a legal concept with a fixed content
or susceptible of scientific verification. Its utilization is the resultant
of many subtle pressures, including the appropriateness of the issues

40. *Cf.* Bartemeyer v. Iowa, 18 Wall. 129, 134–35 (1874). [F.F.]

41. See *Ex parte* La Prade, 289 U.S. 444, 458 (1933). [F.F.]

42. C.I.O. v. McAdory, 325 U.S. 472, 475 (1945). [F.F.]

43. See, *e.g.*, Truax v. Raich, 239 US. 33 (1915); Pierce v. Society of Sisters,
268 U.S. 510 (1925). [F.F.]

for decision by this Court and the actual hardship to the litigants of denying them the relief sought. Both these factors justify withholding adjudication of the constitutional issue raised under the circumstances and in the manner in which they are now before the Court.

The rules for assuring the existence of a case or controversy within the jurisdiction of the Supreme Court were no less applicable in cases arising in federal courts than in those originating in state courts. Frankfurter spelled out his views at length in *Joint Anti-Fascist Refugee Committee v. McGrath*,[44] where he found jurisdiction present although some of his brethren did not. The essential question proffered was whether due process had been accorded to organizations labeled as subversive by the Attorney General of the United States. In the course of his opinion he expounded some of his notions of the demands made by due process of law on the national government by the terms of the Fifth Amendment: [45]

The more issues of law are inescapably entangled in political controversies, especially those that touch the passions of the day, the more the Court is under duty to dispose of a controversy within the narrowest confines that intellectual integrity permits. And so I sympathize with the endeavor of my brother BURTON to decide these cases on a ground as limited as that which has commended itself to him. Unfortunately, I am unable to read the pleadings as he does. Therefore I must face up to larger issues. But in a case raising delicate constitutional questions it is particularly incumbent first to satisfy the threshold inquiry whether we have any business to decide the case at all. Is there, in short, a litigant before us who has a claim presented in a form and under conditions "appropriate for judicial determination"? [46]

Limitation on "the judicial Power of the United States" is expressed by the requirement that a litigant must have "standing to sue" or, more comprehensively, that a federal court may entertain a controversy only if it is "justiciable." Both characterizations mean that a court will not decide a question unless the nature of the action challenged, the kind of injury inflicted, and the relationship between the parties are such that judicial determination is consonant with what was, generally speaking, the business of the Colonial courts and the courts of Westminster when the Constitution was framed. The jurisdiction of the federal courts can be invoked only under circum-

44. 341 U.S. 123 (1951).

45. *Id.* at 149–57, 159–60, 162–65, 170–72.

46. Aetna Life Ins. Co. v. Haworth, 300 U.S. 227, 240 (1937). [F.F.]

stances which to the expert feel of lawyers constitute a "case or controversy." The scope and consequences of the review with which the judiciary is entrusted over executive and legislative action require us to observe these bounds fastidiously.[47] These generalities have had myriad applications. Each application, even to a situation not directly pertinent to what is before us, reflects considerations relevant to decision here. I shall confine my inquiry, however, by limiting it to suits seeking relief from governmental action.

(1) The simplest application of the concept of "standing" is to situations in which there is no real controversy between the parties. Regard for the separation of powers,[48] and for the importance to correct decision of adequate presentation of issues by clashing interests,[49] restricts the courts of the United States to issues presented in an adversary manner. A petitioner does not have standing to sue unless he is "interested in and affected adversely by the decision" of which he seeks review. His "interest must be of a personal and not of an official nature." [50] The interest must not be wholly negligible, as that of a taxpayer of the Federal Government is considered to be.[51] A litigant must show more than that "he suffers in some indefinite way in common with people generally." [52]

Adverse personal interest, even of such an indirect sort as arises from competition, is ordinarily sufficient to meet constitutional standards of justiciability. The courts may therefore by statute be given jurisdiction over claims based on such interests.[53]

(2) To require a court to intervene in the absence of a statute, however, either on constitutional grounds or in the exercise of inherent equitable powers, something more than adverse personal interest is needed. This additional element is usually defined in terms which assume the answer. It is said that the injury must be "a wrong which directly results in the violation of a legal right." [54] Or that the con-

---

47. See the course of decisions beginning with Hayburn's Case, 2 Dall. 409 (1792), through Parker v. Los Angeles County, 338 U.S. 327 (1949). [F.F.]

48. See Muskrat v. United States, 219 U.S. 346 (1911). [F.F.]

49. See Chicago & G.T. Ry. v. Wellman, 143 U.S. 339 (1891). [F.F.]

50. Braxton County Court v. West Virginia, 208 U.S. 192, 197 (1908); see also Massachusetts v. Mellon, 262 U.S. 447 (1923). [F.F.]

51. Frothingham v. Mellon, 262 U.S. 447 (1923); cf. Crampton v. Zabriskie, 101 U.S. 601 (1880). [F.F.]

52. Frothingham v. Mellon, *supra*, at 488. [F.F.] For a more "modern view," see Flast v. Cohen, 392 U.S. 83 (1968).

53. F.C.C. v. Sanders Radio Station, 309 U.S. 470 (1940); cf. I.C.C. v. Oregon-Washington R.R., 288 U.S. 14 (1933). [F.F.]

54. Alabama Power Co. v. Ickes, 302 U.S. 464, 479 (1938). [F.F.]

troversy "must be definite and concrete, touching the legal relations of parties having adverse legal interests."[55] These terms have meaning only when contained by the facts to which they have been applied. In seeking to determine whether in the case before us the standards they reflect are met, therefore, we must go to the decisions. They show that the existence of "legal" injury has turned on the answer to one or more of these questions: (a) Will the action challenged at any time substantially affect the "legal" interests of any person? (b) Does the action challenged affect the petitioner with sufficient "directness"? (c) Is the action challenged sufficiently "final"? Since each of these questions itself contains a word of art, we must look to experience to find their meaning.

(a) *Will the action challenged at any time substantially affect the "legal" interests of any person?* A litigant ordinarily has standing to challenge governmental action of a sort that, if taken by a private person, would create a right of action cognizable by the courts.[56] Or standing may be based on an interest created by the Constitution or a statute.[57] But if no comparable common-law right exists and no such constitutional or statutory interest has been created, relief is not available judicially. Thus, at least unless capricious discrimination is asserted, there is no protected interest in contracting with the Government. A litigant therefore has no standing to object that an official has misinterpreted his instructions in requiring a particular clause to be included in a contract.[58] Similarly, a determination whether the Government is within its powers in distributing electric power may be of enormous financial consequence to a private power company, but it has no standing to raise the issue.[59] The common law does not recognize an interest in freedom from honest competition; a court will give protection from competition by the Government, therefore, only when the Constitution or a statute creates such a right.

(b) *Does the action challenged affect petitioner with sufficient "directness"?* Frequently governmental action directly affects the legal interests of some person, and causes only a consequential detriment to another. Whether the person consequentially harmed can challenge the action is said to depend on the "directness" of the impact of the action on him. A shipper has no standing to attack a rate not applicable

55. Aetna Life Ins. Co. v. Haworth, 300 U.S. 227, 240–41 (1937). [F.F.]

56. United States v. Lee, 106 U.S. 196 (1882). [F.F.]

57. *E.g.*, Parker v. Fleming, 329 U.S. 531 (1947); Coleman v. Miller, 307 U.S. 433 (1939); *cf.* Bell v. Hood, 327 U.S. 678 (1946). [F.F.]

58. Perkins v. Lukens Steel Co., 310 U.S. 113 (1940). [F.F.]

59. Tennessee Power Co. v. T.V.A., 306 U.S. 118 (1939); *cf.* Alabama Power Co. v. Ickes, 302 U.S. 464 (1938). [F.F.]

to him but merely affecting his previous competitive advantage over shippers subject to the rate.[60] When those consequentially affected may resort to an administrative agency charged with their protection, courts are especially reluctant to give them "standing" to claim judicial review.[61]

But it is not always true that only the person immediately affected can challenge the action. The fact that an advantageous relationship is terminable at will does not prevent a litigant from asserting that improper interference with it gives him "standing" to assert a right of action.[62] On this principle an alien employee was allowed to challenge a State law requiring his employer to discharge all but a specified proportion of alien employees,[63] and a private school to enjoin enforcement of a statute requiring parents to send their children to public schools.[64] The likelihood that the interests of the petitioner will be adequately protected by the person directly affected is a relevant consideration,[65] as is, probably, the nature of the relationship involved.[66]

(c) *Is the action challenged sufficiently final?* Although a litigant is the person most directly affected by the challenged action of the Government, he may not have "standing" to raise his objections in a court if the action has not, as it were, come to rest. Courts do not review issues, especially constitutional issues, until they have to.[67] In part, this practice reflects the tradition that courts, having final power, can exercise it most wisely by restricting themselves to situations in which decision is necessary. In part, it is founded on the practical wisdom of not coming prematurely or needlessly in conflict with the executive or legislature.[68] Controversies, therefore, are often held

60. Hines Trustees v. United States, 263 U.S. 143, 148 (1923); Sprunt & Son v. United States, 281 U.S. 249, 255, 257 (1930). [F.F.]

61. See Atlanta v. Ickes, 308 U.S. 517 (1939); *cf.* Associated Industries v. Ickes, 134 F.2d 694 (2d Cir. 1943). [F.F.]

62. Hitchman Coal & Coke Co. v. Mitchell, 245 U.S. 229 (1917). [F.F.]

63. Truax v. Raich, 239 U.S. 33 (1915). [F.F.]

64. Pierce v. Society of Sisters, 268 U.S. 510 (1925). [F.F.]

65. *Compare* Columbia Broadcasting System v. United States, 316 U.S. 407, 423–24 (1942), *with* Schenley Corp. v. United States, 326 U.S. 432, 435 (1946). [F.F.]

66. See Davis & Farnum Mfg. v. Los Angeles, 189 U.S. 207, 220 (1903); Truax v. Raich, 239 U.S. 33, 38–39 (1915). [F.F.]

67. See Parker v. Los Angeles County, 338 U.S. 327 (1949); and see Brandeis, J., concurring, in Ashwander v. T.V.A., 297 U.S. 288, 341 (1936). [F.F.]

68. See Rochester Tel. Corp. v. United States, 307 US. 125, 130–31 (1939). [F.F.]

nonjusticiable "[w]here the action sought to be reviewed may have
the effect of forbidding or compelling conduct on the part of the person
seeking to review it, but only if some further action is taken by the
Commission." [69] There is no "standing" to challenge a preliminary
administrative determination, although the determination itself causes
some detriment to the litigant.[70] Nor does the reservation of authority
to act to a petitioner's detriment entitle him to challenge the reservation when it is conceded that the authority will be exercised only
on a contingency which appears not to be imminent.[71] Lack of finality
also explains the decision in *Standard Scale Co.* v. *Farrell.*[72] There
the Court was faced by an advisory "specification" of characteristics
desirable in ordinary measuring scales. The specification could be
enforced only by independent local officers' withholding their approval
of the equipment. Justiciability was denied.

"Finality" is not, however, a principle inflexibly applied. If the
ultimate impact of the challenged action on the petitioner is sufficiently
probable and not too distant, and if the procedure by which that
ultimate action may be questioned is too onerous or hazardous,
"standing" is given to challenge the action at a preliminary stage.[73]
It is well settled that equity will enjoin enforcement of criminal statutes
found to be unconstitutional "when it is found to be essential to the
protection of the property rights, as to which the jurisdiction of a
court of equity has been invoked." [74] And if the determination challenged creates a status which enforces a course of conduct through
penal sanctions, a litigant need not subject himself to the penalties to
challenge the determination.[75]

(3) Whether "justiciability" exists, therefore, has most often turned
on evaluating both the appropriateness of the issues for decision by
courts and the hardship of denying judicial relief. This explains the
inference to be drawn from the cases that "standing" to challenge
official action is more apt to exist when that action is not within the
scope of official authority than when the objection to the administrative

69. *Id.* at 129; and see Chicago & S. Air Lines v. Waterman S.S. Corp., 333
U.S. 103 (1948). [F.F.]

70. United States v. Los Angeles & S. L. R.R., 273 U.S. 299 (1927); *cf. Ex
parte* Williams, 277 U.S. 267 (1928). [F.F.]

71. Eccles v. Peoples Bank, 333 U.S. 426 (1948). [F.F.]

72. 249 U.S. 571 (1919). [F.F.]

73. Terrace v. Thompson, 263 U.S. 197 (1923); Santa Fe Pac. R.R. v. Lane,
244 U.S. 492 (1917); see Waite v. Macy, 246 U.S. 606 (1918). [F.F.]

74. *E.g.,* Philadelphia Co. v. Stimson, 223 U.S. 605, 621 (1912). [F.F.]

75. La Crosse Tel. Corp. v. Wisconsin Board, 336 US. 18 (1949); Shields v.
Utah Idaho R.R., 305 U.S. 177 (1938). [F.F.]

decision goes only to its correctness.[76] The objection to judicial restraint of an unauthorized exercise of powers is not weighty. . . .

The novelty of the injuries described in these petitions does not alter the fact that they present the characteristics which have in the past led this Court to recognize justiciability. They are unlike claims which the courts have hitherto found incompatible with the judicial process. No lack of finality can be urged. Designation works an immediate substantial harm to the reputations of petitioners. The threat which it carries for those members who are, or propose to become, federal employees makes it not a finicky or tenuous claim to object to the inference with their opportunities to retain or secure such employees as members. The membership relation is as substantial as that protected in *Truax* v. *Raich* and *Pierce* v. *Society of Sisters.* And it is at least doubtful that the members could or would adequately present the organizations' objections to the designation provisions of the Order.

Only on the ground that the organizations assert no interest protected in analogous situations at common law, by statute, or by the Constitution, therefore, can plausible challenge to their "standing" here be made. But the reasons which made an exercise of judicial power inappropriate in *Perkins* v. *Lukens Steel Co., Tennessee Power Co.* v. *T.V.A.,* and *Alabama Power Co.* v. *Ickes* are not apposite here. There the injuries were such that, had they not been inflicted by the Government, they clearly could not have been redressed. In *Perkins* v. *Lukens Steel Co.,* it was not asserted that the authority under which the Government acted was invalid; only the correctness of an interpretation of a statute in the course of the exercise of an admitted power was challenged. In the *Power* cases protection from competition was sought; but the thrust of the law is to preserve competition, not to give protection from it. The action there challenged, furthermore, was not directed at named individuals. Here, on the other hand, petitioners seek to challenge governmental action stigmatizing them individually. They object, not to a particular erroneous application of a valid power, but to the validity of the regulation authorizing the action. They point to two types of injury, each of a sort which, were it not for principles of governmental immunity, would be clearly actionable at common law.

This controversy is therefore amenable to the judicial process. Its justiciability does not depend solely on the fact that the action challenged is defamatory. Not every injury inflicted by a defamatory statement of a government officer can be redressed in court. On the

76. See United States v. Los Angeles & S. L. R.R., 273 U.S. 299, 314–15 (1927); Pennsylvania R.R. v. Labor Board, 261 U.S. 72 (1923); *Ex parte* Williams, 277 U.S. 267, 271 (1928). [F.F.]

balance of all considerations, the exercise here of judicial power accords with traditional canons for access to courts without inroads on the effective conduct of government. . . .

The requirement of "due process" is not a fair-weather or timid assurance. It must be respected in periods of calm and in times of trouble; it protects aliens as well as citizens. But "due process," unlike some legal rules, is not a technical conception with a fixed content unrelated to time, place and circumstances. Expressing as it does in its ultimate analysis respect enforced by law for that feeling of just treatment which has been evolved through centuries of Anglo-American constitutional history and civilization, "due process" cannot be imprisoned within the treacherous limits of any formula. Representing a profound attitude of fairness between man and man, and more particularly between the individual and government, "due process" is compounded of history, reason, the past course of decisions, and stout confidence in the strength of the democratic faith which we profess. Due process is not a mechanical instrument. It is not a yardstick. It is a process. It is a delicate process of adjustment inescapably involving the exercise of judgment by those whom the Constitution entrusted with the unfolding of the process.

Fully aware of the enormous powers thus given to the judiciary and especially to its Supreme Court, those who founded this Nation put their trust in a judiciary truly independent — in judges not subject to the fears or allurements of a limited tenure and by the very nature of their function detached from passing and partisan influences.

It may fairly be said that, barring only occasional and temporary lapses, this Court has not sought unduly to confine those who have the responsibility of governing by giving the great concept of due process doctrinaire scope. The Court has responded to the infinite variety and perplexity of the tasks of government by recognizing that what is unfair in one situation may be fair in another.[77] Whether the *ex parte* procedure to which the petitioners were subjected duly observed "the rudiments of fair play,"[78] cannot, therefore, be tested by mere generalities or sentiments abstractly appealing. The precise nature of the interest that has been adversely affected, the manner in which this was done, the reasons for doing it, the available alternatives to the procedure that was followed, the protection implicit in the office of the functionary whose conduct is challenged, the balance of hurt complained of and good accomplished — these are some of the considerations that must enter into the judicial judgment.

77. *Compare*, for instance, Murray's Lessee v. Hoboken Land & Improvement Co., 18 How. 272 (1856), *with* Ng Fung Ho v. White, 259 U.S. 276 (1921), and see F.C.C. v. WJR, 337 U.S. 265, 275 (1949). [F.F.]

78. Chicago, M. & St. P. Ry. v. Polt, 232 U.S. 165, 168 (1914). [F.F.]

Applying them to the immediate situation, we note that publicly designating an organization as within the proscribed categories of the Loyalty Order does not directly deprive anyone of liberty or property. Weight must also be given to the fact that such designation is not made by a minor official but by the highest law officer of the Government. Again, it is fair to emphasize that the individual's interest is here to be weighed against a claim of the greatest of all public interests, that of national security. In striking the balance the relevant considerations must be fairly, which means coolly, weighed with due regard to the fact that this Court is not exercising a primary judgment but is sitting in judgment upon those who also have taken the oath to observe the Constitution and who have the responsibility for carrying on government.

But the significance we attach to general principles may turn the scale when competing claims appeal for supremacy. Achievements of our civilization as precious as they were hard won were summarized by Mr. Justice Brandeis when he wrote that "in the development of our liberty insistence upon procedural regularity has been a large factor." [79] It is noteworthy that procedural safeguards constitute the major portion of our Bill of Rights. And so, no one now doubts that in the criminal law a "person's right to reasonable notice of a charge against him, and an opportunity to be heard in his defense — a right to his day in court — are basic in our system of jurisprudence." [80] "The hearing, moreover, must be a real one, not a sham or a pretense." [81] Nor is there doubt that notice and hearing are prerequisite to due process in civil proceedings. [82] Only the narrowest exceptions, justified by history become part of the habits of our people or by obvious necessity, are tolerated. [83]

It is against this background of guiding considerations that we must view the rather novel aspects of the situation at hand. It is not true that the evils against which the Loyalty Order was directed are wholly devoid of analogy in our own history. The circumstances attending the Napoleonic conflicts, which gave rise to the Sedition Act of 1798, [84] readily come to mind. But it is true that the executive action now under scrutiny is of a sort not heretofore challenged in this Court.

---

79. Burdeau v. McDowell, 256 U.S. 465, 477 (1921) (dissenting). [F.F.]

80. *In re* Oliver, 333 U.S. 257, 273 (1948). [F.F.]

81. Palko v. Connecticut, 302 U.S. 319, 327 (1937). [F.F.]

82. *E.g.*, Coe v. Armour Fertilizer Works, 237 U.S. 413 (1915). [F.F.]

83. Ownbey v. Morgan, 256 U.S. 94 (1921); Endicott Johnson Corp. v. Encyclopedia Press, 266 U.S. 285 (1924); see Cooke v. United States, 267 U.S. 517, 536 (1925). [F.F.]

84. 1 Stat. 596 (1798). [F.F.]

That of itself does not justify the *ex parte* summary designation procedure. It does make it necessary to consider its validity when judged by our whole experience with the Due Process Clause. . . .

The heart of the matter is that democracy implies respect for the elementary rights of men, however suspect or unworthy; a democratic government must therefore practice fairness; and fairness can rarely be obtained by secret, one-sided determination of facts decisive of rights.

An opportunity to be heard may not seem vital when an issue relates only to technical questions susceptible of demonstrable proof on which evidence is not likely to be overlooked and argument on the meaning and worth of conflicting and cloudy data not apt to be helpful. But in other situations an admonition of Mr. Justice Holmes becomes relevant. "One has to remember that when one's interest is keenly excited evidence gathers from all sides around the magnetic point. . . ." It should be particularly heeded at times of agitation and anxiety, when fear and suspicion impregnate the air we breathe.[85] "The plea that evidence of guilt must be secret is abhorrent to free men, because it provides a cloak for the malevolent, the misinformed, the meddlesome, and the corrupt to play the role of informer undetected and uncorrected." [86] Appearances in the dark are apt to look different in the light of day.

Man being what he is cannot safely be trusted with complete immunity from outward responsibility in depriving others of their rights. At least such is the conviction underlying our Bill of Rights. That a conclusion satisfies one's private conscience does not attest its reliability. The validity and moral authority of a conclusion largely depend on the mode by which it was reached. Secrecy is not congenial to truth-seeking and self-righteousness gives too slender an assurance of rightness. No better instrument has been devised for arriving at truth than to give a person in jeopardy of serious loss notice of the case against him and opportunity to meet it. Nor has a better way been found for generating the feeling, so important to a popular government, that justice has been done.

Avoidance of the exercise of the power of judicial review over national legislation was, nevertheless, a value to be achieved where it was reasonably possible to do so. In *United States v. United Auto Workers*,[87] Frankfurter wrote the opinion for the Court expressing this ob-

85. Compare BROWN, THE FRENCH REVOLUTION IN ENGLISH HISTORY (1965). [F.F.]

86. United States *ex rel.* Knauff v. Shaughnessy, 338 U.S. 537, 551 (1950) (dissenting). [F.F.]

87. 352 U.S. 567 (1957).

jective. It is only one of many instances in which he invoked this tenet of judicial behavior: [88]

> The impressive lesson of history confirms the wisdom of the repeated enunciation, the variously expressed admonition, of self-imposed inhibition against passing on the validity of an Act of Congress "unless absolutely necessary to a decision of the case." [89] Observance of this principle makes for the minimum tension within our democratic political system where "Scarcely any question arises . . . which does not become, sooner or later, a subject of judicial debate." [90]

The wisdom of refraining from avoidable constitutional pronouncements has been most vividly demonstrated on the rare occasions when the Court, forgetting "the fallibility of the human judgment," has departed from its own practice. The Court's failure in *Dred Scott v. Sanford* [91] "to take the smooth handle for the sake of repose" by disposing of the case solely upon "the outside issue" and the effects of its attempt "to settle the agitation" are familiar history. *Dred Scott* does not stand alone. These exceptions have rightly been characterized as among the Court's notable "self-inflicted wounds." [92]

Clearly in this case it is not "absolutely necessary to a decision," [93] to canvass the constitutional issues. The case came here under the Criminal Appeals Act because the District Court blocked the prosecution on the ground that the indictment failed to state an offense within § 313 of the Corrupt Practices Act. Our reversal of the district judge's erroneous construction clears the way for the prosecution to proceed.

Refusal to anticipate constitutional questions is peculiarly appropriate in the circumstances of this case. First of all, these questions come to us unillumined by the consideration of a single judge — we are asked to decide them in the first instance. Again, only an adjudication on the merits can provide the concrete factual setting that sharpens the deliberative process especially demanded for constitutional decision. Finally, by remanding the case for trial it may well be that the Court will not be called upon to pass on the questions now raised.[94]

88. *Id.* at 590–92.

89. Burton v. United States, 196 U.S. 283, 295 (1904). [F.F.]

90. 1 Tocqueville, Democracy in America 306 (4th Am. ed. 1843). [F.F.]

91. 19 How. 393 (1857). [F.F.]

92. Hughes, The Supreme Court of the United States 50 (1928). [F.F.]

93. Burton v. United States, *supra* note 89. [F.F.]

94. *Compare* United States v. Petrillo, 332 U.S. 1, 9 *et seq.* (1947), *with* the subsequent adjudication on the merits in United States v. Petrillo, 75 F. Supp. 176 (N.D. Ill. 1948). [F.F.]

Counsel are prone to shape litigation, so far as it is within their control, in order to secure comprehensive rulings. This is true both of counsel for defendants and for the Government. Such desire on their part is not difficult to appreciate. But the Court has its responsibility. Matter now buried under abstract constitutional issues may, by the elucidation of a trial, be brought to the surface, and in the outcome constitutional questions may disappear. Allegations of the indictment hypothetically framed to elicit a ruling from this Court or based upon misunderstanding of the facts may not survive the test of proof. For example, was the broadcast paid for out of the general dues of the union membership or may the funds be fairly said to have been obtained on a voluntary basis? Did the broadcast reach the public at large or only those affiliated with appellee? Did it constitute active electioneering or simply state the record of particular candidates on economic issues? Did the union sponsor the broadcast with the intent to affect the results of the election? As Senator Taft repeatedly recognized in the debate on § 304, prosecutions under the Act may present difficult questions of fact.[95] We suggest the possibility of such questions, not to imply answers to problems of statutory construction, but merely to indicate the covert issues that may be involved in this case.

The cases set forth in this chapter represent an era that became moribund during the years of the Warren Court, when the considerations put forth by Justice Frankfurter in favor of judicial husbandry and jurisdictional limitations were rejected. It was to be expected that, in a period when the judiciary was so avidly expanding its ken, restraints of this nature on the developing power would not be kindly received. Whether a new and less ambitious judicial Caesar will succeed to power, one more cognizant of the merits of the Frankfurter approach, is only for the future to tell.

95. See 352 U.S. at 585–87, n.1. [F.F.]

4   Stare Decisis

Mr. Justice Frankfurter was not given to dogmas and so, for him, stare decisis was not a doctrine of rigid simplicity. There was reason in adherence to created rules, but there were other factors that must also be taken into account. Stability was important to the life of the law; so, too, was change. Nor did he suggest that the personal equation was absent: "The extent to which judges should feel in duty bound not to innovate is a perennial problem, and the pull of the past is different among different judges as it is in the same judge about different aspects of the past."[1]

Frankfurter was, of course, reluctant to reject earlier decisions of the Court, even on constitutional issues, except on a demonstration of compelling reasons. Nevertheless, in his first Term, in *Graves v. New York* ex rel. *O'Keefe*,[2] he joined the Court in reversing the judicial grant of national tax immunity to state officials' salaries. He felt constrained, however, to express his own reasons for doing so:[3]

I join in the Court's opinion but deem it appropriate to add a few remarks. The volume of the Court's business has long since made impossible the early healthy practice whereby the Justices gave expression to the individual opinions. But the old tradition still has relevance when an important shift in constitutional doctrine is announced after a reconstruction of the membership of the Court. Such shifts of opinion should not derive from mere private judgment. They must be mindful of the necessary demands of continuity in a civilized society. A reversal of a long current of decisions can be justified only if rooted in the Constitution itself as an historic document for a developing nation. . . .

The judicial history of this doctrine of immunity is a striking illustration of an occasional tendency to encrust unwarranted interpretations upon the Constitution and thereafter to consider merely what has been judicially said about the Constitution, rather than to be primarily controlled by a fair conception of the Constitution. Judicial

1. Commissioner v. Church, 335 U.S. 632, 677 (1949).
2. 306 U.S. 466 (1939).
3. *Id*. at 487, 491–92.

exegesis is unavoidable with reference to an organic act like our Constitution, drawn in many particulars with purposed vagueness so as to leave room for the unfolding future. But the ultimate touchstone of constitutionality is the Constitution itself and not what we have said about it.

For Frankfurter there were some earlier decisions that had ceased to have relevancy even before the Court had the chance to declare them officially dead. Time and circumstances had so sapped their vitality that they could no longer be considered controlling. This was the case, according to Frankfurter's opinion for the Court, in *Tigner v. Texas.*[4] There a Texas statute had made certain combinations and conspiracies illegal, but exempted agricultural activities from the section imposing criminal penalties. A similar exemption in an Illinois statute had been held to be offensive to the Equal Protection Clause in *Connolly v. Union Sewer Pipe Co.*[5] The Supreme Court agreed with the lower courts that had found *Connolly* no longer viable: [6]

> Since *Connolly's* case was decided, nearly forty years ago, an impressive legislative movement bears witness to general acceptance of the view that the differences between agriculture and industry call for differentiation in the formulation of public policy. . . .
>
> At the core of all these enactments lies a conception of price and production policy for agriculture very different from that which underlies the demands made upon industry and commerce by the anti-trust laws. These various measures are manifestations of the fact that in our national economy agriculture expresses functions and forces different from the other elements in the total economic process. Certainly these are differences which may be acted upon by the lawmakers. The equality at which the "equal protection" clause aims is not a disembodied equality. The Fourteenth Amendment enjoins the "equal protection of the laws," and laws are not abstract propositions. They do not relate to abstract units A, B and C, but are expressions of policy arising out of specific difficulties, addressed to the attainment of specific ends by the use of specific remedies. The Constitution does not require things which are different in fact or opinion to be treated in law as though they were the same. And so we conclude that to write into law the differences between agriculture and other economic pursuits was within the power of the Texas legislature.

4. 310 U.S. 141 (1940).

5. 184 U.S. 540 (1902).

6. 310 U.S. at 145–47.

Connolly's case has been worn away by the erosion of time, and we are of opinion that it is no longer controlling.

One is nevertheless left with the feeling that it was not so much a change in circumstances as in judicial attitudes that justified the rejection of *Connolly*. For, if anything, the disappearance of family farms had made agriculture more like manufacturing in the interval between *Connolly* and *Tigner*.

In *United States v. Raines*,[7] Frankfurter announced his abandonment of a long-cherished precedent in light of the Court's frequent disregard of it and the presumption of constitutional validity due to congressional action.[8]

The weighty presumptive validity with which the Civil Rights Act of 1957, like every enactment of Congress, comes here is not overborne by any claim urged against it. To deal with legislation so as to find unconstitutionality is to reverse the duty of courts to apply a statute so as to save it. Here this measure is sustained under familiar principles of constitutional law. Nor is there any procedural hurdle left to be cleared to sustain the suit of the United States. Whatever may have been the original force of *Barney* v. *New York*,[9] that decision has long ceased to be an obstruction, nor is any other decision in the way of our result in this case. And so I find it needless to canvass the multitude of opinions that may generally touch on, but do not govern, the issues now before us.

On the other hand, intervening events may have made it undesirable to reverse an earlier and erroneous precedent, especially where correction lies in the power of Congress. Thus, in *Davis v. Department of Labor*.[10] Frankfurter declined to suggest the overruling of the despised *Jensen* doctrine:[11]

Any legislative scheme that compensates workmen or their families for industrial mishaps should be capable of simple and dependable enforcement. That was the aim of Congress when, with due regard for the diverse conditions in the several States, it afforded to harborworkers the benefits of state workmen's compensation laws.[12] But

7. 362 U.S. 17 (1960).

8. *Id.* at 28.

9. 193 U.S. 430 (1904). [F.F.]

10. 317 U.S. 249 (1942).

11. *Id.* at 258–59.

12. Act of 6 October 1917, c. 97, 40 Stat. 395, as amended by the Act of 10 June 1922, c. 216, 42 Stat. 634. [F.F.]

Southern Pacific Co. v. *Jensen,*[13] and cases following, frustrated this purpose.

Such a desirable end cannot now be achieved merely by judicial repudiation of the *Jensen* doctrine. Too much has happened in the twenty-five years since that ill-starred decision. Federal and state enactments have so accommodated themselves to the complexity and confusion introduced by the *Jensen* rulings that the resources of adjudication can no longer bring relief from the difficulties which the judicial process itself brought into being. Therefore, until Congress sees fit to attempt another comprehensive solution of the problem, this Court can do no more than bring some order out of the remaining judicial chaos as marginal situations come before us. Because it contributes to that end, I join in the Court's opinion.

Then, too, a precedent was controlling, for Mr. Justice Frankfurter, only if the earlier decision had in fact resulted from a deliberative consideration of the question by the Court that passed it. *Sub silentio* resolution was not enough. Among other places, he made this point in *Florida Lime Growers v. Jacobsen*:[14]

The statute providing for three-judge Federal District Courts, with direct appeal to this Court, in cases seeking interlocutory injunctions against the operation of state statutes on constitutional grounds, was enacted in 1910.[15] It was amended in 1925 to apply to applications for final as well as interlocutory injunctive relief.[16] Since that time this Court has taken jurisdiction by way of direct appeal in several cases like the present one, where a state statute was sought to be enjoined both on federal constitutional and non-constitutional grounds.[17] In none of these cases, however, was our jurisdiction challenged by the litigants because non-constitutional as well as constitutional relief was sought, nor did the Court notice the existence of a question as to our jurisdiction on that score. We should therefore feel free to apply Mr. Chief Justice Marshall's approach in a similar situation to unconsidered assumptions of jurisdiction: "No question was made, in that case, as to the jurisdiction. It passed *sub silentio*,

13. 244 U.S. 205 (1917). [F.F.]

14. 362 U.S. 73, 86–88 (1960).

15. 36 Stat. 557 (1910). [F.F.]

16. 43 Stat. 938 (1925). [F.F.]

17. See Herkness v. Irion, 278 U.S. 92 (1928); Sterling v. Constantin, 287 U.S. 378, 393 (1932) (limited in Phillips v. United States, 312 U.S. 246 [1941]); Spielman Motor Sales Co. v. Dodge, 295 U.S. 89 (1935); Parker v. Brown, 317 U.S. 341 (1943). [F.F.]

and the court does not consider itself as bound by that case." [18] I therefore approach the question of our jurisdiction in the present case as open, calling for a thorough canvass of the relevant jurisdictional factors.

Nor were precedents to be read for all they were worth. Instead, they had to be utilized with an understanding that differences in issues might call for differences in results. In *Dennis v. United States*, [19] Frankfurter would have rejected the proposition that because government employees were held to be qualified to sit as jurors in some cases in which the United States was a party, they should also be allowed to sit in a case involving a charge of disloyalty to the United States. Frankfurter's opinion, written during the McCarthy era, reveals more than his attitude toward precedents: [20]

Acquiescence in a precedent does not require approval of its extension. Although I adhere to the views expressed by Mr. Justice Jackson for the minority in *Frazier* v. *United States*, [21] I do not urge that it be overruled. But in abiding by it I need not assent to enlarging the areas of its undesirability. The constitutional command for trial by an "impartial jury" casts upon the judiciary the exercise of judgment in determining the circumstances which precluded that free, fearless and disinterested capacity in analyzing evidence which is indispensable if jurymen are to deal impartially with an accusation. The judgment that a court must thus exercise in finding "disqualification for bias" of persons who belong to a particular class is a psychological judgment. It is a judgment founded on human experience and not on technical learning. And so it does not follow that merely because government employees are not automatically disqualified as jurors in every prosecution in the District of Columbia they should not be disqualified in prosecutions that are deemed to concern the security of the nation.

The reason for disqualifying a whole class on the ground of bias is the law's recognition that if the circumstances of that class in the run

---

18. United States v. More, 3 Cranch 159, 172 (1798). See also Mr. Chief Justice Marshall, in Durousseau v. United States, 6 Cranch 307 (1810), and Mr. Justice Brandeis, dissenting, in King Mfg. Co. v. Augusta, 277 U.S. 100, 135 n.21 (1928): "It is well settled that the exercise of jurisdiction under such circumstances [where counsel did not question our jurisdiction] is not to be deemed a precedent when the question is finally brought before us for determination." [F.F.]

19. 339 U.S. 162 (1950).

20. *Id.* at 181–85.

21. 335 U.S. 497, 514 (1948). [F.F.]

of instances are likely to generate bias, consciously or unconsciously, it would be a hopeless endeavor to search out the impact of these circumstances on the mind and judgment of a particular individual. That is the reason why the influences of consanguinity or of financial interest are not individually canvassed. Law as a response to life recognizes the operation of such influences even though not consciously or clearly entertained. The appearance of impartiality is an essential manifestation of its reality. This is the basic psychological reason why the Founders of this country gave the judiciary an unlimited tenure. Impartiality requires independence, and independence, the Framers realized, requires freedom from the effect of those "occasional ill-humors in the society," which as Alexander Hamilton put it in The Federalist are "the influence of particular conjectures." [22]

One of the greatest judges has assured us that "Judges are apt to be naif, simple-minded men." [23] Only naiveté could be unmindful of the force of the considerations set forth by MR. JUSTICE BLACK, and known of all men. There is a pervasiveness of atmosphere in Washington whereby forces are released in relation to jurors who may be deemed supporters of an accused under a cloud of disloyalty that are emotionally different from those which come into play in relation to jurors dealing with offenses which in their implications do not touch the security of the nation. Considering the situation in which men of power and influence find themselves through such alleged associations, it is asking more of human nature in ordinary government employees than history warrants to ask them to exercise that "uncommon portion of fortitude" which the Founders of this nation thought judges could exercise only if given a life tenure.[24]

A government employee ought not to be asked whether he would feel free to decide against the Government in cases that to the common understanding involve disloyalty to this country. Questions ought not to be put to prospective jurors that offer no fair choice for answer. Men ought not to be asked in effect whether they are brave or wholly indifferent to the enveloping atmosphere. They should not be asked to confess that they are weaklings nor should it be assumed that they are fully conscious of all the pressures that may move them. They may not know what judges of considerable forensic experience know, that one cannot have confident knowledge of influences that may play and prey unconsciously upon judgment.[25] The well-known observa-

22. THE FEDERALIST No. 78, at 400 (Beloff ed. 1948). [F.F.]

23. HOLMES, COLLECTED LEGAL PAPERS 295 (1920). [F.F.]

24. THE FEDERALIST, note 22 *supra*. [F.F.]

25. See, *e.g.*, Mr. Justice Oliver, in Rex v. Davies, [1945] 1 K.B. 435, 445. [F.F.]

tions of Mr. Justice Holmes on these psychological influences are here pertinent: "This is not a matter for polite presumptions; we must look facts in the face. Any judge who has sat with juries knows that in spite of forms they are extremely likely to be impregnated by the environing atmosphere." [26] Nor is it irrelevant to note that we are living in a time when inroads have been made on the secrecy of the jury room so that, upon failure to agree, jurors are subjected to harassment to disclose their position in the jury room. Ought we to expose our administration of criminal justice to situations whereby federal employees must contemplate inquisitions into the manner in which they discharged their juror's oath?

To conclude that government employees are not disqualified in prosecutions inherently touching the security of the Government, at a time when public feeling on these matters is notoriously running high, because they are not *ipso facto* disqualified from sitting in a prosecution against a drug addict or a petty thief, is to say that things that are very different are the same. The doctrine of the *Frazier* case does not require such disregard of the relevant. To recognize the existence of what is characterized as a phobia against a particular group is not to discriminate in its favor. If a particular group, no matter what its beliefs, is under pressure of popular hostility, exclusion of potential jurors peculiarly susceptible to such pressure is not an expression of regard for political opinions but recognition by law of the facts of life. It does not follow that because members of different but respected political parties can sit in judgment upon one another where punishment is involved, all members of such parties, no matter what their relation to an operating bias, can freely and fairly sit in judgment upon those belonging to an ostracized group.

Let there be no misunderstanding. To recognize the existence of a group whose views are feared and despised by the community at large does not even remotely imply any support of that group. To take appropriate measures in order to avert injustice even towards a member of a despised group is to enforce justice. It is not to play favorites. The boast of our criminal procedure is that it protects an accused, so far as legal procedure can, from a bias operating against such a group to which he belongs. This principle should be enforced whatever the tenets of the group — whether the old Locofocos or the Know-Nothings, the Ku Klux Klan or the Communists. This is not to coddle Communists but to respect our professions of equal justice to all. It was a wise man who said that there is no greater inequality than the equal treatment of unequals.

We are concerned with something far more important than sustaining a particular conviction. Many and conflicting are the criteria by

26. Frank v. Mangum, 237 U.S. 309, 345, 349 (1915). [F.F.]

which a society is to be deemed good, but perhaps no test is more revealing than the characteristics of its punitive justice. No single aspect of our society is more precious and more distinctive than that we seek to administer criminal justice according to morally fastidious standards. These reveal confidence in our institutions, respect for reason, and loyalty to our professions of fairness. The powerful claim in behalf of our civilization represented by our system of criminal justice will be vindicated and strengthened if those who in the popular mind appear to threaten the very existence of the Government are tried by citizens other than those in the immediate employ of the Government at the seat of Government.

The theme stated in the last paragraph was a guiding principle in Frankfurter's jurisprudence. It is a theme reflecting the first-hand knowledge of oppression revealed by such examples as Sacco and Vanzetti and Tom Mooney, by the Cleveland Crime Survey, and by the Wickersham reports. It was a theme that was reiterated over and over again in Frankfurter's opinions. And it is a theme not very well understood by some of Frankfurter's self-proclaimed followers of today.

5   Separation of Powers

It was typical of Mr. Justice Frankfurter that in *Youngstown Sheet & Tube Co. v. Sawyer*,[1] which presented the Court on which he sat with its most serious and perhaps its most difficult challenge to define the limits of executive power, he began his opinion not with the question of the scope of presidential authority but rather with the question of the propriety of judicial intervention. In the midst of the Korean War, President Truman had assumed the right to "seize" the steel mills to prevent a shutdown that would result from a threatened strike. In a series of opinions, the Justices of the Court announced their respective positions about the limits of presidential dominion. Not untypically, Mr. Justice Black found the letter of the Constitution specified the ban on the presidential action. Other members of the majority, although purporting to join in Black's opinion, wrote opinions of their own expressing more flexibility than the opinion for the Court purported to allow. Frankfurter's was among them:[2]

Before the cares of the White House were his own, President Harding is reported to have said that government after all is a very simple thing. He must have said that, if he said it, as a fleeting inhabitant of fairyland. The opposite is the truth. A constitutional democracy like ours is perhaps the most difficult of man's social arrangements to manage successfully. Our scheme of society is more dependent than any other form of government on knowledge and wisdom and self-discipline for the achievement of its aims. For our democracy implies the reign of reason on the most extensive scale. The Founders of this Nation were not imbued with the modern cynicism that the only thing that history teaches is that it teaches nothing. They acted on the conviction that the experience of man sheds a good deal of light on his nature. It sheds a good deal of light not merely on the need for effective power, if a society is to be at once cohesive and civilized, but also on the need for limitations on the power of governors over the governed.

To that end they rested the structure of our central government

1. 343 U.S. 579 (1952).

2. *Id.* at 593–98, 602–04, 609–11, 613–14.

on the system of checks and balances. For them the doctrine of separation of powers was not mere theory; it was a felt necessity. Not so long ago it was fashionable to find our system of checks and balances obstructive to effective government. It was easy to ridicule that system as outmoded — too easy. The experience through which the world has passed in our own day has made vivid the realization that the Framers of our Constitution were not inexperienced doctrinaires. These long-headed statesmen had no illusion that our people enjoyed biological or psychological or sociological immunities from the hazards of concentrated power. It is absurd to see a dictator in a representative product of the sturdy democratic traditions of the Mississippi Valley. The accretion of dangerous power does not come in a day. It does come, however slowly, from the generative force of unchecked disregard of the restrictions that fence in even the most disinterested assertion of authority.

The Framers, however, did not make the judiciary the overseer of our government. They were familiar with the revisory functions entrusted to judges in a few of the States and refused to lodge such powers in this Court. Judicial power can be exercised only as to matters that were the traditional concern of the courts at Westminster, and only if they arise in ways that to the expert feel of lawyers constitute "Cases" or "Controversies." Even as to question that were the staple of judicial business, it is not for the courts to pass upon them unless they are indispensably involved in a conventional litigation — and then, only to the extent that they are so involved. Rigorous adherence to the narrow scope of the judicial function is especially demanded in controversies that arouse appeals to the Constitution. The attitude with which this Court must approach its duty when confronted with such issues is precisely the opposite of that normally manifested by the general public. So-called constitutional questions seem to exercise a mesmeric influence over the popular mind. This eagerness to settle — preferably forever — a specific problem on the basis of the broadest possible constitutional pronouncements may not unfairly be called one of our minor national traits. An English observer of our scene has acutely described it: "At the first sound of a new argument over the United States Constitution and its interpretation the hearts of Americans leap with a fearful joy. The blood stirs powerfully in their veins and a new lustre brightens their eyes. Like King Harry's men before Harfleur, they stand like greyhounds in the slips, straining upon the start." [3]

The path of duty for this Court, it bears repetition, lies in the opposite direction. Due regard for the implications of the distribution

3. The Economist, 10 May 1952, p. 370. [F.F.]

of powers in our Constitution and for the nature of the judicial process as the ultimate authority in interpreting the Constitution, has not only confined the Court within the narrow domain of appropriate adjudication. It has also led to "a series of rules under which it has avoided passing upon a large part of all the constitutional questions pressed upon it for decision." [4] A basic rule is the duty of the Court not to pass on a constitutional issue at all, however narrowly it may be confined, if the case may, as a matter of intellectual honesty, be decided without even considering delicate problems of power under the Constitution. It ought to be, but apparently is not, a matter of common understanding that clashes between different branches of the government should be avoided if a legal ground of less explosive potentialities is properly available. Constitutional adjudications are apt by exposing differences to exacerbate them.

So here our first inquiry must be not into the powers of the President, but into the powers of a District Judge to issue a temporary injunction in the circumstances of this case. Familiar as that remedy is, it remains an extraordinary remedy. To start with a consideration of the relation between the President's powers and those of Congress — a most delicate matter that has occupied the thoughts of statesman and judges since the Nation was founded and will continue to occupy their thoughts as long as our democracy lasts — is to start at the wrong end. A plaintiff is not entitled to an injunction if money damages would fairly compensate him for any wrong he may have suffered. The same considerations by which the Steelworkers, in their brief *amicus*, demonstrate, from the seizure here in controversy, consequences that cannot be translated into dollars and cents, preclude a holding that only compensable damage for the plaintiffs is involved. Again, a court of equity ought not to issue an injunction, even though a plaintiff otherwise makes out a case for it, if the plaintiff's right to an injunction is overborne by a commanding public interest against it. One need not resort to a large epigrammatic generalization that the evils of industrial dislocation are to be preferred to allowing illegality to go unchecked. To deny inquiry into the President's power in a case like this, because of the damage to the public interest to be feared from upsetting its exercise by him, would in effect always preclude inquiry into challenged power, which presumably only avowed great public interest brings into action. And so, with the utmost unwillingness, with every desire to avoid judicial inquiry into the powers and duties of the other two branches of the government, I cannot escape consideration of the legality of Executive Order No. 10340.

The pole-star for constitutional adjudications is John Marshall's

4. Brandeis, J., in Ashwander v. T.V.A., 297 U.S. 288, 341, 346 (1936). [F.F.]

greatest judicial utterance that "it is a *constitution* we are expounding." [5] That requires both a spacious view in applying an instrument of government "made for an undefined and expanding future," [6] and as narrow a delimitation of the constitutional issues as the circumstances permit. Not the least characteristic of great statesmanship which the Framers manifested was the extent to which they did not attempt to bind the future. It is no less incumbent upon this Court to avoid putting fetters upon the future by needless pronouncements today.

Marshall's admonition that "it is a *constitution* we are expounding" is especially relevant when the Court is required to give legal sanctions to an underlying principle of the Constitution — that of separation of powers. "The great ordinances of the Constitution do not establish and divide fields of black and white." [7]

The issue before us can be met, and therefore should be, without attempting to define the President's powers comprehensively. I shall not attempt to delineate what belongs to him by virtue of his office beyond the power even of Congress to contract; what authority belongs to him until Congress acts; what kind of problems may be dealt with either by the Congress or by the President or by both; [8] what power must be exercised by the Congress and cannot be delegated to the President. It is as unprofitable to lump together in an undiscriminating hotch-potch past presidential actions claimed to be derived from occupancy of the office, as it is to conjure up hypothetical future cases. The judiciary may, as this case proves, have to intervene in determining where authority lies as between the democratic forces in our scheme of government. But in doing so we should be wary and humble. Such is the teaching of this Court's rôle in the history of the country.

It is in this mood and with this perspective that the issue before the Court must be approached. We must therefore put to one side consideration of what powers the President would have had if there had been no legislation whatever bearing on the authority asserted by the seizure, or if the seizure had been only for a short, explicitly temporary period, to be terminated automatically unless Congressional approval were given. These and other questions, like or unlike, are not now here. I would exceed my authority were I to say anything about them.

The question before the Court comes in this setting. Congress has

5. McCulloch v. Maryland, 4 Wheat. 316, 407 (1819). [F.F.]

6. Hurtado v. California, 110 U.S. 516, 530 (1834). [F.F.]

7. Holmes, J., dissenting, in Springer v. Philippine Islands, 277 U.S. 189, 209 (1928). [F.F.]

8. *Cf.* LaAbra Silver Mng. Co. v. United States, 175 U.S. 423 (1899). [F.F.]

frequently — at least 16 times since 1916 — specifically provided for executive seizure of production, transportation, communications, or storage facilities. In every case it has qualified this grant of power with limitations and safeguards. . . .

Congress in 1947 was again called upon to consider whether governmental seizure should be used to avoid serious industrial shutdowns. Congress decided against conferring such power generally and in advance, without special Congressional enactment to meet each particular need.

In any event, nothing can be plainer than that Congress made a conscious choice of policy in a field full of perplexity and peculiarly within legislative responsibility for choice. In formulating legislation for dealing with industrial conflicts, Congress could not more clearly and emphatically have withheld authority than it did in 1947. Perhaps as much so as is true of any piece of modern legislation, Congress acted with full consciousness of what it was doing and in the light of much recent history. Previous seizure legislation had subjected the powers granted to the President to restrictions of varying degrees of stringency. Instead of giving him even limited powers, Congress in 1947 deemed it wise to require the President, upon failure of attempts to reach a voluntary settlement, to report to Congress if he deemed the power of seizure a needed shot for his locker. The President could not ignore the specific limitations of prior seizure statutes. No more could he act in disregard of the limitation put upon seizure by the 1947 Act.

It cannot be contended that the President would have had power to issue this order had Congress explicitly negated such authority in formal legislation. Congress has expressed its will to withhold this power from the President as though it had said so in so many words. The authoritatively expressed purpose of Congress to disallow such power to the President and to require him, when in his mind the occasion arose for such a seizure, to put the matter to Congress and ask for specific authority from it, could not be more decisive if it had been written into §§ 206–210 of the Labor Management Relations Act of 1947. Only the other day, we treated the Congressional gloss upon those sections as part of the Act.[9] Grafting upon the words a purpose of Congress thus unequivocally expressed is the regular legislative mode for defining the scope of an Act of Congress. It would be not merely infelicitous draftsmanship but almost offensive gaucherie to write such a restriction upon the President's power in terms into a statute rather than to have it authoritatively expounded, as it was, by controlling legislative history. . . .

9. Bus Employees v. Wisconsin Board, 340 U.S. 383, 395–96 (1951). [F.F.]

No authority that has since been given to the President can by any fair process of statutory construction be deemed to withdraw the restriction or change the will of Congress as expressed by a body of enactments, culminating in the Labor Management Relations Act of 1947. . . .

It is one thing to draw an intention of Congress from general language and to say that Congress would have explicitly written what is inferred, where Congress has not addressed itself to a specific situation. It is quite impossible, however, when Congress did specifically address itself to a problem, as Congress did to that of seizure, to find secreted in the interstices of legislation the very grant of power which Congress consciously withheld. To find authority so explicitly withheld is not merely to disregard in a particular instance the clear will of Congress. It is to disrespect the whole legislative process and the constitutional division of authority between President and Congress.

The legislative history here canvassed is relevant to yet another of the issues before us, namely, the Government's argument that overriding public interest prevents the issuance of the injunction despite the illegality of the seizure. I cannot accept that contention. "Balancing the equities" when considering whether an injunction should issue, is lawyers' jargon for choosing between conflicting public interests. When Congress itself has struck the balance, has defined the weight to be given the competing interests, a court of equity is not justified in ignoring that pronouncement under the guise of exercising equitable discretion.

Apart from his vast share of responsibility for the conduct of our foreign relations, the embracing function of the President is that "he shall take Care that the Laws be faithfully executed. . . ." Art. II, § 3. The nature of that authority has for me been comprehensively indicated by Mr. Justice Holmes. "The duty of the President to see that the laws be executed is a duty that does not go beyond the laws or require him to achieve more than Congress sees fit to leave within his power." [10] The powers of the President are not as particularized as are those of Congress. But unenumerated powers do not mean undefined powers. The separation of powers built into our Constitution gives essential content to undefined provisions in the frame of our government.

To be sure, the content of the three authorities of government is not to be derived from an abstract analysis. The areas are partly interacting, not wholly disjointed. The Constitution is a framework for government. Therefore the way the framework has consistently operated fairly establishes that it has operated according to its true

10. Myers v. United States, 272 U.S. 52, 177 (1926). [F.F.]

nature. Deeply embedded traditional ways of conducting government cannot supplant the Constitution or legislation, but they give meaning to the words of a text or supply them. It is an inadmissibly narrow conception of American constitutional law to confine it to the words of the Constitution and to disregard the gloss which life has written upon them. In short, a systematic, unbroken, executive practice, long pursued to the knowledge of the Congress and never before questioned, engaged in by Presidents who have also sworn to uphold the Constitution, making as it were such exercise of power part of the structure of our government, may be treated as a gloss on "executive Power" vested in the President by § 1 of Art. II. . . . .

A scheme of government like ours no doubt at times feels the lack of power to act with complete, all-embracing, swiftly moving authority. No doubt a government with distributed authority, subject to be challenged in the courts of law, at least long enough to consider and adjudicate the challenge, labors under restrictions from which other governments are free. It has not been our tradition to envy such governments. In any event our government was designed to have such restrictions. The price was deemed not too high in view of the safeguards which these restrictions afford. I know no more impressive words on this subject than those of Mr. Justice Brandeis:[11]

"The doctrine of the separation of powers was adopted by the Convention of 1787, not to promote efficiency but to preclude the exercise of arbitrary power. The purpose was, not to avoid friction, but, by means of the inevitable friction incident to the distribution of the governmental powers among three departments, to save the people from autocracy."

It is not a pleasant judicial duty to find that the President has exceeded his powers and still less so when his purposes were dictated by concern for the Nation's well-being, in the assured conviction that he acted to avert danger. But it would stultify one's faith in our people to entertain even a momentary fear that the patriotism and the wisdom of the President and the Congress, as well as the long view of the immediate parties in interest, will not find ready accommodation for differences on matters which, however close to their concern and however intrinsically important, are overshadowed by the awesome issues which confront the world. When at a moment of utmost anxiety President Washington turned to this Court for advice, and he had to be denied it as beyond the Court's competence to give, Chief Justice Jay, on behalf of the Court, wrote thus to the Father of his Country: [12]

11. *Id.* at 240, 293. [F.F.]

12. Letter of 8 August 1793, 3 JOHNSTON, CORRESPONDENCE AND PUBLIC PA-PERS OF JOHN JAY 489 (1891). [F.F.]

"We exceedingly regret every event that may cause embarrassment to your administration, but we derive consolation from the reflection that your judgment will discern what is right, and that your usual prudence, decision, and firmness will surmount every obstacle to the preservation of the rights, peace, and dignity of the United States."

In reaching the conclusion that conscience compels, I too derive consolation from the reflection that the President and the Congress between them will continue to safeguard the heritage which comes to them straight from George Washington.

Frankfurter was again to write in denial of executive authority in *Wiener v. United States*,[13] where the issue was the power of the President to remove a member of the War Claims Commission without cause. This time it was not Truman but Eisenhower whose actions were questioned. Frankfurter, in denying the power, invoked the authority of *Humphrey*, probably the single most disliked judgment of his friend and hero, Franklin D. Roosevelt:[14]

Controversy pertaining to the scope and limits of the President's power of removal fills a thick chapter of our political and judicial history. The long stretches of its history, beginning with the very first Congress, with early echoes in the Reports of this Court, were laboriously traversed in *Myers* v. *United States*,[15] and need not be retraced. President Roosevelt's reliance upon the pronouncements of the Court in that case in removing a member of the Federal Trade Commission on the ground that "the aims and purposes of the Administration with respect to the work of the Commission can be carried out most effectively with personnel of my own selection" reflected contemporaneous professional opinion regarding the significance of the *Myers* decision. Speaking through a Chief Justice who himself had been President, the Court did not restrict itself to the immediate issue before it, the President's inherent power to remove a postmaster, obviously an executive official. As of set purpose and not by way of parenthetic casualness, the Court announced that the President had inherent constitutional power of removal also of officials who had "duties of a quasi-judicial character . . . whose decisions after hearing affect interests of individuals, the discharge of which the President can not in a particular case properly influence or control."[16]

13. 357 U.S. 349 (1958).

14. *Id.* at 351–54.

15. 272 U.S. 52 (1926). [F.F.]

16. *Id.* at 135. [F.F.]

This view of presidential power was deemed to flow from his "constitutional duty of seeing that the laws be faithfully executed." [17]

The assumption was short-lived that the *Myers* case recognized the President's inherent constitutional power to remove officials, no matter what the relation of the executive to the discharge of their duties and no matter what restrictions Congress may have imposed regarding the nature of their tenure. The versatility of circumstances often mocks a natural desire for definitiveness. Within less than ten years a unanimous Court, in *Humphrey's Executor* v. *United States*,[18] narrowly confined the scope of the *Myers* decision to include only "all purely executive officers." [19] The Court explicitly "disapproved" the expressions in *Myers* supporting the President's inherent constitutional power to remove members of quasi-judicial bodies.[20] Congress had given members of the Federal Trade Commission a seven-year term and also provided for the removal of a Commissioner by the President for inefficiency, neglect of duty or malfeasance in office. In the present case, Congress provided for a tenure defined by the relatively short period of time during which the War Claims Commission was to operate — that is, it was to wind up not later than three years after the expiration of the time for filing of claims. But nothing was said in the Act about removal.

This is another instance in which the most appropriate legal significance must be drawn from congressional failure of explicitness. Necessarily this is a problem in probabilities. We start with one certainty. The problem of the President's power to remove members of agencies entrusted with duties of the kind with which the War Claims Commission was charged was within the lively knowledge of Congress. Few contests between Congress and the President have so recurringly had the attention of Congress as that pertaining to the power of removal. Not the least significant aspect of the *Myers* case is that on the Court's special invitation Senator George Wharton Pepper, of Pennsylvania, presented the position of Congress at the bar of this Court.

Humphrey's case was a *cause célèbre* — and not least in halls of Congress. And what is the essence of the decision in Humphrey's case? It drew a sharp line of cleavage between officials who were part of the Executive establishment and were thus removable by virtue of the President's constitutional powers, and those who are members of a body "to exercise its judgment without the leave or hindrance of

17. *Ibid.* [F.F.]
18. 295 U.S. 602 (1935). [F.F.]
19. *Id.* at 628. [F.F.]
20. *Id.* at 626–27. [F.F.]

any other official or any department of the government,"[21] as to whom a power or removal exists only if Congress may fairly be said to have conferred it. This sharp differentiation derives from the difference in functions between those who are part of the Executive establishment and those whose tasks require absolute freedom from Executive interference. "For it is quite evident," again to quote *Humphrey's Executor*, "that one who holds his office only during the pleasure of another, cannot be depended upon to maintain an attitude of independence against the latter's will."[22]

Thus, the most reliable factor for drawing an inference regarding the President's power of removal in our case is the nature of the function that Congress vested in the War Claims Commission. What were the duties that Congress confided to this Commission? And can the inference fairly be drawn from the failure of Congress to provide for removal that these Commissioners were to remain in office at the will of the President? For such is the assertion of power on which petitioner's removal must rest. The ground of President Eisenhower's removal of petitioner was precisely the same as President Roosevelt's removal of Humphrey. Both Presidents desired to have Commissioners, one on the Federal Trade Commission, the other on the War Claims Commission, "of my own selection." They wanted these Commissioners to be their men. The terms of removal in the two cases are identic and express the assumption that the agencies of which the two Commissioners were members were subject in the discharge of their duties to the control of the Executive. An analysis of the Federal Trade Commission Act left this Court in no doubt that such was not the conception of Congress in creating the Federal Trade Commission. The terms of the War Claims Act of 1948 leave no doubt that such was not the conception of Congress regarding the War Claims Commission.

In the realm of foreign affairs, however, Frankfurter would allow more latitude to the chief executive in framing the controlling rules. In *United States v. Pink*,[23] the question was whether the presidential agreement by which the United States agreed to recognize Russia would take precedence over the state law in the disposition of assets claimed by creditors of the Russian regime. Against a telling dissent by Mr. Justice Stone, Frankfurter wrote his concurring opinion:[24]

21. *Id.* at 625–26. [F.F.]
22. *Id.* at 629. [F.F.]
23. 315 U.S. 203 (1942).
24. *Id.* at 240–42.

That the President's control of foreign relations includes the settlement of claims is indisputable. Thus, referring to the adhesion of the United States to the Dawes Plan, Secretary of State Hughes reported that "this agreement was negotiated under the long-recognized authority of the President to arrange for the payment of claims in favor of the United States and its nationals. The exercise of this authority has many illustrations, one of which is the Agreement of 1901 for the so-called Boxer Indemnity." [25] The President's power to negotiate such a settlement is the same whether it is an isolated transaction between this country and a friendly nation, or is part of a complicated negotiation to restore normal relations, as was the case with Russia.

That the power to establish such normal relations with a foreign country belongs to the President is equally indisputable. Recognition of a foreign country is not a theoretical problem or an exercise in abstract symbolism. It is the assertion of national power directed towards safeguarding and promoting our interests and those of civilization. Recognition of a revolutionary government normally involves the removal of areas of friction. As often as not, areas of friction are removed by the adjustment of claims pressed by this country on behalf of its nationals against a new regime.

Such a settlement was made by the President when this country resumed normal relations with Russia. The two chief barriers to renewed friendship with Russia — intrusive propaganda and the effects of expropriation decrees upon our nationals — were at the core of our negotiations in 1933, as they had been for a good many years. The exchanges between the President and M. Litvinov must be read not in isolation but as the culmination of difficulties and dealings extending over fifteen years. And they must be read not as self-contained technical documents, like a marine insurance contract or a bill of lading, but as characteristically delicate and elusive expressions of diplomacy. The draftsmen of such notes must save sensibilities and avoid the explicitness on which diplomatic negotiations so easily founder.

The controlling history of the Soviet regime and of this country's relations with it must be read between the lines of the Roosevelt-Litvinov Agreement. One needs to be no expert in Russian law to know that the expropriation decrees intended to sweep the assets of Russian companies taken over by that government into Russia's control no matter where those assets were credited. Equally clear is it that the assignment by Russia meant to give the United States, as

25. Secretary Hughes to President Coolidge, 3 February 1925, MS, Department of State, quoted in 5 HACKWORTH, DIGEST OF INTERNATIONAL LAW, c. 16, § 514 (1940–44). [F.F.]

part of the comprehensive settlement, everything that Russia claimed under its laws against Russians. It does violence to the course of negotiations between the United States and Russia, and to the scope of the final adjustment, to assume that a settlement thus made on behalf of the United States — to settle both money claims and to soothe feelings — was to be qualified by the variant notions of the courts of the forty-eight states regarding "situs" or "jurisdiction" over intangibles or the survival of extinct Russian corporations. In our dealings with the outside world, the United States speaks with one voice and acts as one, unembarrassed by the complications as to domestic issues which are inherent in the distribution of political power between the national government and the individual states.

So, too, when the question was whether a war had been terminated, so that the stringencies of the Alien Enemy Act might be relieved, as was the case in *Ludecke v. Watkins*,[26] executive authority was held paramount, at least within the latitude provided by the statute: [27]

And so we reach the claim that while the President had summary power under the Act, it did not survive cessation of actual hostilities. This claim in effect nullifies the power to deport alien enemies, for such deportations are hardly practicable during the pendency of what is colloquially known as the shooting war. Nor does law lag behind common sense. War does not cease with a cease-fire order, and power to be exercised by the President such as that conferred by the Act of 1798 is a process which begins when war is declared but is not exhausted when the shooting stops.[28] "The state of war" may be terminated by treaty or legislation or Presidential proclamation. Whatever the mode, its termination is a political act.[29] Whether and when it would be open to this Court to find that a war though merely formally kept alive had in fact ended, is a question too fraught with gravity even to be adequately formulated when not compelled. Only a few months ago the Court rejected the contention that the state of war in relation to which the President has exercised the authority now challenged was terminated.[30] Nothing that has happened since calls for a qualification of that view. It is still true, as was said in the opinion in that case which eyed the war power most jealously, "We have armies abroad

26. 335 U.S. 160 (1948).

27. *Id.* at 166–73.

28. See United States v. Anderson, 9 Wall. 56, 70 (1870); The Protector, 12 Wall. 700 (1872); McElrath v. United States, 102 U.S. 426, 438 (1880); Hamilton v. Kentucky Distilleries Co., 251 U.S. 146, 167 (1919). [F.F.]

29. *Ibid.* [F.F.]

30. Woods v. Miller Co., 333 U.S. 138 (1948). [F.F.]

exercising our war power and have made no peace terms with our allies, not to mention our principal enemies." [31] . . .

The political branch of the Government has not brought the war with Germany to an end. On the contrary, it has proclaimed that "a state of war still exists." [32] The Court would be assuming the functions of the political agencies of the Government to yield to the suggestion that the unconditional surrender of Germany and the disintegration of the Nazi Reich have left Germany without a government capable of negotiating a treaty of peace. It is not for us to question a belief by the President that enemy aliens who were justifiably deemed fit subjects for internment during active hostilities do not lose their potency for mischief during the period of confusion and conflict which is characteristic of a state of war even when the guns are silent but the peace of Peace has not come. These are matters of political judgment for which judges have neither technical competence nor official responsibility.

This brings us to the final question. Is the statute valid as we have construed it? The same considerations of reason, authority, and history, that led us to reject reading the statutory language "declared war" to mean "actual hostilities," support the validity of the statute. The war power is the war power. If the war, as we have held, has not in fact ended, so as to justify local rent control, *a fortiori*, it validly supports the power given to the President by the Act of 1798 in relation to alien enemies. Nor does it require protracted argument to find defect in the Act because resort to the courts may be had only to challenge the construction and validity of the statute and to question the existence of the "declared war," as has been done in this case. The Act is almost as old as the Constitution, and it would savor of doctrinaire audacity now to find the statute offensive to some emanation of the Bill of Rights. The fact that hearings are utilized by the Executive to secure an informed basis for the exercise of summary power does not argue the right of courts to retry such hearings, nor bespeak denial of due process to withhold such power from the courts.

Such great war powers may be abused, no doubt, but that is a bad reason for having judges supervise their exercise, whatever the legal formulas within which such supervision would nominally be confined. In relation to the distribution of constitutional powers among the three branches of the Government, the optimistic Eighteenth

---

31. *Id.* at 147 (concurring opinion). [F.F.]

32. Presidential Proclamation 2714, 12 Fed. Reg. 1 (1946); Woods v. Miller Co., note 30 *supra*, at 140; Fleming v. Mohawk Wrecking & Lumber Co., 331 U.S. 111, 116 (1947). [F.F]

Century language of Mr. Justice Iredell, speaking of this very Act, is still pertinent: [33]

"All systems of government suppose they are to be administered by men of common sense and common honesty. In our country, as all ultimately depends on the voice of the people, they have it in their power, and it is to be presumed they generally will choose men of this description; but if they will not, the case, to be sure, is without remedy. If they choose fools, they will have foolish laws. If they chose knaves, they will have knavish ones. But this can never be the case until they are generally fools or knaves themselves, which, thank God, is not likely ever to become the character of the American people."

Accordingly, we hold that full responsibility for the just exercise of this great power may validly be left where the Congress has constitutionally placed it — on the President of the United States. The Founders in their wisdom made him not only the Commander-in-Chief but also the guiding organ in the conduct of our foreign affairs. He who was entrusted with such vast powers in relation to the outside world was also entrusted by Congress, almost throughout the whole life of the nation, with the disposition of alien enemies during a state of war. Such a page of history is worth more than a volume of rhetoric.

33. Case of Fries, 9 Fed. Cas. No. 5126, 826, at 836 (1799). [F.F.]

6

The Political Thicket

From his first Term on the Court to his last, Mr. Justice Frankfurter was adamant that it was not part of the judicial function to control the behavior or makeup of legislatures except insofar as the legislative action impinged on the defined rights of individuals. Whether the objection took the label of "lack of standing" to sue or of "political question," it was one that would confine the judiciary more severely than either the earlier Court or the late one was willing to accept.

In 1939 the issue was presented by Kansas legislators objecting to the procedures of the Kansas legislature, including the role of the lieutenant governor, in approving the proposed Child Labor Amendment. Frankfurter's personal predilections with regard to national power to regulate and prohibit child labor were well known. That power was to be justified by other judicial decisions. In *Coleman v. Miller*[1] he announced principles of judicial behavior to which he remained true throughout his tenure. He was joined there by Justices Roberts, Black, and Douglas:[2]

In endowing this Court with "judicial Power" the Constitution presupposed an historic content for that phrase and relied on assumption by the judiciary of authority only over issues which are appropriate for disposition by judges. The Constitution further explicitly indicated the limited area within which judicial action was to move — however far-reaching the consequences of action within that area — by extending "judicial Power" only to "Cases" and "Controversies." Both by what they said and by what they implied, the framers of the Judiciary Article gave merely the outlines of what were to them the familiar operations of the English judicial system and its manifestations on this side of the ocean before the Union. Judicial power could come into play only in matters that were the traditional concern of the courts at Westminster and only if they arose in ways that to the expert feel of lawyers constituted "Cases" or "Controversies." It was not for courts to meddle with matters that required no subtlety to be identified as political issues. And even as to the kinds

1. 307 U.S. 433 (1939).
2. *Id.* at 460–65, 467, 469–70.

61

of questions which were the staple of judicial business, it was not for courts to pass upon them as abstract, intellectual problems but only if a concrete, living contest between adversaries called for the arbitrament of law. . . .

As abstractions, these generalities represent common ground among judges. Since, however, considerations governing the exercise of judicial power are not mechanical criteria but derive from conceptions regarding the distribution of governmental powers in their manifold, changing guises, differences in the applications of canons of jurisdiction have arisen from the beginning of the Court's history. Conscious or unconscious leanings toward the serviceability of the judicial process in the adjustment of public controversies clothed in the form of private litigation inevitably affect decisions. For they influence awareness in recognizing the relevance of conceded doctrines of judicial self-limitation and rigor in enforcing them. . . .

Our power to [review the Kansas judgment sustaining the vote of the lieutenant governor] is explicitly challenged by the United States as *amicus curiae*, but would in any event have to be faced. . . . To whom and for what causes the courts of Kansas are open are matters for Kansas to determine. But Kansas cannot define the contours of the authority of the federal courts, and more particularly of this Court. It is our ultimate responsibility to determine who may invoke our judgment and under what circumstances. . . .

It is not our function, and it is beyond our power, to write legal essays or to give legal opinions, however solemnly requested and however great the national emergency. . . . Unlike the rôle allowed to judges in a few state courts and to the Supreme Court of Canada, our exclusive business is litigation. The requisites of litigation are not satisfied when questions of constitutionality though conveyed through the outward forms of a conventional court proceeding do not bear special relation to a particular litigant. The scope and consequences of our doctrine of judicial review over executive and legislative action should make us observe fastidiously the bounds of the litigious process within which we are confined. No matter how seriously infringement of the Constitution may be called into question, this is not the tribunal for its challenge except by those who have some specialized interest of their own to vindicate, apart from a political concern which belongs to all. . . .

Indeed the claim that the Amendment was dead or that it was no longer open to Kansas to ratify, is not only not an interest which belongs uniquely to these Kansas legislators; it is not even an interest special to Kansas. For it is the common concern of every citizen of the United States whether the Amendment is still alive, or whether

Kansas could be included among the necessary "three-fourths of the several States."

These legislators have no more standing on these claims of unconstitutionality to attack "Senate Concurrent Resolution No. 3" than they would have standing here to attack some Kansas statute claimed by them to offend the Commerce Clause. By as much right could a member of Congress who had voted against the passage of a bill because moved by constitutional scruples urge before this Court our duty to consider his arguments of unconstitutionality. . . .

We can only adjudicate an issue as to which there is a claimant before us who has a special, individualized stake in it. One who is merely the self-constituted spokesman of the constitutional point of view can not ask us to pass on it. . . .

The right of the Kansas senators to be here is rested on recognition by *Leser* v. *Garnett*,[3] of a voter's right to protect his franchise. The historic source of this doctrine and the reasons for it were explained in *Nixon* v. *Herndon*.[4] That was an action for $5,000 damages against the Judges of Elections for refusing to permit the plaintiff to vote at a primary election in Texas. In disposing of the objection that the plaintiff had no cause of action because the subject matter of the suit was political, Mr. Justice Holmes thus spoke for the Court: "Of course the petition concerns political action but it alleges and seeks to recover for private damage. That private damage may be caused by such political action and may be recovered for in a suit at law hardly has been doubted for over two hundred years, since *Ashby* v. *White*,[5] and has been recognized by this Court." "Private damage" is the clue to the famous ruling in *Ashby* v. *White*, and determines its scope as well as that of cases in this Court of which it is the justification. The judgment of Lord Holt is permeated with the conception that a voter's franchise is a personal right, assessable in money damages, of which the exact amount "is peculiarly appropriate for the determination of a jury,"[6] and for which there is no remedy outside the law courts. "Although this matter relates to the parliament," said Lord Holt, "yet it is an injury precedaneous to the parliament," as my Lord Hale said in the case of *Bernadiston* v. *Soame*, 2 Lev. 114, 116.[7] The parliament cannot judge of this injury, nor give damage to the plaintiff for it: they cannot make him a recompense."[8]

---

3. 258 U.S. 130 (1922). [F.F.]

4. 273 U.S. 536, 540 (1927). [F.F.]

5. 2 Ld. Raym. 938, 3 *id.* 32. (1703). [F.F.]

6. See Wiley v. Sinkler, 179 U.S. 58, 65 (1900). [F.F.]

7. (1674). [F.F.]

8. 2 Ld. Raym. 938, 958 (1703). [F.F.]

The reasoning of *Ashby* v. *White* and the practice which has followed it leave intra-parliamentary controversies to parliaments and outside the scrutiny of law courts. The procedures for voting in legislative assemblies — who are members, how and when they should vote, what is the requisite number of votes for different phases of legislative activity, what votes were cast and how they were counted — surely are matters that not merely concern political action but are of the very essence of political action, if "political" has any connotation at all. . . . In no sense are they matters of "private damage." They pertain to legislators not as individuals but as political representatives executing the legislative process. To open the law courts to such controversies is to have courts sit in judgment on the manifold disputes engendered by procedures for voting in legislative assemblies. If the doctrine of *Ashby* v. *White* vindicating the private rights of a voting citizen has not been doubted in over two hundred years, it is equally significant that for over two hundred years *Ashby* v. *White* has not been sought to be put to purposes like the present. In seeking redress here these Kansas senators have wholly misconceived the functions of this Court. The writ of *certiorari* to the Kansas Supreme Court should therefore be dismissed.

Mr. Justice Frankfurter's last major constitutional pronouncement was rendered in *Baker* v. *Carr*[9] in which he spelled out in dissent the case for judicial abstention from the reapportionment of state and federal legislatures. That the Court had never before ventured on such an effort was clear. The essential argument against leaving this political problem for political resolution was that the legislators would never impinge on their own prerogatives. And certain it was that the mandates of the state constitutions for decennial or regular reapportionment had been treated by the state legislatures as if they did not exist. On the other hand, the history of the development of the franchise in this country and in England reveals that when the populace demands democratization, it has been forthcoming, whatever adverse effects it might have on incumbent officeholders. The fact was that, except for a few crusaders, the public was rather unconcerned with the issue. No political contests were waged over the problem. There was no popular movement for reapportionment.

Frankfurter's grim forebodings about the effect of judicial intervention have been proved false. The decisions have received not so much public acclaim as public disdain. Legislative reapportionment has proved irrelevant to the major issues of our time. Those who con-

9. 369 U.S. 186 (1962).

trolled state legislatures in the past still control state legislatures. New legislators have not brought about new legislation. The impotence of state government may be one reason for the miniscule change in fact brought about by what promised, in theory, to be a major break with the past.

It is not possible to measure the contribution of the reapportionment decisions to the decline of the Court's popularity recorded by the Gallup and Harris polls. One is inclined to believe that this fall from grace is attributable more to the Court's decisions in the areas of criminal procedure, obscenity regulation, and school prayers. But the reapportionment decisions may have provided one more straw to the burden of opprobrium that the Court now carries.

Frankfurter's last cry for leaving responsibility for political change with the political processes was an elegant one. To say that it will not emerge triumphant when a new Court in a new era reconsiders the role of the judiciary in the apportionment of state legislatures would be to indulge prognosis no less dubious than the Justice's own: [10]

The Court today reverses a uniform course of decision established by a dozen cases, including one by which the very claim now sustained was unanimously rejected only five years ago. The impressive body of rulings thus cast aside reflected the equally uniform course of our political history regarding the relationship between population and legislative representation — a wholly different matter from denial of the franchise to individuals because of race, color, religion or sex. Such a massive repudiation of the experience of our whole past in asserting destructively novel judicial power demands a detailed analysis of the role of this Court in our constitutional scheme. Disregard of inherent limits in the effective exercise of the Court's "judicial Power" not only presages the futility of judicial intervention in the essentially political conflict of forces by which the relation between population and representation has time out of mind been and now is determined. It may well impair the Court's position as the ultimate organ of "the supreme Law of the Land" in that vast range of legal problems, often strongly entangled in popular feeling, on which this Court must pronounce. The Court's authority — possessed of neither the purse nor the sword — ultimately rests on sustained public confidence in its moral sanction. Such feeling must be nourished by the Court's complete detachment, in fact and in appearance, from political entanglements and by abstention from injecting itself into the clash of political forces in political settlements. . . .

. . . In effect, today's decision empowers the courts of the country

10. *Id.* at 266–67, 269–70, 297, 299–302, 323–24.

to devise what should constitute the proper composition of the legislatures of the fifty States. If state courts should for one reason or another
find themselves unable to discharge this task, the duty of doing so
is put on the federal courts or on this Court, if State views do not
satisfy this Court's notion of what is proper districting.

. . . The Framers carefully and with deliberate forethought refused
so to enthrone the judiciary. In this situation, as in others of like
nature, appeal for relief does not belong here. Appeal must be to an
informed, civically militant electorate. In a democratic society like
ours, relief must come through an aroused popular conscience that
sears the conscience of the people's representatives. In any event there
is nothing judicially more unseemly nor more self-defeating than
for this Court to make *in terrorem* pronouncements, to indulge in
merely empty rhetoric, sounding a word of promise to the ear, sure
to be disappointing to the hope. . . .

The present case involves all of the elements that have made the
Guarantee Clause cases non-justiciable. It is, in effect, a Guarantee
Clause claim masquerading under a different label. But it cannot
make the case more fit for judicial action that appellants invoke the
Fourteenth Amendment rather than Art. IV, § 4, where, in fact, the
gist of their complaint is the same — unless it can be found that the
Fourteenth Amendment speaks with greater particularity to their
situation. . . .

What, then, is this question of legislative apportionment? Appellants invoke the right to vote and to have their votes counted. But
they are permitted to vote and their votes are counted. They go to
the polls, they cast their ballots, they send their representatives to the
state councils. Their complaint is simply that the representatives are
not sufficiently numerous or powerful — in short, that Tennessee
has adopted a basis of representation with which they are dissatisfied.
Talk of "debasement" or "dilution" is circular talk. One cannot
speak of "debasement" or "dilution" of the value of a vote until there
is first defined a standard of reference as to what a vote should be
worth. What is actually asked of the Court in this case is to choose
among competing bases of representation — ultimately, really, among
competing theories of political philosophy — in order to establish
an appropriate frame of government for the State of Tennessee and
thereby for all the States of the Union.

In such a matter, abstract analogies which ignore the facts of history
deal in unrealities; they betray reason. This is not a case in which a
State has, through a device however oblique and sophisticated, denied
Negroes or Jews or redheaded persons a vote, or given them only
a third or a sixth of a vote. That was *Gomillion* v. *Lightfoot*.[11] What

11. 364 U.S. 339 (1960).

Tennessee illustrates is an old and still widespread method of representation — representation by local geographical division, only in part respective of population — in preference to others, others, forsooth, more appealing. Appellants contest this choice and seek to make this Court the arbiter of the disagreement. They would make the Equal Protection Clause the charter of adjudication, asserting that the equality which it guarantees comports, if not the assurance of equal weight to every voter's vote, at least the basic conception that representation ought to be proportionate to population, a standard by reference to which the reasonableness of apportionment plans may be judged.

To find such a political conception legally enforceable in the broad and unspecific guarantee of equal protection is to rewrite the Constitution.[12] Certainly, "equal protection" is no more secure a foundation for judicial judgment of the permissibility of varying forms of representative government than is "Republican Form." Indeed since "equal protection of the laws" can only mean an equality of persons standing in the same relation to whatever governmental action is challenged, the determination whether treatment is equal presupposes a determination concerning the nature of the relationship. This, with respect to apportionment, means an inquiry into the theoretic base of representation in an acceptably republican state. For a court could not determine the equal-protection issue without in fact first determining the Republican-Form issue, simply because what is reasonable for equal-protection purposes will depend upon what frame of government, basically, is allowed. To divorce "equal protection" from "Republican Form" is to talk about half a question.

The notion that representation proportioned to the geographic spread of population is so universally accepted as a necessary element of equality between man and man that it must be taken to be the standard of a political equality preserved by the Fourteenth Amendment — that it is, in appellants' words "the basic principle of representative government" — is, to put it bluntly, not true. However desirable and however desired by some among the great political thinkers and framers of our government, it has never been generally practiced, today or in the past. It was not the English system, it was not the colonial system, it was not the system chosen for the national government by the Constitution, it was not the system exclusively or even predominantly practiced by the States at the time of adoption of the Fourteenth Amendment, it is not predominantly practiced by the States today. Unless judges, the judges of this Court, are to make their private views of political wisdom the measure of the Constitution — views which in all honesty cannot but give the appearance, if not

12. Luther v. Borden, 7 How. 1 (1849). [F.F.]

reflect the reality, of involvement with the business of partisan politics so inescapably a part of apportionment controversies — the Fourteenth Amendment, "itself a historical product," [13] provides no guide for judicial oversight of the representation problem. . . .

Manifestly, the Equal Protection Clause supplies no clearer guide for judicial examination of apportionment methods than would the Guarantee Clause itself. Apportionment, by its character, is a subject of extraordinary complexity, involving — even after the fundamental theoretical issues concerning what is to be represented in a representative legislature have been fought out or compromised — considerations of geography, demography, electoral convenience, economic and social cohesions or divergencies among particular local groups, communications, the practical effects of political institutions like the lobby and the city machine, ancient traditions and ties of settled usage, respect for proven incumbents of long experience and senior status, mathematical mechanics, censuses compiling relevant data, and a host of others. Legislative responses throughout the country to the reapportionment demands of the 1960 Census have glaringly confirmed that these are not factors that lend themselves to evaluations of a nature that are the staple of judicial determinations or for which judges are equipped to adjudicate by legal training or experience or native wit. And this is the more so true because in every strand of this complicated, intricate web of values meet the contending forces of partisan politics. The practical significance of apportionment is that the next election results may differ because of it. Apportionment battles are overwhelmingly party or intra-party contests. It will add a virulent source of friction and tension in federal-state relations to embroil the federal judiciary in them.

It was not that the Court was not available to invoke the protection of the Equal Protection Clause for an individual deprived of his rights to participate in the political processes. Thus, Frankfurter wrote in his concurring opinion in *Snowden v. Hughes*: [14]

All questions pertaining to the political arrangements of state governments are, no doubt, peculiarly outside the domain of federal authority. The disposition of state offices, the manner in which they should be filled and contests concerning them, are solely for state determination, always provided that the equality of treatment required by the Civil War Amendments is respected. And so I appreciate that there are strong considerations of policy which make federal courts inhospitable toward litigation involving the enforcement of state

13. Jackman v. Rosenbaum Co., 260 U.S. 22, 31 (1922). [F.F.]
14. 321 U.S. 1, 14–15 (1944).

election laws. But I do not think that the criteria for establishing a denial of the equal protection of the laws are any different in cases of discrimination in granting opportunities for presenting oneself as a candidate for office "as one of the nominees of the Republican Party" than those that are relevant when claim is made that a state has discriminated in regulating the pursuit of a private calling.

The hard problem was rather that of *Colegrove v. Green*,[15] which was overruled by *Baker v. Carr*, where the injury complained of was an injury to the polity not to the individual. Cures for such wrongs should be sought elsewhere than in the judiciary:[16]

We are of opinion that the appellants ask of this Court what is beyond its competence to grant. This is one of those demands on judicial power which cannot be met by verbal fencing about "jurisdiction." It must be resolved by considerations on the basis of which this Court, from time to time, has refused to intervene in controversies. It has refused to do so because due regard for the effective working of our Government revealed this issue to be of a peculiarly political nature and therefore not meet for judicial determination.

This is not an action to recover for damage because of the discriminatory exclusion of a plaintiff from rights enjoyed by other citizens. The basis for the suit is not a private wrong, but a wrong suffered by Illinois as a polity.[17] In effect this is an appeal to the federal courts to reconstruct the electoral process of Illinois in order that it may be adequately represented in the councils of the Nation. Because the Illinois legislature has failed to revise its Congressional Representative districts in order to reflect great changes, during more than a generation, in the distribution of its population, we are asked to do this, as it were, for Illinois.

. . . Nothing is clearer than that this controversy concerns matters that bring courts into immediate and active relations with party contests. From the determination of such issues this Court has traditionally held aloof. It is hostile to a democratic system to involve the judiciary in the politics of the people. And it is not less pernicious if such judicial intervention in an essentially political contest be dressed up in the abstract phrases of the law. . . .

To sustain this action would cut very deep into the very being of Congress. Courts ought not to enter this political thicket. The remedy for unfairness in districting is to secure State legislatures that will

15. 328 U.S. 549 (1946).

16. *Id.* at 552–54, 556.

17. *Compare* Nixon v. Herndon, 273 U.S. 536 (1927), and Lane v. Wilson, 307 U.S. 268 (1939), *with* Giles v. Harris, 189 U.S. 475 (1903). [F.F.]

apportion properly, or to invoke the ample powers of Congress. The Constitution has many commands that are not enforceable by courts because they clearly fall outside the conditions and purposes that circumscribe judicial action. Thus, "on Demand of the executive Authority," Art. IV, § 2, of a State it is the duty of a sister State to deliver up a fugitive from justice. But the fulfilment of this duty cannot be judicially enforced.[18] The duty to see to it that the laws are faithfully executed cannot be brought under legal compulsion.[19] Violation of the great guaranty of a republican form of government in States cannot be challenged in the courts.[20] The Constitution has left the performance of many duties in our government scheme to depend on the fidelity of the executive and legislative action and, ultimately, on the vigilance of the people in exercising their political rights.

This language sounds old-fashioned at a time when the Court's duty to act purports to rest at least as much on the defaults of the other branches of government as on the power delegated by the Constitution. Perhaps, if the reins of government are once again taken in hand by the political branches, the Court may surrender them, voluntarily or otherwise.

The mandate of the Fifteenth Amendment, however, was clearer for Mr. Justice Frankfurter than those of the Fourteenth Amendment. And because the objective of the rule was so pellucid, he was the more ready to use the Court's power to effectuate it. Even so, there were troublesome questions. For him, the Fifteenth Amendment was still a limitation on state action and not on that of individuals. When a group organized for purposes of seizing political power excludes Negroes from its membership, has it violated the Fifteenth Amendment because the primaries that it runs are, in fact, decisive of the subsequent elections? The Justice, not without recognizing the difficulties, decided in *Terry v. Adams*[21] that the Fifteenth Amendment had been breached by this conduct:[22]

This case is for me by no means free of difficulty. Whenever the law draws a line between permissive and forbidden conduct cases are bound to arise which are not obviously on one side or the other. These dubious situations disclose the limited utility of the figure of

18. Kentucky v. Denison, 24 How. 66 (1861). [F.F.]
19. Mississippi v. Johnson, 4 Wall. 475 (1867). [F.F.]
20. Pacific Telephone Co. v. Oregon, 223 U.S. 118 (1912). [F.F.]
21. 345 U.S. 461 (1953).
22. *Id.* at 472–77.

speech, a "line," in the law. Drawing a "line" is necessarily exercising a judgment, however confined the conscientious judgment may be within the bounds of constitutional and statutory provisions, the course of decisions, and the presuppositions of the judicial process. If "line" is in the main a fruitful tool for dividing the sheep from the goats, it must not be forgotten that since the "line" is figuratively the place of this or that case in relation to it cannot be ascertained externally but is a matter of the mind.

Close analysis of what it is that the Fifteenth Amendment prohibits must be made before it can be determined what the relevant line is in the situation presented by this case. The Fifteenth Amendment, not the Fourteenth, outlawed discrimination on the basis of race or color with respect to the right to vote. Concretely, of course, it was directed against attempts to bar Negroes from having the same political franchise as white folk. "The right of citizens of the United States to vote shall not be denied or abridged by the United States or by any State on account of race, color, or previous condition of servitude." U.S. Const., Amend. XV, § 1. The command against such denial or abridgment is directed to the United States and to the individual States. Therefore, violation of this Amendment and the enactments passed in enforcement of it must involve the United States or a State. In this case the conduct that is assailed pertains to the election of local Texas officials. To find a denial or abridgment of the guaranteed voting right to colored citizens of Texas solely because they are colored, one must find that the State has had a hand in it.

The State, in these situations, must mean not private citizens but those clothed with the authority and the influence which official position affords. The application of the prohibition of the Fifteenth Amendment to "any State" is translated by legal jargon to read "State action." This phrase gives rise to a false direction in that it implies some impressive machinery or deliberative conduct normally associated with what orators call a sovereign state. The vital requirement is State responsibility — that somewhere, somehow, to some extent, there be an infusion of conduct by officials, panoplied with State power, into any scheme by which colored citizens are denied voting rights merely because they are colored.

As the action of the entire white voting community, the Jaybird primary is as a practical matter the instrument of those few in this small county who are politically active — the officials of the local Democratic party and, we may assume, the elected officials of the county. As a matter of practical politics, those charged by State law with the duty of assuring all eligible voters an opportunity to participate in the selection of candidates at the primary — the county election officials who are normally leaders in their communities —

participate by voting in the Jaybird primary. They join the white voting community in proceeding with elaborate formality, in almost all respects parallel to the procedures dictated by Texas law for the primary itself, to express their preferences in a wholly successful effort to withdraw significance from the State-prescribed primary, to subvert the operation of what is formally the law of the State for primaries in this county. . . .

The State of Texas has entered into a comprehensive scheme of regulation of political primaries, including procedures by which election officials shall be chosen. The county election officials are thus clothed with the authority of the State to secure observance of the State's interest in "fair methods and a fair expression" of preferences in the selection of nominees.[23] If the Jaybird Association, although not a political party, is a device to defeat the law of Texas regulating primaries, and if the electoral officials, clothed with State power in the county, share in that subversion, they cannot divest themselves of the State authority and help as participants in the scheme. Unlawful administration of a State statute fair on its face may be shown "by extrinsic evidence showing a discriminatory design to favor one individual or class over another not to be inferred from the action itself";[24] here, the county election officials aid in this subversion of the State's official scheme of which they are trustees, by helping as participants in the scheme.

This is not a case of occasional efforts to mass voting strength. Nor is this a case of boss-control, whether crudely or subtly exercised. Nor is this a case of spontaneous efforts by citizens to influence votes or even continued efforts by a fraction of the electorate in support of good government. This is a case in which county election officials have participated in and condoned a continued effort effectively to exclude Negroes from voting. Though the action of the Association as such may not be proscribed by the Fifteenth Amendment, its role in the entire scheme to subvert the operation of the official primary brings it "within reach of the law. . . . [T]hey are bound together as the parts of a single plan. The plan may make the parts unlawful."[25]

The State here devised a process for primary elections. The right of all citizens to share in it, and not to be excluded by unconstitutional bars, is emphasized by the fact that in Texas nomination in the Democratic primary is tantamount to election. The exclusion of the

23. *Cf.* Waples v. Marrast, 108 Tex. 5, 12, 184 S.W. 180, 183 (1916). [F.F.]

24. Snowden v. Hughes, 321 U.S. 1, 8 (1944). [F.F.]

25. Mr. Justice Holmes, speaking for the Court, in Swift & Company v. United States, 196 U.S. 375, 396 (1905). [F.F.]

Negroes from meaningful participation in the only primary scheme
set up by the State was not an accidental, unsought consequence of
the exercise of civic rights by voters to make their common viewpoint
count. It was the design, the very purpose of this arrangement that
the Jaybird primary in May exclude Negro participation in July.
That it was the action in part of the election officials charged by Texas
law with the fair administration of the primaries, brings it within the
reach of the law. The officials made themselves party to means
whereby the machinery with which they are entrusted does not
discharge the functions for which it was designed.

Again, when the city of Tuskegee, Alabama, redrew its boundaries,
converting it "from a square to an uncouth twenty-eight-sided figure,"
with the sole result of excluding all but a few Negroes from participation in municipal elections, Frankfurter found a situation clearly dis-
tinguishable from the "political question" he would have eschewed
in *Colegrove v. Green* and *Baker v. Carr. Gomillion v. Lightfoot*[26]
presented a gerrymander that violated the Fifteenth Amendment:[27]

When a legislature thus singles out a readily isolated segment of a
racial minority for special discriminatory treatment, it violates the
Fifteenth Amendment. In no case involving unequal weight in voting
distribution that has come before the Court did the decision sanction
a differentiation on racial lines whereby approval was given to
unequivocal withdrawal of the vote solely from colored citizens.
Apart from all else, these considerations lift this controversy out of
the so-called "political" arena and into the conventional sphere of
constitutional litigation.

In sum, as Mr. Justice Holmes remarked, when dealing with a
related situation, "Of course the petition concerns political action,"
but "The objection that the subject matter of the suit is political is
little more than a play upon words."[28] A statute which is alleged to
have worked unconstitutional deprivations of petitioners' rights is
not immune to attack simply because the mechanism employed by
the legislature is a redefinition of municipal boundaries. According
to the allegations here made, the Alabama Legislature has not merely
redrawn the Tuskegee city limits with incidental inconvenience to
the petitioners; it is more accurate to say that it has deprived the
petitioners of the municipal franchise and consequent rights and to
that end it has incidentally changed the city's boundaries. While in
form this is merely an act redefining metes and bounds, if the allegations

26. 364 U.S. 339 (1960).

27. *Id.* at 346–48.

28. Nixon v. Herndon, 273 U.S. 536, 540 (1927). [F.F.]

are established, the inescapable human effect of this essay in geometry and geography is to despoil colored citizens, and only colored citizens, of their theretofore enjoyed voting rights. . . .

When a State exercises power wholly within the domain of state interest, it is insulated from federal judicial review. But such insulation is not carried over when state power is used as an instrument for circumventing a federally protected right. This principle has had many applications. It has long been recognized in cases which have prohibited a State from exploiting a power acknowledged to be absolute in an isolated context to justify the imposition of an "unconstitutional condition." What the Court has said in those cases is equally applicable here, *viz.*, that "Acts generally lawful may become unlawful when done to accomplish an unlawful end,[29] and a constitutional power cannot be used by way of condition to attain an unconstitutional result."[30]

What Mr. Justice Frankfurter was unwilling to recognize was the fact that differences that were evident to him were not evident to all his brethren. *Gomillion* as surely led to *Baker v. Carr* as Pavlov's bells led to his dogs' salivation.

29. United States v. Reading Co., 226 U.S. 324, 357 (1912). [F.F.]
30. Western Union Telegraph Co. v. Foster, 247 U.S. 105, 114 (1918). [F.F.]

7 Freedom of Speech and Association

The essential shift in judicial doctrine that marked Mr. Justice Frankfurter's tenure on the Court — the period between the fall of the Nine Old Men and the rise of the Warren Court — was one from substantive due process in the economic area to substantive due process and substantive equal protection in the area of civil liberties. In this day, the phrase "freedom of association" rings truer and louder as a solution to difficult problems than the answer formed by the words "freedom of contract." And the Court is regarded as more competent to act as guardian of the former than of the latter.

The shift was not so easy for Frankfurter as for some of his brethren. Certainly he rejected the notion of the Court as the master economist and social planner of its time. "It is equally immaterial that such state action may run counter to the economic wisdom either of Adam Smith or J. Maynard Keynes, or be ultimately mischievous even from the point of view of avowed state policy."[1] And he recognized that "the right to free discussion . . . is to be guarded with a jealous eye."[2] But, for him, this still left great problems in the resolution of the difficult cases involving the Bill of Rights. For he refused to be bemused by simplistic construction of the First Amendment or the rationalization of a hierarchy of constitutional rights. These cases, therefore, however simple for some of the Justices, remained always, for him, deep problems of judicial statesmanship.

Frankfurter was never able to accommodate to the notion of the Constitution's grand clauses as fixed and unbending formulas that meant the same thing regardless of the circumstances that called forth their application. And this was true whether the constitutional provisions involved were those of the Commerce Clause or of the First Amendment. As he said in *Martin v. Struthers*:[3]

From generation to generation, fresh vindication is given to the prophetic wisdom of the framers of the Constitution in casting it in

1. Osborn v. Ozlin, 310 U.S. 53, 62 (1940).

2. A. F. of L. v. Swing, 312 U.S. 321, 325 (1941).

3. 319 U.S. 141, 152 (1943).

75

terms so broad that it has adaptable vitality for the drastic changes in our society which they knew to be inevitable, even though they could not foresee them. Thus it has come to be that the transforming consequences resulting from the pervasive industrialization of life find the Commerce Clause appropriate, for instance, for national regulation of an aircraft flight wholly within a single state. Such exertion of power by the national government over what might seem a purely local transaction would, as a matter of abstract law, have been as unimaginable to Marshall as to Jefferson, precisely because neither could have foreseen the present conquest of the air by man. But law, whether derived from acts of Congress or the Constitution, is not an abstraction. The Constitution cannot be applied in disregard of the external circumstances in which men live and move and have their being. Therefore, neither the First nor the Fourteenth Amendment is to be treated by judges as though it were a mathematical abstraction, an absolute having no relation to the lives of men.

Nor was he prepared to accept the notion of a "preferred position" for the provisions of the Bill of Rights. He traced the history of that notion in his opinion in *Kovacs v. Cooper*[4] and explained why he would not accede to it:[5]

Wise accommodation between liberty and order always has been, and ever will be, indispensable for a democratic society. Insofar as the Constitution commits the duty of making this accommodation to this Court, it demands vigilant judicial self-restraint. A single decision by a closely divided court, unsupported by the confirmation of time, cannot check the living process of striking a wise balance between liberty and order as new cases come here for adjudication. . . .

The opinions in this case prompt me to make some additional observations. My brother REED speaks of "the preferred position of freedom of speech," though, to be sure, he finds that the Trenton ordinance does not disregard it. This is a phrase that has uncritically crept into some recent opinions of this Court. I deem it a mischievous phrase, if it carries the thought, which it may subtly imply, that any law touching communication is infected with presumptive invalidity. It is not the first time in the history of constitutional adjudication that such a doctrinaire attitude has disregarded the admonition most to be observed in exercising the Court's reviewing power over legislation, "that it is a *constitution* we are expounding."[6] I say the phrase is mischievous because it radiates a constitutional doctrine

4. 336 U.S. 77 (1949).

5. *Id.* at 89–90, 94–96.

6. McCulloch v. Maryland, 4 Wheat. 316, 407 (1819). [F.F.]

without avowing it. Clarity and candor in these matters, so as to avoid gliding unwittingly into error, make it appropriate to trace the history of the phrase "preferred position." . . .

In short, the claim that any legislation is presumptively unconstitutional which touches the field of the First Amendment and the Fourteenth Amendment, insofar as the latter's concept of "liberty" contains what is specifically protected by the First, has never commended itself to a majority of this Court.

Behind the notion sought to be expressed by the formula as to "the preferred position of freedom of speech" lies a relevant consideration in determining whether an enactment relating to the liberties protected by the Due Process Clause of the Fourteenth Amendment is violative of it. In law also, doctrine is illuminated by history. The ideas now governing the constitutional protection of freedom of speech derive essentially from the opinions of Mr. Justice Holmes.

The philosophy of his opinions on that subject arose from a deep awareness of the extent to which sociological conclusions are conditioned by time and circumstance. Because of this awareness Mr. Justice Holmes seldom felt justified in opposing his own opinion to economic views which the legislature embodied in law. But since he also realized that the progress of civilization is to a considerable extent the displacement of error which once held sway as official truth by beliefs which in turn have yielded to other beliefs, for him the right to search for truth was of a different order than some transient economic dogma. And without freedom of expression, thought becomes checked and atrophied. Therefore, in considering what interests are so fundamental as to be enshrined in the Due Process Clause, those liberties of the individual which history has attested as the indispensable conditions of an open as against a closed society come to this Court with a momentum for respect lacking when appeal is made to liberties which derive merely from shifting economic arrangements. Accordingly, Mr. Justice Holmes was far more ready to find legislative invasion where free inquiry was involved than in the debatable area of economics.[7]

The objection to summarizing this line of thought by the phrase "the preferred position of freedom of speech" is that it expresses a complicated process of constitutional adjudication by a deceptive formula. And it was Mr. Justice Holmes who admonished us that "To rest upon a formula is a slumber that, prolonged, means death."[8] Such a formula makes for mechanical jurisprudence.

---

7. See FRANKFURTER, MR. JUSTICE HOLMES AND THE SUPREME COURT 58 *et seq.* (1938). [F.F.]

8. HOLMES, COLLECTED LEGAL PAPERS 306 (1920). [F.F.]

In the realm of political activity, Frankfurter, in weighing claims for freedom of speech, recognized the nation's interest in self-preservation as a valid competing factor against a claim of freedom of speech. Probably no attitude that he displayed on the Court caused greater alienation of Frankfurter's "liberal" friends than his willingness to balance, as he did in *Dennis v. United States*,[9] claims for the right to political advocacy of the overthrow of the government against claims for national security, and then to concede what was a determining influence to the judgment of the national legislature. Again, agreement or disagreement with his conclusion, however, is not so important as the revelation of Frankfurter's methods of dealing with what he regarded as complex, if basic, constitutional issues. For him, there were no simple, no less simplistic, answers:[10]

"The law is perfectly well settled," this Court said over fifty years ago, "that the first ten amendments to the Constitution, commonly known as the Bill of Rights, were not intended to lay down any novel principles of government, but simply to embody certain guaranties and immunities which we had inherited from our English ancestors, and which had from time immemorial been subject to certain well-recognized exceptions arising from the necessities of the case. In incorporating these principles into the fundamental law there was no intention of disregarding the exceptions, which continued to be recognized as if they had been formally expressed."[11] That this represents the authentic view of the Bill of Rights and the spirit in which it must be construed has been recognized again and again in cases that have come here within the last fifty years.[12] Absolute rules would inevitably lead to absolute exceptions, and such exceptions would eventually corrode the rules. The demands of free speech in a democratic society as well as the interest in national security are better served by candid and informed weighing of the competing interests, within the confines of the judicial process, than by announcing dogmas too inflexible for the non-Euclidian problems to be solved.

But how are competing interests to be assessed? Since they are not subject to quantitative ascertainment, the issue necessarily resolves itself into asking, who is to make the adjustment? — who is to balance the relevant factors and ascertain which interest is in the circumstances to prevail? Full responsibility for the choice cannot

---

9. 341 U.S. 494 (1951).

10. *Id.* at 524–25, 542–53, 555–56.

11. Robertson v. Baldwin, 165 U.S. 275, 281 (1897). [F.F.]

12. See, *e.g.*, Gompers v. United States, 233 U.S. 604, 610 (1914). [F.F.]

be given to the courts. Courts are not representative bodies. They are not designed to be a good reflex of a democratic society. Their judgment is best informed, and therefore most dependable, within narrow limits. Their essential quality is detachment, founded on independence. History teaches that the independence of the judiciary is jeopardized when courts become embroiled in the passions of the day and assume primary responsibility in choosing between competing political, economic and social pressures. . . .

. . . A survey of the relevant decisions indicates that the results which we have reached are on the whole those that would ensue from careful weighing of conflicting interests. The complex issues presented by regulation of speech in public places, by picketing, and by legislation prohibiting advocacy of crime have been resolved by scrutiny of many factors besides the imminence and gravity of the evil threatened. The matter has been well summarized by a reflective student of the Court's work. "The truth is that the clear-and-present-danger test is an oversimplified judgment unless it takes account also of a number of other factors: the relative seriousness of the danger in comparison with the value of the occasion for speech or political activity; the availability of more moderate controls than those which the state has imposed; and perhaps the specific intent with which the speech or activity is launched. No matter how rapidly we utter the phrase 'clear and present danger,' or how closely we hyphenate the words, they are not a substitute for the weighing of values. They tend to convey a delusion of certitude when what is most certain is the complexity of the strands in the web of freedoms which the judge must disentangle." [13]

It is a familiar experience in the law that new situations do not fit neatly into legal conceptions that arose under different circumstances to satisfy different needs. So it was when the injunction was tortured into an instrument of oppression against labor in industrial conflicts. So it is with the attempt to use the direction of thought lying behind the criterion of "clear and present danger" wholly out of the context in which it originated, and to make of it an absolute dogma and definitive measuring rod for the power of Congress to deal with assaults against security through devices other than overt physical attempts.

Bearing in mind that Mr. Justice Holmes regarded questions under the First Amendment as questions of "proximity and degree," [14] it would be a distortion, indeed a mockery, of his reasoning to compare the "puny anonymities," [15] to which he was addressing

13. FREUND, ON UNDERSTANDING THE SUPREME COURT 27–28 (1949). [F.F.]

14. Schenck v. United States, 249 U.S. 47, 52 (1919). [F.F.]

15. Abrams v. United States, 250 U.S. 616, 629 (1919). [F.F.]

himself in the *Abrams* case in 1919 or the publication that was "futile and too remote from possible consequences,"[16] in the *Gitlow* case in 1925 with the setting of events in this case in 1950.

It does an ill-service to the author of the most quoted judicial phrases regarding freedom of speech, to make him the victim of a tendency which he fought all his life, whereby phrases are made to do service for critical analysis by being turned into dogma. "It is one of the misfortunes of the law that ideas become encysted in phrases and thereafter for a long time cease to provoke further analysis."[17] The phrase "clear and present danger," in its origin, "served to indicate the importance of freedom of speech to a free society but also to emphasize that its exercise must be compatible with the preservation of other freedoms essential to a democracy and guaranteed by our Constitution."[18] It were far better that the phrase be abandoned than that it be sounded once more to hide from the believers in an absolute right of free speech the plain fact that the interest in speech, profoundly important as it is, is no more conclusive in judicial review than other attributes of democracy or than a determination of the people's representatives that a measure is necessary to assure the safety of government itself. . . .

The defendants have been convicted of conspiring to organize a party of persons who advocate the overthrow of the Government by force and violence. The jury has found that the object of the conspiracy is advocacy as "a rule or principle of action," "by language reasonably and ordinarily calculated to incite persons to such action," and with the intent to cause the overthrow "as speedily as circumstances would permit."

On any scale of values which we have hitherto recognized, speech of this sort ranks low.

Throughout our decisions there has recurred a distinction between the statement of an idea which may prompt its hearers to take unlawful action, and advocacy that such action be taken. The distinction has its root in the conception of the common law, supported by principles of morality, that a person who procures another to do an act is responsible for that act as though he had done it himself. . . .

It is true that there is no divining rod by which we may locate "advocacy." Exposition of ideas readily merges into advocacy. The same Justice who gave currency to application of the incitement doctrine in this field dissented four times from what he thought was

16. Gitlow v. New York, 268 U.S. 652, 673 (1925). [F.F.]

17. Holmes, J., dissenting, in Hyde v. United States, 225 U.S. 347, 391 (1912). [F.F.]

18. Pennekamp v. Florida, 328 U.S. 331, 352–53 (1946) (concurring opinion). [F.F.]

its misapplication. As he said in the *Gitlow* dissent, "Every idea is an incitement." [19] Even though advocacy of overthrow deserves little protection, we should hesitate to prohibit it if we thereby inhibit the interchange of rational ideas so essential to representative government and free society.

But there is underlying validity in the distinction between advocacy and the interchange of ideas, and we do not discard a useful tool because it may be misused. That such a distinction could be used unreasonably by those in power against hostile or unorthodox views does not negate the fact that it may be used reasonably against an organization wielding the power of the centrally controlled international Communist movement. The object of the conspiracy before us is so clear that the chance of error in saying that the defendants conspired to advocate rather than to express ideas is slight. MR. JUSTICE DOUGLAS quite properly points out that the conspiracy before us is not a conspiracy to overthrow the Government. But it would be equally wrong to treat it as a seminar in political theory.

These general considerations underlie decision of the case before us.

On the one hand is the interest in security. The Communist Party was not designed by these defendants as an ordinary political party. For the circumstances of its organization, its aim and methods, and the relation of the defendants to its organization and aims we are concluded by the jury's verdict. The jury found that the Party rejects the basic premise of our political system — that change is to be brought about by nonviolent constitutional process. The jury found that the Party advocates the theory that there is a duty and necessity to overthrow the Government by force and violence. It found that the Party entertains and promotes this view, not as a prophetic insight or as a bit of unworldly speculation, but as a program for winning adherents and as a policy to be translated into action.

In finding that the defendants violated the statute, we may not treat as established fact that the Communist Party in this country is of significant size, well-organized, well-disciplined, conditioned to embark on unlawful activity when given the command. But in determining whether application of the statute to the defendants is within the constitutional powers of Congress, we are not limited to the facts found by the jury. We must view such a question in the light of whatever is relevant to a legislative judgment. We may take judicial notice that the Communist doctrines which these defendants have conspired to advocate are in the ascendency in powerful nations who cannot be acquitted of unfriendliness to the institutions of this country. We may take account of evidence brought forward at this trial and elsewhere, much of which has long been common knowledge.

19. 268 U.S. at 673. [F.F.]

In sum, it would amply justify a legislature in concluding that recruitment of additional members for the Party would create a substantial danger to national security. . . .

On the other hand is the interest in free speech. The right to exert all governmental powers in aid of maintaining our institutions and resisting their physical overthrow does not include intolerance of opinions and speech that cannot do harm although opposed and perhaps alien to dominant, traditional opinion. The treatment of its minorities, especially their legal position, is among the most searching tests of the level of civilization attained by a society. It is better for those who have almost unlimited power of government in their hands to err on the side of freedom. We have enjoyed so much freedom for so long that we are perhaps in danger of forgetting how much blood it cost to establish the Bill of Rights.

Of course, no government can recognize a "right" of revolution, or a "right" to incite revolution if the incitement has no other purpose or effect. But speech is seldom restricted to a single purpose, and its effects may be manifold. A public interest is not wanting in granting freedom to speak their minds even to those who advocate the overthrow of the Government by force. For, as the evidence in this case abundantly illustrates, coupled with such advocacy is criticism of defects in our society. Criticism is the spur to reform; and Burke's admonition that a healthy society must reform in order to conserve has not lost its force. Astute observers have remarked that one of the characteristics of the American Republic is indifference to fundamental criticism.[20] It is a commonplace that there may be a grain of truth in the most uncouth doctrine, however false and repellent the balance may be. Suppressing advocates of overthrow inevitably will also silence critics who do not advocate overthrow but fear that their criticism may be so construed. No matter how clear we may be that the defendants now before us are preparing to overthrow our Government at the propitious moment, it is self-delusion to think that we can punish them for their advocacy without adding to the risks run by loyal citizens who honestly believe in some of the reforms these defendants advance. It is a sobering fact that in sustaining the convictions before us we can hardly escape restriction on the interchange of ideas.

We must not overlook the value of that interchange. Freedom of expression is the well-spring of our civilization — the civilization we seek to maintain and further by recognizing the right of Congress to put some limitation upon expression. Such are the paradoxes of life. For social development of trial and error, the fullest possible opportunity for the free play of the human mind is an indispensable

20. BRYCE, THE AMERICAN COMMONWEALTH c. 84 (3d ed. 1906). [F.F.]

prerequisite. The history of civilization is in considerable measure the displacement of error which once held sway as official truth by beliefs which in turn have yielded to other truths. Therefore the liberty of man to search for truth ought not to be fettered, no matter what orthodoxies he may challenge. Liberty of thought soon shrivels without freedom of expression. Nor can truth be pursued in an atmosphere hostile to the endeavor or under dangers which are hazarded only by heroes. . . .

It is not for us to decide how we would adjust the clash of interests which this case presents were the primary responsibility for reconciling it ours. Congress has determined that the danger created by advocacy of overthrow justifies the ensuing restriction of freedom of speech. The determination was made after due deliberation, and the seriousness of the congressional purpose is attested by the volume of legislation passed to effectuate the same ends.

Can we then say that the judgment Congress exercised was denied it by the Constitution? Can we establish a constitutional doctrine which forbids the elected representatives of the people to make this choice? Can we hold that the First Amendment deprives Congress of what it deemed necessary for the Government's protection?

To make validity of legislation depend on judicial reading of events still in the womb of time — a forecast, that is, of the outcome of forces at best appreciated only with knowledge of the topmost secrets of nations — is to charge the judiciary with duties beyond its equipment. We do not expect courts to pronounce historic verdicts on bygone events. Even historians have conflicting views to this day on the origins and conduct of the French Revolution, or, for that matter, varying interpretations of "the glorious Revolution" of 1688. It is as absurd to be confident that we can measure the present clash of forces and their outcome as to ask us to read history still enveloped in clouds of controversy.

In the light of their experience, the Framers of the Constitution chose to keep the judiciary dissociated from direct participation in the legislative process. In asserting the power to pass on the constitutionality of legislation, Marshall and his Court expressed the purposes of the Founders.[21] But the extent to which the exercise of this power would interpenetrate matters of policy could hardly have been foreseen by the most prescient. The distinction which the Founders drew between the Court's duty to pass on the power of Congress and its complementary duty not to enter directly the domain of policy is fundamental. But in its actual operation it is rather subtle, certainly to the common understanding. Our duty to abstain from confounding policy with constitutionality demands perceptive

21. See BEARD, THE SUPREME COURT AND THE CONSTITUTION (1938). [F.F.]

humility as well as self-restraint in not declaring unconstitutional what in a judge's private judgment is deemed unwise and even dangerous.

Even when moving strictly within the limits of constitutional adjudication, judges are concerned with issues that may be said to involve vital finalities. The too easy transition from disapproval of what is undesirable to condemnation as unconstitutional, has led some of the wisest judges to question the wisdom of our scheme in lodging such authority in courts. But it is relevant to remind that in sustaining the power of Congress in a case like this nothing irrevocable is done. The democratic process at all events is not impaired or restricted. Power and responsibility remain with the people and immediately with their representatives. All the Court says is that Congress was not forbidden by the Constitution to pass this enactment and that a prosecution under it may be brought against a conspiracy such as the one before us.

The wisdom of the assumptions underlying the legislation and prosecution is another matter. In finding that Congress has acted within its power, a judge does not remotely imply that he favors the implications that lie beneath the legal issues. Considerations there enter which go beyond the criteria that are binding upon judges within the narrow confines of their legitimate authority. The legislation we are here considering is but a truncated aspect of a deeper issue. . . .

Civil liberties draw at best only limited strength from legal guaranties. Preoccupation by our people with the constitutionality, instead of with the wisdom, of legislation or of executive action is preoccupation with a false value. Even those who would most freely use the judicial brake on the democratic process by invalidating legislation that goes deeply against their grain, acknowledge, at least by paying lip service, that constitutionality does not exact a sense of proportion or the sanity of humor or an absence of fear. Focusing attention on constitutionality tends to make constitutionality synony-mous with wisdom. When legislation touches freedom of thought and freedom of speech, such a tendency is a formidable enemy of the free spirit. Much that should be rejected as illiberal, because repressive and envenoming, may well be not unconstitutional. The ultimate reliance for the deepest needs of civilization must be found outside their vindication in courts of law; apart from all else, judges, howsoever they may conscientiously seek to discipline themselves against it, unconsciously are too apt to be moved by the deep undercurrents of public feeling. A persistent, positive translation of the liberating faith into the feelings and thoughts and actions of men and women is the real protection against attempts to strait-jacket the human mind. Such temptations will have their way, if fear and hatred are not exorcized. The mark of a truly civilized man is confidence in the strength and security derived from the inquiring mind. We may be grateful for such honest comforts as it supports, but we must be unafraid of its incertitudes. Without open minds there can be no open society. And if society be not open the spirit of man is mutilated and becomes enslaved.

The same balancing of vital interests — albeit without congressional judgment in the balance — had to be made by Frankfurter in weighing the values of a free press against incursions by that press on the possibilities of a fair trial. The Justice again felt called upon to point out that freedom of the press was not an absolute and that some preventative measures other than reversal of a tainted conviction must be tolerated. In each of the major cases on which he spoke to this issue, Frankfurter concurred in the judgment of the Court refusing to sustain the use of the contempt power. But he would make clear that such a sanction did exist. His opinion on this issue was cogently stated in *Pennekamp v. Florida*: [22]

. . . This Court sits to interpret, in appropriate judicial controversies, a Constitution which in its Bill of Rights formulates the conditions of a democracy. But democracy is the least static form of society. Its basis is reason not authority. Formulas embodying vague and uncritical generalizations offer tempting opportunities to evade the need for continuous thought. But so long as men want freedom they resist this temptation. Such formulas are most beguiling and most mischievous when contending claims are those not of right and wrong but of two rights, each highly important to the well-being of society. Seldom is there available a pat formula that adequately analyzes such a problem, least of all solves it. Certainly no such formula furnishes a ready answer to the question now here for decision or even exposes its true elements. The precise issue is whether, and to what extent, a State can protect the administration of justice by authorizing prompt punishment, without the intervention of a jury, of publications out of court that may interfere with a court's disposition of pending litigation. . . .

Without a free press there can be no free society. Freedom of the press, however, is not an end in itself but a means to the end of a free society. The scope and nature of the constitutional protection of freedom of speech must be viewed in that light and in that light applied. The independence of the judiciary is no less a means to the end of a free society, and the proper functioning of an independent

22. 328 U.S. 331, 350–51, 354–57, 365–66 (1946).

judiciary puts the freedom of the press in its proper perspective. For the judiciary cannot function properly if what the press does is reasonably calculated to disturb the judicial judgment in its duty and capacity to act solely on the basis of what is before the court. A judiciary is not independent unless courts of justice are enabled to administer law by absence of pressure from without, whether exerted through the blandishments of reward or the menace of disfavor. In the noble words, penned by John Adams, of the First Constitution of Massachusetts: "It is essential to the preservation of the rights of every individual, his life, liberty, property, and character, that there be an impartial interpretation of the laws, and administration of justice. It is the right of every citizen to be tried by judges as free, impartial and independent as the lot of humanity will admit." A free press is not to be preferred to an independent judiciary through which that freedom may, if necessary, be vindicated. And one of the potent means for assuring judges their independence is a free press.

A free press is vital to a democratic society because its freedom gives it power. Power in a democracy implies responsibility in its exercise. No institution in a democracy, either governmental or private, can have the limits of power which enforce responsibility be finally determined by the limited power itself.[23] In plain English, freedom carries with it responsibility even for the press; freedom of the press is not a freedom from responsibility for its exercise. Most State constitutions expressly provide for liability for abuse of the press's freedom. That there was such legal liability was so taken for granted by the framers of the First Amendment that it was not spelled out. Responsibility for its abuse was imbedded in the law. The First Amendment safeguarded the right.

These are generalities. But they are generalities of the most practical importance in achieving a proper adjustment between a free press and an independent judiciary.

Especially in the administration of the criminal law — that most awesome aspect of government — society needs independent courts of justice. This means judges free from control by the executive, free from all ties with political interests, free from all fears of reprisal or hopes of reward. The safety of society and the security of the innocent alike depend upon wise and impartial criminal justice. Misuse of its machinery may undermine the safety of the State; its misuse may deprive the individual of all that makes a free man's life dear.

Criticism therefore must not feel cramped, even criticism of the administration of criminal justice. Weak characters ought not to be

23. See BECKER, FREEDOM AND RESPONSIBILITY IN THE AMERICAN WAY OF LIFE (1945). [F.F.]

judges, and the scope allowed to the press for society's sake may assume that they are not. No judge fit to be one is likely to be influenced consciously except by what he sees and hears in court and by what is judicially appropriate for his deliberations. However, judges are also human, and we know better than did our forbears how powerful is the pull of the unconscious and how treacherous the rational process. While the ramparts of reason have been found to be more fragile than the Age of Enlightenment had supposed, the means for arousing passion and confusing judgment have been reinforced. And since judges, however stalwart, are human, the delicate task of administering justice ought not to be made unduly difficult by irresponsible print. . . .

The press does have the right, which is its professional function, to criticize and to advocate. The whole gamut of public affairs is the domain for fearless and critical comment, and not least the administration of justice. But the public function which belongs to the press makes it an obligation of honor to exercise this function only with the fullest sense of responsibility. Without such a lively sense of responsibility a free press may readily become a powerful instrument of injustice. It should not and may not attempt to influence judges or juries before they have made up their minds on pending controversies. Such a restriction, which merely bars the operation of extraneous influence specifically directed to a concrete case, in no wise curtails the fullest discussion of public issues generally. It is not suggested that generalized discussion of a particular topic should be forbidden, or run the hazard of contempt proceedings, merely because some phases of such a general topic may be involved in a pending litigation. It is the focused attempt to influence a particular decision that may have a corroding effect on the process of justice, and it is such comment that justifies the corrective process.

The administration of law, particularly that of the criminal law, normally operates in an environment that is not universal or even general but individual. The distinctive circumstances of a particular case determine whether law is fairly administered in that case, through a disinterested judgment on the basis of what has been formally presented inside the courtroom on explicit considerations, instead of being subjected to extraneous factors psychologically calculated to disturb the exercise of an impartial and equitable judgment.

If men, including judges and journalists, were angels, there would be no problems of contempt of court. Angelic judges would be undisturbed by extraneous influences and angelic journalists would not seek to influence them. The power to punish for contempt, as a means of safeguarding judges in deciding on behalf of the community as impartially as is given to the lot of men to decide, is not a privilege accorded to judges. The power to punish for contempt of court is a safeguard not for judges as persons but for the function which they exercise. It is a condition of that function — indispensable for a free society — that in a particular controversy pending before a court and awaiting judgment, human beings, however strong, should not be torn from their moorings of impartiality by the undertow of extraneous influence. In securing freedom of speech, the Constitution hardly meant to create the right to influence judges or juries. That is no more freedom of speech than stuffing a ballot box is an exercise of the right to vote.

It must be acknowledged that here, as elsewhere, Frankfurter's views were not accepted by his brethren. After he left the Court, it decided in favor of the press's right to be irresponsible about the material it published, so long as it was not malicious.[24]

It was during the era of the Warren Court that the issue of censorship of obscenity reached its climax. Again Frankfurter was unable to join those who would ban all censorship. Nor would he deny that there were limits within which the states' authority had to be confined. His general attitude that each case was unique made it especially difficult to determine in advance whether a particular book or film could be suppressed. For him the authority to act in this way would depend upon the book or film in question and its audience, so long as the state acted in accordance with the demands of proper procedure. Frankfurter detailed some of his views on censorship in the case involving New York's ban on the showing of the movie *Lady Chatterley's Lover*:[25]

As one whose taste in art and literature hardly qualifies him for the *avant-garde*, I am more than surprised, after viewing the picture, that the New York authorities should have banned "Lady Chatterley's Lover." To assume that this motion picture would have offended Victorian moral sensibilities is to rely only on the stuffiest of Victorian conventions. Whatever one's personal preferences may be about such matters, the refusal to license the exhibition of this picture, on the basis of the 1954 amendment to the New York State Education Law, can only mean that that enactment forbids the public showing

24. See New York Times Co. v. Sullivan, 376 U.S. 254 (1964), and its now prevalent rationalization in Kalven, *The New York Times Case: A Note on "the Central Meaning of the First Amendment,"* 1964 SUPREME COURT RE-VIEW 191.

25. Kingsley Pictures Corp. v. Regents, 360 U.S. 684, 691–96 (1959).

of any film that deals with adultery except by way of sermonizing condemnation or depicts any physical manifestation of an illicit amorous relation. Since the denial of a license by the Board of Regents was confirmed by the highest court of the State, I have no choice but to agree with this Court's judgment in holding that the State exceeded the bounds of free expression protected by the "Liberty" of the Fourteenth Amendment. But I also believe that the Court's opinion takes ground that exceeds the appropriate limits for decision. . . .

Even the author of "Lady Chatterley's Lover" did not altogether rule out censorship, nor was his passionate zeal on behalf of society's profound interest in the endeavors of true artists so doctrinaire as to be unmindful of the facts of life regarding the sordid exploitation of man's nature and impulses. He knew there was such a thing as pornography, dirt for dirt's sake, or, to be more accurate, dirt for money's sake. This is what D. H. Lawrence wrote: [26]

"But even I would censor genuine pornography, rigorously. It would not be very difficult. In the first place, genuine pornography is almost always underworld, it doesn't come into the open. In the second, you can recognize it by the insult it offers invariably, to sex, and to the human spirit.

"Pornography is the attempt to insult sex, to do dirt on it. This is unpardonable. Take the very lowest instance, the picture post-card sold underhand, by the underworld, in most cities. What I have seen of them have been of an ugliness to make you cry. The insult to the human body, the insult to a vital human relationship! Ugly and cheap they make the human nudity, ugly and degraded they make the sexual act, trivial and cheap and nasty." . . .

In short, there is an evil against which a State may constitutionally protect itself, whatever we may think about the questions involved. The real problem is the formulation of constitutionally allowable safeguards which society may take against evil without impinging upon the necessary dependence of a free society upon the fullest scope of free expression. One cannot read the debates in the House of Commons and the House of Lords and not realize the difficulty of reconciling these conflicting interests, in the framing of legislation on the ends of which there was agreement, even for those who most generously espouse that freedom of expression without which all freedom gradually withers.

It is not our province to meet these recalcitrant problems of legislative drafting. Ours is the vital but very limited task of scrutinizing the work of the draftsmen in order to determine whether they have kept within the narrow limits of the kind of censorship which even D. H. Lawrence deemed necessary. The legislation must

26. LAWRENCE, PORNOGRAPHY AND OBSCENITY 12–13 (1929). [F.F.]

not be so vague, the language so loose, as to leave to those who have to apply it too wide a discretion for sweeping within its condemnation what is permissible expression as well as what society may permissibly prohibit. Always remembering that the widest scope of freedom is to be given to the adventurous and imaginative exercise of the human spirit, we have struck down legislation phrased in language intrinsically vague, unless it be responsive to the common understanding of men even though not susceptible of explicit definition. The ultimate reason for invalidating such laws is that they lead to timidity and inertia and thereby discourage the boldness of expression indispensable for a progressive society.

Unless I misread the opinion of the Court, it strikes down the New York legislation in order to escape the task of deciding whether a particular picture is entitled to the protection of expression under the Fourteenth Amendment. Such an exercise of the judicial function, however onerous or ungrateful, inheres in the very nature of the judicial enforcement of the Due Process Clause. We cannot escape such instance-by-instance, case-by-case application of that clause in all the varieties of situations that come before this Court. . . .

While, like the Court, Frankfurter did not reach the issue of obscenity in *Smith v. California*,[27] he did deal with some of the attendant problems in his concurring opinion and took the opportunity once again to reject notions of "doctrinaire absolutism" in this area:[28]

The Court does not reach, and neither do I, the issue of obscenity. The Court disposes of the case exclusively by sustaining the appellant's claim that the "liberty" protected by the Due Process Clause of the Fourteenth Amendment precludes a State from making the dissemination of obscene books an offense merely because a book in a bookshop is found to be obscene without some proof of the bookseller's knowledge touching the obscenity of its contents.

The Court accepts the settled principle of constitutional law that traffic in obscene literature may be outlawed as a crime. But it holds that one cannot be made amenable to such criminal outlawry unless he is chargeable with knowledge of the obscenity. Obviously the Court is not holding that a bookseller must familiarize himself with the contents of every book in his shop. No less obviously, the Court does not hold that a bookseller who insulates himself against knowledge about an offending book is thereby free to maintain an emporium for smut. How much or how little awareness that a book may be found to be obscene suffices to establish scienter, or what

27. 361 U.S. 147 (1959).

28. *Id.* at 161–67.

kind of evidence may satisfy the how much or the how little, the Court leaves for another day.

I am no friend of deciding a case beyond what the immediate controversy requires, particularly when the limits of constitutional power are at stake. On the other hand, a case before this Court is not just a case. Inevitably its disposition carries implications and gives directions beyond its particular facts. Were the Court holding that this kind of prosecution for obscenity requires proof of the guilty mind associated with the concept of crimes deemed infamous, that would be that and no further elucidation would be needed. But if the requirement of scienter in obscenity cases plays a role different from the normal role of *mens rea* in the definition of crime, a different problem confronts the Court. If, as I assume, the requirement of scienter in an obscenity prosecution like the one before us does not mean that the bookseller must have read the book or must substantially know its contents on the one hand, nor on the other that he can exculpate himself by studious avoidance of knowledge about its contents, then, I submit, invalidating an obscenity statute because a State dispenses altogether with the requirement of scienter does require some indication of the scope and quality of scienter that is required. It ought at least to be made clear, and not left for future litigation, that the Court's decision in its practical effect is not intended to nullify the conceded power of the State to prohibit booksellers from trafficking in obscene literature.

Of course there is an important difference in the scope of the power of a State to regulate what feeds the belly and what feeds the brain. The doctrine of *United States* v. *Balint*[29] has its appropriate limits. The rule that scienter is not required in prosecutions for so-called public welfare offenses is a limitation on the general principle that awareness of what one is doing is a prerequisite for the infliction of punishment.[30] The balance that is struck between this vital principle and the overriding public menace inherent in the trafficking of noxious food and drugs cannot be carried over in balancing the vital role of free speech as against society's interest in dealing with pornography. On the other hand, the constitutional protection of non-obscene speech cannot absorb the constitutional power of the States to deal with obscenity. It would certainly wrong them to attribute to Jefferson or Madison a doctrinaire absolutism that would bar legal restriction against obscenity as a denial of free speech. We have not yet been told that all laws against defamation and against inciting crime by speech[31] are unconstitutional as impermissible

29. 258 U.S. 250 (1922). [F.F.]

30. Morissette v. United States, 342 U.S. 246 (1952). [F.F.]

31. See Fox v. Washington, 236 U.S. 273 (1915). [F.F.]

curbs upon unrestrictable utterance. We know this was not Jefferson's view, any more than it was the view of Holmes and Brandeis, JJ., the originating architects of our prevailing constitutional law protective of freedom of speech.

Accordingly, the proof of scienter that is required to make prosecutions for obscenity constitutional cannot be of a nature to nullify for all practical purposes the power of the State to deal with obscenity. Out of regard for the State's interest, the Court suggests an unguiding, vague standard for establishing "awareness" by the bookseller of the contents of a challenged book in contradiction of his disclaimer of knowledge of its contents. A bookseller may, of course, be well aware of the nature of the book and its appeal without having opened its cover, or, in any true sense, having knowledge of the book. As a practical matter therefore the exercise of the constitutional right of a State to regulate obscenity will carry with it some hazard to the dissemination by a bookseller of non-obscene literature. Such difficulties or hazards are inherent in many domains of the law for the simple reason that law cannot avail itself of factors ascertained quantitatively or even wholly impersonally.

The uncertainties pertaining to the scope of scienter requisite for an obscenity prosecution and the speculative proof that the issue is likely to entail, are considerations that reinforce the right of one charged with obscenity — a right implicit in the very nature of the legal concept of obscenity — to enlighten the judgment of the tribunal, be it the jury or as in this case the judge, regarding the prevailing literary and moral community standards and to do so through qualified experts. It is immaterial whether the basis of the exclusion of such testimony is irrelevance, or the incompetence of experts to testify to such matters. The two reasons coalesce, for community standards or the psychological or physiological consequences of questioned literature can as a matter of fact hardly be established except through experts. Therefore, to exclude such expert testimony is in effect to exclude as irrelevant evidence that goes to the very essence of the defense and therefore to the constitutional safeguards of due process. The determination of obscenity no doubt rests with judge or jury. Of course the testimony of experts would not displace judge or jury in determining the ultimate question whether the particular book is obscene, any more than the testimony of experts relating to the state of the art in patent suits determines the patentability of a controverted device.

There is no external measuring rod for obscenity. Neither, on the other hand, is its ascertainment a merely subjective reflection of the taste or moral outlook of individual jurors or individual judges. Since the law through its functionaries is "applying contemporary community standards" in determining what constitutes obscenity,[32] it surely must be deemed rational, and therefore relevant to the issue of obscenity, to allow light to be shed on what those "contemporary community standards" are. Their interpretation ought not to depend solely on the necessarily limited, hit-or-miss, subjective view of what they are believed to be by the individual juror or judge. It bears repetition that the determination of obscenity is for juror or judge not on the basis of his personal upbringing or restricted reflection or particular experience of life, but on the basis of "contemporary community standards." Can it be doubted that there is a great difference in what is to be deemed obscene in 1959 compared with what was deemed obscene in 1859? The difference derives from a shift in community feeling regarding what is to be deemed prurient or not prurient by reason of the effects attributable to this or that particular writing. Changes in the intellectual and moral climate of society, in part doubtless due to the views and findings of specialists, afford shifting foundations for the atttribution. What may well have been consonant "with mid-Victorian morals, does not seem to me to answer to the understanding and morality of the present time." [33] This was the view of Judge Learned Hand decades ago reflecting an atmosphere of propriety much closer to mid-Victorian days than is ours. Unless we disbelieve that the literary, psychological or moral standards of a community can be made fruitful and illuminating subjects of inquiry by those who give their life to such inquiries, it was violative of "due process" to exclude the constitutionally relevant evidence proffered in this case. The importance of this type of evidence in prosecutions for obscenity has been impressively attested by the recent debates in the House of Commons dealing with the insertion of such a provision in the enactment of the Obscene Publications Act,[34] as well as by the most considered thinking on this subject in the proposed Model Penal Code of the American Law Institute.[35] For the reasons I have indicated, I would make the right to introduce such evidence a requirement of due process in obscenity prosecutions.

The alleged conflict between a requirement of lawful behavior in public places and the right of free speech is — despite the beliefs of some — not a novel one. It has arisen in many contexts in the past,

32. Roth v. United States, 354 U.S. 476, 489 (1957). [F.F.]

33. United States v. Kennerley, 209 Fed. 119, 120 (S.D. N.Y. 1913). [F.F.]

34. 7 & 8 Eliz. II c. 66 (1959) (see 597 Parliamentary Debates, H. Comm., No. 36 [16 December 1958] cols. 1009–10, 1042–43; 604 Parliamentary Debates, H. Comm., No. 100 [24 April 1959] col. 803). [F.F.]

35. See A.L.I., Model Penal Code § 207.10 (Tent. Draft No. 6 1957). [F.F.]

and the future will supply new and different forms of this confrontation. Frankfurter spoke to the general issues in the contexts of three different cases under the appellation of *Niemotko v. Maryland*.[36] Not surprisingly, he did not offer a formula by way of solution:[37]

Due regard for the interests that were adjusted in the decisions just canvassed affords guidance for deciding the cases before us.

1. In the *Niemotko* case, neither danger to the public peace, nor consideration of time and convenience to the public, appears to have entered into denial of the permit. Rumors that there would be violence by those opposed to the meeting appeared only after the Council made its decision, and in fact never materialized. The city allowed other religious groups to use the park. To allow expression of religious views by some and deny the same privilege to others merely because they or their views are unpopular, even deeply so, is a denial of equal protection of the law forbidden by the Fourteenth Amendment.

2. The *Kunz* case presents a very different situation. We must be mindful of the enormous difficulties confronting those charged with the task of enabling the polyglot millions in the City of New York to live in peace and tolerance. Street-preaching in Columbus Circle is done in a milieu quite different from preaching on a New England village green. Again, religious polemic does not touch the merely ratiocinative nature of man, and the ugly facts disclosed by the record of this case show that Kunz was not reluctant to offend the deepest religious feelings of frequenters of Columbus Circle. Especially in such situations, this Court should not substitute its abstract views for the informed judgment of local authorities confirmed by local courts.

I cannot make too explicit my conviction that the City of New York is not restrained by anything in the Constitution of the United States from protecting completely the community's interests in relation to its streets. But if a municipality conditions holding street meetings on the granting of a permit by the police, the basis which guides licensing officials in granting or denying a permit must not give them a free hand, or a hand effectively free when the actualities of police administration are taken into account. It is not for this Court to formulate with particularity the terms of a permit system which would satisfy the Fourteenth Amendment. No doubt, finding a want of such standards presupposes some conception of what is necessary to meet the constitutional requirement we draw from the Fourteenth

36. 340 U.S. 268 (1951). The other cases were Kunz v. New York, 340 U.S. 290 (1951), and Feiner v. New York, 340 U.S. 315 (1951).

37. *Id.* at 284–89.

Amendment. But many a decision of this Court rests on some inarticulate major premise and is none the worse for it. A standard may be found inadequate without the necessity of explicit delineation of the standards that would be adequate, just as doggerel may be felt not to be poetry without the need of writing an essay on what poetry is.

Administrative control over the right to speak must be based on appropriate standards, whether the speaking be done indoors or out-of-doors. The vice to be guarded against is arbitrary action by officials. The fact that in a particular instance an action appears not arbitrary does not save the validity of the authority under which the action was taken.

In the present case, Kunz was not arrested for what he said on the night of arrest, nor because at that time he was disturbing the peace or interfering with traffic. He was arrested because he spoke without a license, and the license was refused because the police commission thought it likely on the basis of past performance that Kunz would outrage the religious sensibilities of others. If such had been the supportable finding on the basis of fair standards in safeguarding peace in one of the most populous centers of New York City, this Court would not be justified in upsetting it. It would not be censorship in advance. But here the standards are defined neither by language nor by settled construction to preclude discriminatory or arbitrary action by officials. The ordinance, as judicially construed, provides that anyone who, in the judgment of the licensing officials, would "ridicule" or "denounce" religion creates such a danger of public disturbance that he cannot speak in any park or street in the City of New York. Such a standard, considering the informal procedure under which it is applied, too readily permits censorship of religion by the licensing authorities.[38] The situation here disclosed is not, to reiterate, beyond control on the basis of regulation appropriately directed to the evil.

3. Feiner was convicted under New York Penal Law, § 722, which provides:

"Any person who with intent to provoke a breach of the peace, or whereby a breach of the peace may be occasioned, commits any of the following acts shall be deemed to have committed the offense of disorderly conduct: . . .

"2. Acts in such a manner as to annoy, disturb, interfere with, obstruct, or be offensive to others; . . . ."

A State court cannot of course preclude review of due process questions merely by phrasing its opinion in terms of an ultimate

---

38. Cantwell v. Connecticut, 310 U.S. 296 (1940). [F.F.]

standard which in itself satisfies due process.[39] But this Court should not re-examine determinations of the State courts on "those matters which are usually termed issues of fact."[40] And it should not overturn a fair appraisal of facts made by State courts in the light of their knowledge of local conditions.

Here, Feiner forced pedestrians to walk in the street by collecting a crowd on the public sidewalks, he attracted additional attention by using sound amplifiers, he indulged in name-calling, he told part of his audience that it should rise up in arms. In the crowd of 75 to 80 persons, there was angry muttering and pushing. Under these circumstances, and in order to prevent a disturbance of the peace, an officer asked Feiner to stop speaking. When he had twice ignored the request, Feiner was arrested. The trial judge concluded that "the officers were fully justified in feeling that a situation was developing which could very, very easily result in a serious disorder." His view was sustained by an intermediate appellate court and by a unanimous decision of the New York Court of Appeals.[41] The estimate of a particular local situation thus comes here with the momentum of the weightiest judicial authority of New York.

This Court has often emphasized that in the exercise of our authority over state court decisions the Due Process Clause must not be construed in an abstract and doctrinaire way by disregarding local conditions. In considering the degree of respect to be given findings by the highest court of a State in cases involving the Due Process Clause, the course of decisions by that court should be taken into account. Particularly within the area of due process colloquially called "civil liberties," it is important whether such a course of decisions reflects a cavalier attitude toward civil liberties or real regard for them. Only unfamiliarity with its decisions and the outlook of its judges could generate a notion that the Court of Appeals of New York is inhospitable to claims of civil liberties or is wanting in respect for this Court's decisions in support of them. It is pertinent, therefore, to note that all members of the New York Court accepted the finding that Feiner was stopped not because the listeners or police officers disagreed with his views but because these officers were honestly concerned with preventing a breach of the peace. This unanimity is all the more persuasive since three members of the Court had dissented, only three months earlier, in favor of Kunz, a man whose vituperative utterances must have been highly offensive to them.

39. Watts v. Indiana, 338 U.S. 49, 50 (1949); Baumgartner v. United States, 322 U.S. 665, 670–71 (1944); Norris v. Alabama, 294 U.S. 587, 589–90 (1935). *Cf.* Appleby v. City of New York, 271 U.S. 364, 379–80 (1926). [F.F.]

40. Watts v. Indiana, 338 U.S. at 50. [F.F.]

41. 300 N.Y. 391, 91 N.E.2d 316 (1950). [F.F.]

As was said in *Hague* v. *C.I.O.*,[42] uncontrolled official suppression of the speaker "cannot be made a substitute for the duty to maintain order."[43] Where conduct is within the allowable limits of free speech, the police are peace officers for the speaker as well as for his hearers. But the power effectively to preserve order cannot be displaced by giving a speaker complete immunity. Here, there were two police officers present for 20 minutes. They interfered only when they apprehended imminence of violence. It is not a constitutional principle that, in acting to preserve order, the police must proceed against the crowd, whatever its size and temper, and not against the speaker.

It is true that breach-of-peace statutes, like most tools of government, may be misused. Enforcement of these statutes calls for public tolerance and intelligent police administration. These, in the long run, must give substance to whatever this Court may say about free speech. But the possibility of misuse is not alone a sufficient reason to deny New York the power here asserted or so limit it by constitutional construction as to deny its practical exercise.

The more recent decisions of the Court that have largely relieved speech and press from any obligation to truth and decency run counter to all that Frankfurter found in the First Amendment. For him, freedom invoked a concomitant responsibility that was also of the essence of the First Amendment. His views on the responsibility of the press — the nature of the public trust — were again partially revealed in *Associated Press v. United States*,[44] where the Court held the Sherman Law applicable even to the press barons:[45]

To be sure, the Associated Press is a cooperative organization of members who are "engaged in a commercial business for profit."[46] But in addition to being a commercial enterprise, it has a relation to the public interest unlike that of any other enterprise pursued for profit. A free press is indispensable to the workings of our democratic society. The business of the press, and therefore the business of the Associated Press, is the promotion of truth regarding public matters by furnishing the basis for an understanding of them. Truth and understanding are not wares like peanuts or potatoes. And so, the incidence of restraints upon the promotion of truth through denial

42. 307 U.S. 496 (1939). [F.F]

43. *Id.* at 516.

44. 326 U.S. 1 (1945).

45. *Id.* at 27–29.

46. Associated Press v. N.L.R.B., 301 U.S. 103, 128 (1937). [F.F.]

of access to the basis for understanding calls into play considerations very different from comparable restraints in a cooperative enterprise having merely a commercial aspect. I find myself entirely in agreement with Judge Learned Hand that "neither exclusively, nor even primarily, are the interests of the newspaper industry conclusive; for that industry serves one of the most vital of all general interests: the dissemination of news from as many different sources, and with as many different facets and colors as is possible. That interest is closely akin to, if indeed it is not the same as, the interest protected by the First Amendment; it presupposes that right conclusions are more likely to be gathered out of a multitude of tongues, than through any kind of authoritative selection. To many this is, and always will be, folly; but we have staked upon it our all." [47]

From this point of view it is wholly irrelevant that the Associated Press itself has rival news agencies. As to ordinary commodities, agreements to curtail the supply and to fix prices are in violation of the area of free enterprise which the Sherman Law was designed to protect. The press in its commercial aspects is also subject to the regulation of the Sherman Law. [48] But the freedom of enterprise protected by the Sherman Law necessarily has different aspects in relation to the press than in the case of ordinary commercial pursuits. The interest of the public is to have the flow of news not trammeled by the combined self-interest of those who enjoy a unique constitutional position precisely because of the public dependence on a free press. A public interest so essential to the vitality of our democratic government may be defeated by private restraints no less than by public censorship.

Equally irrelevant is the objection that it turns the Associated Press into a "public utility" to deny to a combination of newspapers the right to treat access to their pooled resources as though they were regulating membership in a social club. The relation of such restraints upon access to news and the relation of such access to the function of a free press in our democratic society must not be obscured by the specialized notions that have gathered around the legal concept of "public utility."

The short of the matter is that the by-laws which the District Court has struck down clearly restrict the commerce which is conducted by the Associated Press, and the restrictions are unreasonable because they offend the basic functions which a constitutionally guaranteed free press serves in our nation.

47. 52 F. Supp. 362, 372 (S.D. N.Y. 1943). [F.F.]

48. Indiana Farmer's Guide Co. v. Prairie Farmer Co., 293 U.S. 268 (1934). [F.F.]

His antipathy to relieving the perpetrators of libel from responsibility for their deeds is to be found in Frankfurter's opinion for the Court sustaining the Illinois "group libel" statute in *Beauharnais v. Illinois.*[49] (It should be noted that the vitality of the *Beauharnais* decision has probably been totally sapped by the more recent decisions of the Court in this area.)

Libel of an individual was a common-law crime, and thus criminal in the colonies. Indeed, at common law, truth or good motives was no defense. In the first decades after the adoption of the Constitution, this was changed by judicial decision, statute or constitution in most States, but nowhere was there any suggestion that the crime of libel be abolished. Today, every American jurisdiction — the forty-eight States, the District of Columbia, Alaska, Hawaii and Puerto Rico — punish libels directed at individuals. "There are certain well-defined and narrowly limited classes of speech, the prevention and punishment of which have never been thought to raise any Constitutional problem. These include the lewd and obscene, the profane, the libelous, and the insulting or 'fighting' words — those which by their very utterance inflict injury or tend to incite an immediate breach of the peace. It has been well observed that such utterances are no essential part of any exposition of ideas, and are of such slight social value as a step to truth that any benefit that may be derived from them is clearly outweighed by the social interest in order and morality. 'Resort to epithets or personal abuse is not in any proper sense communication of information or opinion safeguarded by the Constitution, and its punishment as a criminal act would raise no question under that instrument.' " . . . Such were the views of a unanimous Court in *Chaplinsky* v. *New Hampshire.*[50]

No one will gainsay that it is libelous falsely to charge another with being a rapist, robber, carrier of knives and guns, and user of marijuana. The precise question before us, then, is whether the protection of "liberty" in the Due Process Clause of the Fourteenth Amendment prevents a State from punishing such libels — as criminal libel has been defined, limited and constitutionally recognized time out of mind — directed at designated collectivities and flagrantly disseminated. There is even authority, however dubious, that such utterances were also crimes at common law. It is certainly clear that some American jurisdictions have sanctioned their punishment under ordinary criminal libel statutes. We cannot say, however, that the question is concluded by history and practice. But if an utterance

49. 343 U.S. 250, 254–65 (1952).

50. 315 U.S. 568, 571–72 (1942). [F.F.]

directed at an individual may be the object of criminal sanctions, we cannot deny to a State power to punish the same utterance directed at a defined group, unless we can say that this is a wilful and purposeless restriction unrelated to the peace and well-being of the State.

Illinois did not have to look beyond her own borders or await the tragic experience of the last three decades to conclude that wilful purveyors of falsehood concerning racial and religious groups promote strife and tend powerfully to obstruct the manifold adjustments required for free, ordered life in a metropolitan, polyglot community. From the murder of the abolitionist Lovejoy in 1837 to the Cicero riots of 1951, Illinois has been the scene of exacerbated tension between races, often flaring into violence and destruction. In many of these outbreaks, utterances of the character here in question, so the Illinois legislature could conclude, played a significant part. The law was passed on June 29, 1917, at a time when the State was struggling to assimilate vast numbers of new inhabitants, as yet concentrated in discrete racial or national or religious groups — foreign-born brought to it by the crest of the great wave of immigration, and Negroes attracted by jobs in war plants and the allurements of northern claims. Nine years earlier, in the very city where the legislature sat, what is said to be the first northern race riot had cost the lives of six people, left hundreds of Negroes homeless and shocked citizens into action far beyond the borders of the State. Less than a month before the bill was enacted, East St. Louis had seen a day's rioting, prelude to an outbreak, only four days after the bill became law, so bloody that it led to Congressional investigation. A series of bombings had begun which was to culminate two years later in the awful race riot which held Chicago in its grip for seven days in the summer of 1919. Nor has tension and violence between the groups defined in the statute been limited in Illinois to clashes between whites and Negroes.

In the face of this history and its frequent obligato of extreme racial and religious propaganda, we would deny experience to say that the Illinois legislature was without reason in seeking ways to curb false or malicious defamation of racial and religious groups, made in public places and by means calculated to have a powerful emotional impact on those to whom it was presented. "There are limits to the exercise of these liberties [of speech and of the press]. The danger in these times from the coercive activities of those who in the delusion of racial or religious conceit would incite violence and breaches of the peace in order to deprive others of their equal right to the exercise of their liberties, is emphasized by events familiar to all. These and other transgressions of those limits the States appropriately may punish." This was the conclusion, again of a unanimous Court, in 1940.[51]

It may be argued, and weightily, that this legislation will not help matters; that tension and on occasion violence between racial and religious groups must be traced to causes more deeply embedded in our society than the rantings of modern Know-Nothings. Only those lacking responsible humility will have a confident solution for problems as intractable as the frictions attributable to differences of race, color or religion. This being so, it would be out of bounds for the judiciary to deny the legislature a choice of policy, provided it is not forbidden by some explicit limitation on the State's power. That the legislative remedy might not in practice mitigate the evil, or might itself raise new problems, would only manifest once more the paradox of reform. It is the price to be paid for the trial-and-error inherent in legislative efforts to deal with obstinate social issues. "The science of government is the most abstruse of all sciences; if, indeed, that can be called a science which has but few fixed principles, and practically consists in little more than the exercise of a sound discretion, applied to the exigencies of the state as they arise. It is the science of experiment."[52] Certainly the Due Process Clause does not require the legislature to be in the vanguard of science — especially sciences as young as human ecology and cultural anthropology.[53]

In *Wieman v. Updegraff*,[54] as elsewhere, Frankfurter wrote in defense of a concept of academic freedom, a concept not to be found in any words of the First Amendment: [55]

The case concerns the power of a State to exact from teachers in one of its colleges an oath that they are not, and for the five years immediately preceding the taking of the oath have not been, members of any organization listed by the Attorney General of the United States, prior to the passage of the statute, as "subversive" or "Communist-front." Since the affiliation which must thus be forsworn may well have been for reasons or for purposes as innocent as membership in a club or one of the established political parties, to require such an oath, on pain of a teacher's loss of his position in case of refusal to take the oath, penalizes a teacher for exercising a

51. Cantwell v. Connecticut, 310 U.S. 296, 310 (1940). [F.F.]

52. Anderson v. Dunn, 6 Wheat. 204, 226 (1821). [F.F.]

53. See Tigner v. Texas, 310 U.S. 141, 148 (1940). [F.F.]

54. 344 U.S. 183, 194 (1952).

55. *Id.* at 194–98.

right of association peculiarly characteristic of our people.[56] Such joining is an exercise of the rights of free speech and free inquiry. By limiting the power of the States to interfere with freedom of speech and freedom of inquiry and freedom of association, the Fourteenth Amendment protects all persons, no matter what their calling. But, in view of the nature of the teacher's relation to the effective exercise of the rights which are safeguarded by the Bill of Rights and by the Fourteenth Amendment, inhibition of freedom of thought, and of action upon thought, in the case of teachers brings the safeguards of those amendments vividly into operation. Such unwarranted inhibition upon the free spirit of teachers affects not only those who, like the appellants, are immediately before the Court. It has an unmistakable tendency to chill that free play of the spirit which all teachers ought especially to cultivate and practice; it makes for caution and timidity in their associations by potential teachers.

The Constitution of the United States does not render the United States or the States impotent to guard their governments against destruction by enemies from within. It does not preclude measures of self-protection against anticipated overt acts of violence. Solid threats to our kind of government — manifestations of purposes that reject argument and the free ballot as the means for bringing about changes and promoting progress — may be met by preventive measures before such threats reach fruition. However, in considering the constitutionality of legislation like the statute before us it is necessary to keep steadfastly in mind what it is that is to be secured. Only thus will it be evident why the Court has found that the Oklahoma law violates those fundamental principles of liberty "which lie at the base of all our civil and political institutions" and as such are imbedded in the due process of law which no State may offend.[57]

That our democracy ultimately rests on public opinion is a platitude of speech but not a commonplace in action. Public opinion is the ultimate reliance of our society only if it be disciplined and responsible. It can be disciplined and responsible only if habits of open-mindedness and of critical inquiry are acquired in the formative years of our citizens. The process of education has naturally enough been the basis of hope for the perdurance of our democracy on the part of all our great leaders, from Thomas Jefferson onwards.

To regard teachers — in our entire educational system, from the primary grades to the university — as the priests of our democracy is therefore not to indulge in hyperbole. It is the special task of teachers to foster those habits of open-mindedness and critical

56. See SCHLESINGER, PATHS TO THE PRESENT 23 (1949). [F.F.]

57. Hebert v. Louisiana, 272 U.S. 312, 316 (1926). [F.F.]

inquiry which alone make for responsible citizens, who, in turn, make possible an enlightened and effective public opinion. Teachers must fulfill their function by precept and practice, by the very atmosphere which they generate; they must be exemplars of open-mindedness and free inquiry. They cannot carry out their noble task if the conditions for the practice of a responsible and critical mind are denied to them. They must have the freedom of responsible inquiry, by thought and action, into the meaning of social and economic ideas, into the checkered history of social and economic dogma. They must be free to sift evanescent doctrine, qualified by time and circumstance, from that restless, enduring process of extending the bounds of understanding and wisdom, to assure which the freedoms of thought, of speech, of inquiry, of worship are guaranteed by the Constitution of the United States against infraction by National or State government.

The functions of educational institutions in our national life and the conditions under which alone they can adequately perform them are at the basis of these limitations upon State and National power. These functions and the essential conditions for their effective discharge have been well described by a leading educator:[58]

"Now, a university is a place that is established and will function for the benefit of society, provided it is a center of independent thought. It is a center of independent thought and criticism that is created in the interest of the progress of society, and the one reason that we know that every totalitarian government must fail is that no totalitarian government is prepared to face the consequences of creating free universities.

"It is important for this purpose to attract into the institution men of the greatest capacity, and to encourage them to exercise their independent judgment.

"Education is a kind of continuing dialogue, and a dialogue assumes, in the nature of the case, different points of view.

"The civilization which I work and which I am sure, every American is working toward, could be called a civilization of the dialogue, where instead of shooting one another when you differ, you reason things out together.

"In this dialogue, then, you cannot assume that you are going to have everybody thinking the same way or feeling the same way. It would be unprogressive if that happened. The hope of eventual development would be gone. More than that, of course, it would be very boring.

58. Testimony of Robert M. Hutchins, Associate Director of the Ford Foundation, 25 November 1952, in Hearings before the House Select Committee to Investigate Tax Exempt Foundations and Comparable Organizations, pursuant to H. Res. 561, 82d Cong., 2d Sess. (1952). [F.F.]

"A university, then, is a kind of continuing Socratic conversation on the highest level for the very best people you can think of, you can bring together, about the most important questions, and the thing that you must do to the uttermost possible limits is to guarantee those men the freedom to think and to express themselves.

"Now, the limits on this freedom, the limits of this freedom, cannot be merely prejudice, because although our prejudices might be perfectly satisfactory, the prejudices of our successors or of those who are in a position to bring pressure to bear on the institution, might be subversive in the real sense, subverting the American doctrine of free thought and free speech."

The loyalty oath demanded of teachers in *Wieman v. Updegraff* presented some issues not substantially different from the rights of freedom of association canvassed by Frankfurter in *American Communications Ass'n v. Douds*.[59] There the problem derived from a congressional limitation on benefits to unions whose officers had not taken required non-Communist oaths. The balance, for Frankfurter, was not so easily struck here as in the case of the teachers:[60]

"Scarcely any political question arises in the United States," observed the perceptive de Tocqueville as early as 1835, "that is not resolved, sooner or later, into a judicial question."[61] And so it was to be expected that the conflict of political ideas now dividing the world more pervasively than any since this nation was founded would give rise to controversies for adjudication by this Court. "The judicial Power" with which alone this Court is invested comes into operation only as to issues that the long tradition of our history has made appropriate for disposition by judges. When such questions are properly here they are to be disposed of within those strict confines of legal reasoning which laymen too often deem invidiously technical. This restriction to justiciable issues to be disposed of in the unrhetorical manner of opinion-writing reflects respect by the judiciary for its very limited, however great, function in the proper distribution of authority in our political scheme so as to avoid autocratic rule. No doubt issues like those now before us cannot be completely severed from the political and emotional context out of which they emerge. For that very reason adjudication touching such matters should not go one whit beyond the immediate issues requiring decision, and what is said in support of the adjudication should insulate the Court as far as is rationally possible from the political conflict beneath the legal issues.

59. 339 U.S. 382 (1950).

60. *Id.* at 415–22.

61. 1 TOCQUEVILLE, DEMOCRACY IN AMERICA 280 (Bradley ed. 1948). [F.F.]

The central problem presented by the enactment now challenged is the power of Congress, as part of its comprehensive scheme for industrial peace, to keep Communists out of controlling positions in labor unions as a condition to utilizing the opportunities afforded by the National Labor Relations Act, as amended by the Labor Management Relations Act, 1947. Wrapped up in this problem are two great concerns of our democratic society — the right of association for economic and social betterment and the right of association for political purposes. It is too late in the day to deny to Congress the power to promote industrial peace in all the far-flung range of interstate commerce. To that end, Congress may take appropriate measures to protect interstate commerce against disruptive conduct not fairly related to industrial betterment within our democratic framework. It is one thing to forbid heretical political thought merely as heretical thought. It is quite a different thing for Congress to restrict attempts to bring about another scheme of society, not through appeal to reason and the use of the ballot as democracy has been pursued throughout our history, but through an associated effort to disrupt industry.

Thus stated, it would make undue inroads upon the policy-making power of Congress to deny it the right to protect the industrial peace of the country by excluding from leadership in trade unions which seek to avail themselves of the machinery of the Labor Management Relations Act those who are united for action against our democratic process. This is so not because Congress in affording a facility can subject it to any condition it pleases. It cannot. Congress may withhold all sorts of facilities for a better life but if it affords them it cannot make them available in an obviously arbitrary way or exact surrender of freedoms unrelated to the purpose of the facilities. Congress surely can provide for certain clearly relevant qualifications of responsibility on the part of leaders of trade unions invoking the machinery of the Labor Management Relations Act. The essential question now is whether Congress may determine that membership of union officers in the Communist Party creates such an obvious hazard to the peace-promoting purposes of the Act that access to the machinery of the Act may be denied unions which prefer their freedom to have officers who are Communists to their opportunities under the Act.

When we are dealing with conflicting freedoms, as we are on the issues before us, we are dealing with large concepts that too readily lend themselves to explosive rhetoric. We are also dealing with matters as to which different nuances in phrasing the same conclusion lead to different emphasis and thereby eventually may lead to different conclusions in slightly different situations. From my point of view

these are issues as to which it would be desirable for the members
of the Court to write full-length individual opinions. The Court's
business in our time being what it is precludes this. It must suffice for
me to say that the judgment of Congress that trade unions which
are guided by officers who are committed by ties of membership to
the Communist Party must forego the advantages of the Labor
Management Relations Act is reasonably related to the accomplish-
ment of the purposes which Congress constitutionally had a right
to pursue. To deny that that is a judgment which Congress may, as a
matter of experience, enforce even though it involves the indicated
restrictions upon freedom would be to make naiveté a requirement
in judges. Since the Court's opinion, in the main, expresses the
point of view which I have very inadequately sketched, I join it
except as qualified in what follows. . . .

In my view Congress has cast its net too indiscriminately in some
of the provisions of § 9(h). To ask avowal that one "does not believe
in, and is not a member of or supports any organization that believes
in . . . the overthrow of the United States Government . . . by
any illegal or unconstitutional methods" is to ask assurances from
men regarding matters that open the door too wide to mere speculation
or uncertainty. It is asking more than rightfully may be asked of
ordinary men to take oath that a method is not "unconstitutional"
or "illegal" when constitutionality or legality is frequently determined
by this Court by the chance of a single vote. It does not meet the
difficulty to suggest that the hazard of a prosecution for perjury is
not great since the convictions for perjury must be founded on willful
falsity. To suggest that a judge might not be justified in allowing a
case to go to a jury, or that a jury would not be justified in convicting,
or that, on the possible happening of these events, an appellate
court would be compelled to reverse, or, finally, that resort could be
had to this Court for review on a petition for certiorari, affords
safeguards too tenuous to neutralize the danger.[62] The hazards that
were found to be fatal to the legislation under review in *Winters* v.
New York[63] appear trivial by comparison with what is here involved.

It is not merely the hazard of prosecution for perjury that is
dependent on a correct determination as to the implications of a
man's belief or the belief of others with whom he may be associated
in an organization concerned with political and social issues. It
should not be assumed that oaths will be lightly taken; fastidiously
scrupulous regard for them should be encouraged. Therefore, it
becomes most relevant whether an oath which Congress asks men
to take may or may not be thought to touch matters that may not be

62. Musser v. Utah, 333 U.S. 95 (1948). [F.F.]

63. 333 U.S. 507 (1948). [F.F.]

subjected to compulsory avowal of belief or disbelief. In the uncertainty of the reach of § 9(h), one may withhold an oath because of conscientious scruples that it covers beliefs whose disclosure Congress could not in terms exact. If a man has scruples about taking an oath because of uncertainty as to whether it encompasses some beliefs that are inviolate, the surrender of abstention is invited by the ambiguity of the congressional exaction. As MR. JUSTICE JACKSON's opinion indicates, probing into men's thoughts trenches on those aspects of individual freedom which we rightly regard as the most cherished aspects of Western civilization. The cardinal article of faith of our civilization is the inviolate character of the individual. A man can be regarded as an individual and not as a function of the state only if he is protected to the largest possible extent in his thoughts and in his beliefs as the citadel of his person. Entry into that citadel can be justified, if at all, only if strictly confined so that the belief that a man is asked to reveal is so defined as to leave no fair room for doubt that he is not asked to disclose what he has a right to withhold.

No one could believe more strongly than I do that every rational indulgence should be made in favor of the constitutionality of an enactment by Congress. I deem it my duty to go to the farthest possible limits in so construing legislation as to avoid a finding that Congress has exceeded the limits of its powers.[64]

If I possibly could, to avoid questions of unconstitutionality I would construe the requirements of § 9(h) to be restricted to disavowal of actual membership in the Communist Party, or in an organization that is in fact a controlled cover for that Party or of active belief, as a matter of present policy, in the overthrow of the Government of the United States by force. But what Congress has written does not permit such a gloss nor deletion of what it has written.[65] I cannot deem it within the rightful authority of Congress to probe into opinions that involve only an argumentative demonstration of some coincidental parallelism of belief with some of the beliefs of those who direct the policy of the Communist Party, though without any allegiance to it. To require oaths as to matters that open up such possibilities invades the inner life of men whose compassionate thought or doctrinaire hopes may be as far removed from any dangerous kinship with the Communist creed as were those of the founders of the present orthodox political parties in this country.

64. See, *e.g.*, United States v. Lovett, 328 U.S. 303, 318, 329 (1946); Shapiro v. United States, 335 U.S. 1, 36 (1948); United States v. C.I.O., 335 U.S. 106, 124, 129 (1948). [F.F.]

65. See Yu Cong Eng v. Trinidad, 271 U.S. 500 (1926). [F.F.]

8 Religion: Freedom and Establishment

The religion clauses of the First Amendment are themselves in tension so that almost every question likely to arise thereunder requires an effort at accommodation.[1] Freedom of religion has never, in this country's constitutional history, meant license to disregard the commands of the sovereign. Nor can disestablishment be any more easily reduced to total state abstention from protection of, or ordinary government contributions to, religious interests. Mr. Justice Frankfurter addressed himself on several occasions to the meaning of the disestablishment provision, never so fully as in *McGowan v. Maryland*,[2] the so-called *Sunday Closing Law Cases*:[3]

Because the long colonial struggle for disestablishment — the struggle to free all men, whatever their theological views, from state-compelled obligation to acknowledge and support state-favored faiths — made indisputably fundamental to our American culture the principle that the enforcement of religious belief as such is no legitimate concern of civil government, this Court has held that the Fourteenth Amendment embodies and applies against the States freedoms that are loosely indicated by the not rigidly precise but revealing phrase "separation of church and state."[4] The general principles of church-state separation were found to be included in the Amendment's Due Process Clause in view of the meaning which the presuppositions of our society infuse into the concept of "liberty" protected by the clause. This is the source of the limitations imposed upon the States. To the extent that those limitations are akin to the restrictions which the First Amendment places upon the action of the central government, it is because — as with the freedom of thought and speech of which Mr. Justice Cardozo spoke in *Palko* v. *Connecticut*,[5] — it is accurate to say concerning the principle that a government must neither establish nor suppress religious belief, that "With

1. See KURLAND, RELIGION AND THE LAW (1962).

2. 366 U.S. 420 (1961).

3. *Id* at 460–67.

4. Illinois *ex rel.* McCollum v. Board of Education, 333 U.S. 203 (1948). [F.F.]

5. 302 U.S. 319 (1937). [F.F.]

rare aberrations a pervasive recognition of that truth can be traced in our history, political and legal." [6]

But the several opinions in *Everson* [7] and *McCollum*, [8] and in *Zorach v. Clauson*, [9] make sufficiently clear that "separation" is not a self-defining concept. "[A]greement, in the abstract, that the First Amendment was designed to erect a 'wall of separation between church and State,' does not preclude a clash of views as to what the wall separates." [10] By its nature, religion — in the comprehensive sense in which the Constitution uses that word — is an aspect of human thought and action which profoundly relates the life of man to the world in which he lives. Religious beliefs pervade, and religious institutions have traditionally regulated, virtually all human activity. It is a postulate of American life, reflected specifically in the First Amendment to the Constitution but not there alone, that those beliefs and institutions shall continue, as the needs and longings of the people shall inspire them, to exist, to function, to grow, to wither, and to exert with whatever innate strength they may contain their many influences upon men's conduct, free of the dictates and directions of the state. However, this freedom does not and cannot furnish the adherents of religious creeds entire insulation from every civic obligation. As the state's interest in the individual becomes more comprehensive, its concerns and the concerns of religion perforce overlap. State codes and the dictates of faith touch the same activities. Both aim at human good, and in their respective views of what is good for man they may concur or they may conflict. No constitutional command which leaves religion free can avoid this quality of interplay.

Innumerable civil regulations enforce conduct which harmonizes with religious canons. State prohibitions of murder, theft and adultery reinforce commands of the decalogue. Nor do such regulations, in their coincidence with tenets of faith, always support equally the beliefs of all religious sects: witness the civil laws forbidding usury and enforcing monogamy. Because these laws serve ends which are within the appropriate scope of secular state interest, they may be enforced against those whose religious beliefs do not proscribe, and even sanction, the activity which the law condemns. [11]

6. *Id.* at 327 [F.F.]

7. Everson v. Board of Education, 330 U.S. 1 (1947). [F.F.]

8. Note 4 *supra* [F.F.]

9. 343 U.S. 306 (1952). [F.F.]

10. 333 U.S. at 213 (concurring opinion). [F.F.]

11. Reynolds v. United States, 98 U.S. 145 (1879); Davis v. Beason, 133 U.S. 333 (1890); Cleveland v. United States, 329 U.S. 14 (1946). [F.F.]

This is not to say that governmental regulations which find support in their appropriateness to the achievement of secular, civil ends are invariably valid under the First or Fourteenth Amendment, whatever their effects in the sphere of religion. If the value to society of achieving the object of a particular regulation is demonstrably outweighed by the impediment to which the regulation subjects those whose religious practices are curtailed by it, or if the object sought by the regulation could with equal effect be achieved by alternative means which do not substantially impede those religious practices, the regulation cannot be sustained.[12] This was the ground upon which the Court struck down municipal license taxes as applied to religious colporteurs.[13] In each of those cases it was believed that the State's need for revenue, which could be satisfied by taxing any of a variety of sources, did not justify a levy imposed upon an activity which in the light of history could reasonably be viewed as sacramental.[14]

Within the discriminating phraseology of the First Amendment, distinction has been drawn between cases raising "establishment" and "free exercise" questions. Any attempt to formulate a bright-line distinction is bound to founder. In view of the competition among religious creeds, whatever "establishes" one sect disadvantages another, and vice versa. But it is possible historically, and therefore helpful analytically — no less for problems arising under the Fourteenth Amendment, illuminated as that Amendment is by our national experience, than for problems arising under the First — to isolate in general terms the two largely overlapping areas of concern reflected in the two constitutional phrases, "establishment" and "free exercise," and which emerge more or less clearly from the background of events and impulses which gave those phrases birth.

In assuring the free exercise of religion, the Framers of the First Amendment were sensitive to the then recent history of those persecutions and impositions of civil disability with which sectarian majorities in virtually all of the Colonies had visited deviation in the matter of conscience. This protection of unpopular creeds, however, was not to be the full extent of the Amendment's guarantee of freedom from governmental intrusion in matters of faith. The battle in Virginia, hardly four years won, where James Madison had led the

12. Cantwell v. Connecticut, 310 U.S. 296 (1940). [F.F.]

13. Follett v. Town of McCormick, 321 U.S. 573 (1944); Murdock v. Pennsylvania, 319 U.S. 105 (1943); Jones v. Opelika, 319 U.S. 103 (1943). [F.F.]

14. But see Cox v. New Hampshire, 312 U.S. 569 (1941), in which the Court, balancing the public benefits secured by a regulatory measure against the degree of impairment of individual conduct expressive of religious faith which it entailed, sustained the prohibition of an activity similarly regarded by its practicants as sacramental. And see Prince v. Massachusetts, 321 U.S. 158 (1944). [F.F.]

forces of disestablishment in successful opposition to Patrick Henry's proposed Assessment Bill levying a general tax for the support of Christian teachers, was a vital and compelling memory in 1789. The lesson of that battle, in the words of Jefferson's Act for Establishing Religious Freedom, whose passage was its verbal embodiment, was "that to compel a man to furnish contributions of money for the propagation of opinions which he disbelieves, is sinful and tyrannical; that even the forcing him to support this or that teacher of his own religious persuasion, is depriving him of the comfortable liberty of giving his contributions to the particular pastor, whose morals he would make his pattern, and whose powers he feels most persuasive to righteousness, and is withdrawing from the ministry those temporal rewards, which proceeding from an approbation of their personal conduct, are an additional incitement to earnest and unremitting labours for the instruction of mankind. . . ." What Virginia had long practiced, and what Madison, Jefferson and others fought to end, was the extension of civil government's support to religion in a manner which made the two in some degree interdependent, and thus threatened the freedom of each. The purpose of the Establishment Clause was to assure that the national legislature would not exert its power in the service of any purely religious end; that it would not, as Virginia and virtually all of the Colonies had done, make of religion, as religion, an object of legislation.

Of course, the immediate object of the First Amendment's prohibition was the established church as it had been known in England and in most of the Colonies. But with foresight those who drafted and adopted the words, "Congress shall make no law respecting an establishment of religion," did not limit the constitutional proscription to any particular, dated form of state-supported theological venture. The Establishment Clause withdrew from the sphere of legitimate legislative concern and competence a specific, but comprehensive, area of human conduct: man's belief or disbelief in the verity of some transcendental idea and man's expression in action of that belief or disbelief. Congress may not make these matters, as such, the subject of legislation, nor, now, may any legislature in this country. Neither the National Government nor, under the Due Process Clause of the Fourteenth Amendment, a State may, by any device, support belief or the expression of belief for its own sake, whether from conviction of the truth of that belief, or from conviction that by the propagation of that belief the civil welfare of the State is served, or because a majority of its citizens, holding that belief, are offended when all do not hold it.

With regulations which have other objectives the Establishment

Clause, and the fundamental separationist concept which it expresses, are not concerned. These regulations may fall afoul of the constitutional guarantee against infringement of the free exercise or observance of religion. Where they do, they must be set aside at the instance of those whose faith they prejudice. But once it is determined that a challenged statute is supportable as implementing other substantial interests than the promotion of belief, the guarantee prohibiting religious "establishment" is satisfied.

To ask what interest, what objective, legislation serves, of course, is not to psychoanalyze its legislators, but to examine the necessary effects of what they have enacted. If the primary end achieved by a form of regulation is the affirmation or promotion of religious doctrine — primary, in the sense that all secular ends which it purportedly serves are derivative from, not wholly independent of, the advancement of religion — the regulation is beyond the power of the state. This was the case in *McCollum*. Or if a statute furthers both secular and religious ends by means unnecessary to the effectuation of the secular ends alone — where the same secular ends could equally be attained by means which do not have consequences for promotion of religion — the statute cannot stand. A State may not endow a church although that church might inculcate in its parishioners moral concepts deemed to make them better citizens, because the very *raison d'être* of a church, as opposed to any other school of civilly serviceable morals, is the predication of religious doctrine. However, inasmuch as individuals are free, if they will, to build their own churches and worship in them, the State may guard its people's safety by extending fire and police protection to the churches so built. It was on the reasoning that parents are also at liberty to send their children to parochial schools which meet the reasonable educational standards of the State,[15] that this Court held in the *Everson* case that expenditure of public funds to assure that children attending every kind of school enjoy the relative security of buses, rather than being left to walk or hitchhike, is not an unconstitutional "establishment," even though such an expenditure may cause some children to go to parochial schools who would not otherwise have gone. The close division of the Court in *Everson* serves to show what nice questions are involved in applying to particular governmental action the proposition, undeniable in the abstract, that not every regulation some of whose practical effects may facilitate the observance of a religion by its adherents affronts the requirement of church-state separation.

15. Pierce v. Society of Sisters, 268 U.S. 510 (1925). [F.F.]

Frankfurter, like many of the other Justices, was particularly concerned that the divisiveness of religious differences should not impede the unifying force, as he saw it, of the American public school systems. That was his specific worry as he joined in striking down Illinois's released-time program in *McCollum v. Board of Education*:[16]

This case, in the light of the *Everson* decision, demonstrates anew that the mere formulation of a relevant Constitutional principle is the beginning of the solution of a problem, not its answer. This is so because the meaning of a spacious conception like that of the separation of Church from State is unfolded as appeal is made to the principle from case to case. We are all agreed that the First and the Fourteenth Amendments have a secular reach far more penetrating in the conduct of Government than merely to forbid an "established church." But agreement, in the abstract, that the First Amendment was designed to erect a "wall of separation between church and State," does not preclude a clash of views as to what the wall separates. Involved is not only the Constitutional principle but the implications of judicial review in its enforcement. Accommodation of legislative freedom and Constitutional limitations upon that freedom cannot be achieved by a mere phrase. We cannot illuminatingly apply the "wall-of-separation" metaphor until we have considered the relevant history of religious education in America, the place of the "released time" movement in that history, and its precise manifestation in the case before us.

Separation in the field of education, then, was not imposed upon unwilling States by force of superior law. In this respect the Fourteenth Amendment merely reflected a principle then dominant in our national life. To the extent that the Constitution thus made it binding upon the States, the basis of the restriction is the whole experience of our people. Zealous watchfulness against fusion of secular and religious activities by Government itself, through any of its instruments but especially through its educational agencies, was the democratic response of the American community to the particular needs of a young and growing nation, unique in the composition of its people. A totally different situation elsewhere, as illustrated for instance by the English provisions for religious education in State-maintained schools, only serves to illustrate that free societies are not cast in one mould.[17] Different institutions evolve from different historic circumstances.

It is pertinent to remind that the establishment of this principle of

17. See Education Act of 1944, 7 & 8 Geo. VI, c. 31.
16. 333 U.S. 203, 212–13, 215–17, 231–32 (1948).

Separation in the field of education was not due to any decline in the religious beliefs of the people. Horace Mann was a devout Christian, and the deep religious feeling of James Madison is stamped upon the Remonstrance. The secular public school did not imply indifference to the basic role of religion in the life of the people, nor rejection of religious education as a means of fostering it. The claims of religion were not minimized by refusing to make the public schools agencies for their assertion. The non-sectarian or secular public school was the means of reconciling freedom in general with religious freedom. The sharp confinement of the public schools to secular education was a recognition of the need of a democratic society to educate its children, insofar as the State undertook to do so, in an atmosphere free from pressures in a realm in which pressures are most resisted and where conflicts are most easily and most bitterly engendered. Designed to serve as perhaps the most powerful agency for promoting cohesion among a heterogeneous democratic people, the public school must be kept scrupulously free from entanglement in the strife of sects. The preservation of the community from divisive conflicts, of Government from irreconcilable pressures by religious groups, of religion from censorship and coercion however subtly exercised, requires strict confinement of the State to instruction other than religious, leaving to the individual's church and home, indoctrination in the faith of his choice. . . .

Separation means separation, not something less. Jefferson's metaphor in describing the relaxation between Church and State speaks of a "wall of separation," not of a fine line easily overstepped. The public school is at once the symbol of our democracy and the most pervasive means for promoting our common destiny. In no activity of the State is it more vital to keep out divisive forces than in its schools, to avoid confusing, not to say fusing, what the Constitution sought to keep strictly apart. "The great American principle of eternal separation" — Elihu Root's phrase bears repetition — is one of vital reliances of our Constitutional system for assuring unities among our people stronger than our diversities. It is the Court's duty to enforce this principle in its full integrity.

We renew our conviction that "we have staked the very existence of our country on the faith that complete separation between the state and religion is best for the state and best for religion."[18] If nowhere else, in the relation between Church and State, "good fences make good neighbors."

Frankfurter's closing quotation from Robert Frost manifests his belief that relevance to Supreme Court issues is confined neither to

18. Everson v. Board of Education, 330 U.S. 1, 59 (1947). [F.F.]

the formal documents of law nor even to the more amorphous contributions of the social sciences. Most revealing, perhaps is that Frankfurter found in Frost's poems "variations on the theme of wise humility." [19]

19. FRANKFURTER, OF LAW AND LIFE AND OTHER THINGS THAT MATTER 232 (Kurland ed. 1965).

9   Criminal Justice: Federal Courts

That Felix Frankfurter had little faith in the special capacity of the Supreme Court to design general rules of criminal procedure is attested by his objections to the promulgation of the Federal Rules of Criminal Procedure. On the other hand, in the case-by-case judicial process, he found the appropriate means for establishing such rules. Where possible he eschewed constitutional standards in favor of the exercise of what he termed the Court's supervisory powers over the administration of criminal justice in the federal courts. Most prominent of the cases which fell into this category was *McNabb v. United States*,[1] which involved his notions of the importance of criminal procedure no less than his desire to avoid constitutional rules:[2]

It is true, as the petitioners assert, that a conviction in the federal courts, the foundation of which is evidence obtained in disregard of liberties deemed fundamental by the Constitution, cannot stand.[3] And this Court has, on Constitutional grounds, set aside convictions, both in the federal and state courts, which were based upon confessions "secured by protracted and repeated questioning of ignorant and untutored persons, in whose minds the power of officers was greatly magnified,"[4] or "who have been unlawfully held incommunicado without advice of friends or counsel."[5]

In the view we take of the case, however, it becomes unnecessary to reach the Constitutional issue pressed upon us. For, while the power of this Court to undo convictions in state courts is limited to

1. 318 U.S. 322 (1943).

2. *Id.* at 339–45.

3. Boyd v. United States, 116 U.S. 616 (1886); Weeks v. United States, 232 U.S. 383 (1914); Gouled v. United States, 255 U.S. 298 (1921); Amos v. United States, 255 U.S. 313 (1920); Agnello v. United States, 269 U.S. 20 (1925); Byars v. United States, 273 U.S. 28 (1927); Grau v. United States, 287 U.S. 124 (1932). [F.F.]

4. Lisenba v. California, 314 U.S. 219, 239–40 (1941). [F.F.]

5. Ward v. Texas, 316 U.S. 547, 555 (1942); and see Brown v. Mississippi, 297 U.S. 278 (1936); Chambers v. Florida, 309 U.S. 227 (1940); Canty v. Alabama, 309 U.S. 629 (1940); White v. Texas, 310 U.S. 530 (1940); Lomax v. Texas, 313 U.S. 544 (1941); Vernon v. Alabama, 313 U.S. 547 (1941). [F.F.]

the enforcement of those "fundamental principles of liberty and justice,"[6] which are secured by the Fourteenth Amendment, the scope of our reviewing power over convictions brought here from the federal courts is not confined to ascertainment of Constitutional validity. Judicial supervision of the administration of criminal justice in the federal courts implies the duty of establishing and maintaining civilized standards of procedure and evidence. Such standards are not satisfied by observance of those minimal historical safeguards for securing trial by reason which are summarized as "due process of law" and below which we reach what is really trial by force. Moreover, review by this Court of state action expressing its notion of what will best further its own security in the administration of criminal justice demands appropriate respect for the deliberative judgment of a state in so basic an exercise of its jurisdiction. Consideration of large policy in making the necessary accommodations in our federal system are wholly irrelevant to the formulation and application of proper standards for the enforcement of the federal criminal law in the federal courts.

The principles governing the admissibility of evidence in federal criminal trials have not been restricted, therefore, to those derived solely from the Constitution. In the exercise of its supervisory authority over the administration of criminal justice in the federal courts,[7] this Court has, from the very beginning of its history, formulated rules of evidence to be applied in federal criminal prosecutions.[8] And in formulating such rules of evidence for federal criminal trials the Court has been guided by considerations of justice not limited to the strict canons of evidentiary relevance.

Quite apart from the Constitution, therefore, we are constrained to hold that the evidence elicited from the petitioners in the circumstances disclosed here must be excluded. For in their treatment of the petitioners the arresting officers assumed functions which Congress has explicitly denied them. They subjected the accused to the pressures of a procedure which is wholly incompatible with the vital but very restricted duties of the investigating and arresting officers of the Government and which tends to undermine the integrity of the

6. Hebert v. Louisiana, 272 U.S. 312, 316 (1926). [F.F.]

7. Nardone v. United States, 308 U.S. 338, 341–42 (1939). [F.F.]

8. *E.g., Ex parte* Bollman & Swartwout, 4 Cranch 75, 130–31 (1807); United States v. Palmer, 3 Wheat. 610, 643–44 (1818); United States v. Furlong, 5 Wheat, 184, 199 (1820); United States v. Gooding, 12 Wheat. 460, 468–70 (1827); United States v. Wood, 14 Pet. 430 (1840); United States v. Murphy, 16 Pet. 203 (1842); Funk v. United States, 290 U.S. 371 (1933); Wolfle v. United States, 291 U.S. 7 (1934); see 1 WIGMORE ON EVIDENCE 170–97 (3d ed. 1940); Note, 47 HARV. L. REV. 853 (1934). [F.F.]

criminal proceeding. Congress has explicitly commanded that "It shall be the duty of the marshal, his deputy, or other officer, who may arrest a person charged with any crime or offense, to take the defendant before the nearest United States commissioner or the nearest judicial officer having jurisdiction under existing laws for a hearing, commitment, or taking bail for trial. . . ."[9] Similar legislation, requiring that arrested persons be promptly taken before a committing authority, appears on the statute books of nearly all the states.

The purpose of this impressively pervasive requirement of criminal procedure is plain. A democratic society, in which respect for the dignity of all men is central, naturally guards against the misuse of the law enforcement process. Zeal in tracking down crime is not in itself an assurance of soberness of judgment. Disinterestedness in law enforcement does not alone prevent disregard of cherished liberties. Experience has therefore counseled that safeguards must be provided against the dangers of the overzealous as well as the despotic. The awful instruments of the criminal law cannot be entrusted to a single functionary. The complicated process of criminal justice is therefore divided into different parts, responsibility for which is separately vested in the various participants upon whom the criminal law relies for its vindication. Legislation such as this, requiring that the police must with reasonable promptness show legal cause for detaining arrested persons, constitutes an important safeguard — not only in assuring protection for the innocent but also in securing conviction of the guilty by methods that commend themselves to a progressive and self-confident society. For this procedural requirement checks resort to those reprehensible practices known as the "third degree" which, though universally rejected as indefensible, still find their way into use. It aims to avoid all the evil implications of secret interrogation of persons accused of crime. It reflects a sentimental but a sturdy view of law enforcement. It outlaws easy but self-defeating ways in which brutality is substituted for brains as an instrument of crime detection. A statute carrying such purposes is expressive of a general legislative policy to which courts should not be heedless when appropriate situations call for its application.

The circumstances in which the statements admitted in evidence

9. 18 U.S.C. § 595. Similarly, the Act of 18 June 1934, c. 595, 38 Stat. 1008, 5 U.S.C. § 300a, authorizing officers of the Federal Bureau of Investigation to make arrests, requires that "the person arrested shall be immediately taken before a committing officer." Compare also the Act of 1 March 1879, c. 125, 20 Stat. 327, 341, 18 U.S.C. § 593, which provides that when arrests are made of persons in the act of operating an illicit distillery, the arrested persons shall be taken forthwith before some judicial officer residing in the county where the arrests were made, or if none, in the county nearest the place of arrest. [F.F.]

against the petitioners were secured reveal a plain disregard of the duty enjoined by Congress upon federal law officers. Freeman and Raymond McNabb were arrested in the middle of the night at their home. Instead of being brought before a United States commissioner or a judicial officer, as the law requires, in order to determine the sufficiency of the justification for their detention, they were put in a barren cell and kept there for fourteen hours. For two days they were subjected to unremitting questioning by numerous officers. Benjamin's confession was secured by detaining him unlawfully and questioning him continuously for five or six hours. The McNabbs had to submit to all this without the aid of friends or the benefit of counsel. The record leaves no room for doubt that the questioning of the petitioners took place while they were in the custody of the arresting officers and before any order of commitment was made. Plainly, a conviction resting on evidence secured through such a flagrant disregard of the procedure which Congress has commanded cannot be allowed to stand without making the courts themselves accomplices in willful disobedience of law. Congress has not explicitly forbidden the use of evidence so procured. But to permit such evidence to be made the basis of a conviction in the federal courts would stultify the policy which Congress has enacted into law.

In *McNabb*, Frankfurter was also trying to preach to the state courts by example. Our constitutional history would have taken a different turn if the state courts had voluntarily adopted requirements that later were imposed on them. The flexibility that might have been theirs was dissipated by recalcitrance. A tight yoke was applied by the Warren Court because the loose rein was found inadequate.

Reluctant as he was to resort to constitutional standards, Frankfurter was nevertheless the first among the contemporary Court ready to make the protections of the Fourth Amendment's ban on unreasonable searches and seizures into realities. His dissent in *Davis v. United States*,[10] anticipated much of the Court's more recent efforts in this field: [11]

In its surface aspects this case concerns merely a squalid effort to evade the wartime system of gasoline rationing. But it should not be disposed of in that perspective. It is not the first petty little case to put to the test respect for principles which the founders of this nation deemed essential for a free society. For the case is directly related to one of the great chapters in the historic process whereby

10. 328 U.S. 582 (1946).

11. *Id.* at 594–97, 603–07, 614–16.

civil liberty was achieved and constitutionally protected against
future inroads.

The Court's decision, as I see it, presents this issue: May papers
which an accused could not be compelled to produce even by a
judicial process of a search warrant be taken from him against his
will by officers of the law without such judicial process for use as
evidence in a criminal prosecution against him? Judicial process may
not compel the production of documents either because of the
protection of the Fifth Amendment against self-crimination, or, as
in this case, because the authorization by Congress of search warrants
is withheld in a situation like the present. The Court apparently rules
that because the gasoline business was subject to regulation, the search
and seizure of such documents without a warrant is not an unreasonable search and seizure condemned by the Fourth Amendment. To
hold that the search in this case was legal is to hold that a search which
could not be justified under a search warrant is lawful without it. I
cannot escape the conviction that such a view of the Fourth Amendment makes a travesty of it and of the long course of legislation in
which Congress applied that Amendment.

Where search is made under the authority of a warrant issued from
a judicial source, the scope of the search must be confined to the
specific authorization of the warrant. It cannot be that the Constitution meant to make it legally advantageous not to have a warrant, so
that the police may roam freely and have the courts retrospectively
hold that the search that was made was "reasonable," reasonableness
being judged from the point of view of obtaining relevant evidence. I
had supposed that that was precisely what the Fourth Amendment
was meant to stop. "The Government could desire its possession
only to use it as evidence against the defendant and to search for
and seize it for such purpose was unlawful." [12]

There is indeed a difference between private papers and papers
having also a public bearing. Private papers of an accused cannot
be seized even through legal process because their use would violate
the prohibition of the Fifth Amendment against self-incrimination.
So-called public papers — papers in which the public has an interest
other than that which they may serve as evidence in a case — may
be seized, but like all other things in an individual's possession they
can be seized only upon a properly safeguarded search. The amenability of corporate papers to testimonial compulsion means that a
corporation, because it is a corporation, cannot make claim to the
privilege of self-crimination. Nor can the custodian of corporate books
immunize them against their production in court because they may

12. Gouled v. United States, 255 U.S. 298, 310 (1921). [F.F.]

also carry testimony against him. The Fourth Amendment does not give freedom from testimonial compulsion. Subject to familiar qualifications every man is under obligation to give testimony. But that obligation can be exacted only under judicial sanctions which are deemed precious to Anglo-American civilization. Merely because there may be the duty to make documents available for litigation does not mean that police officers may forcibly or fraudulently obtain them. This protection of the right to be let alone except under responsible judicial compulsion is precisely what the Fourth Amendment meant to express and to safeguard.

An even more fundamental issue lurks in the Court's opinion if a casual but explicit phrase about the locus of the search and seizure as "a place of business, not a private resident" is intended to carry relevant legal implications. If this is an indirect way of saying that the Fourth Amendment only secures homes against unreasonable searches and seizures but not offices — private offices of physicians and lawyers, of trade unions and other organizations, of business and scientific enterprises — then indeed it would constitute a sudden and drastic break with the whole history of the Fourth Amendment and its applications by this Court.[13] I cannot believe that a vast area of civil liberties was thus meant to be wiped out by a few words, without prior argument or consideration.

The course of decision in this Court has thus far jealously enforced the principle of a free society secured by the prohibition of unreasonable searches and seizures. Its safeguards are not to be worn away by a process of devitalizing interpretation. The approval given today to what was done by arresting officers in this case indicates that we are in danger of forgetting that the Bill of Rights reflects the experience with police excesses. It is not only under Nazi rule that police excesses are inimical to freedom. It is easy to make light of insistence on scrupulous regards for the safeguards of civil liberties when invoked on behalf of the unworthy. It is too easy. History bears testimony that by such disregard are the rights of liberty extinguished, heedlessly at first, then stealthily, and brazenly in the end. . . .

. . . [S]o unhappy was the experience with police search for papers and articles "in home or office,"[14] that it was once maintained that no search and seizure is valid. To Lord Coke has been attributed the proposition that warrants could not be secured even for stolen property.[15] Under early English doctrine even search warrants by

13. See Olmstead v. United States, 277 U.S. 438, 477 and cases cited in nn. 5, 6, 7 (1928).

14. Gouled v. United States, 255 U.S. 298, 308, 309 (1921). [F.F.]

15. But see COKE, FOURTH INSTITUTE 176–177 (1644). [F.F.]

appropriate authority could issue only for stolen goods.[16] Certainly warrants lacking strict particularity as to location to be searched or articles to be seized were deemed obnoxious.[17] An attempt to exceed these narrow limits called forth the enduring judgment of Lord Camden, in *Entick* v. *Carrington*,[18] in favor of freedom against police intrusions. And when appeal to the colonial courts on behalf of these requisite safeguards for the liberty of the people failed,[19] a higher tribunal resolved the issue. The familiar comment of John Adams on Otis' argument in *Paxton's Case* can never become stale: "American independence was then and there born; the seeds of patriots and heroes were then and there sown, to defend the vigorous youth, the *non sine Diis animosus infans*. Every man of a crowded audience appeared to me to go away, as I did, ready to take arms against writs of assistance. Then and there was the first scene of the first act of opposition to the arbitrary claims of Great Britain. Then and there the child Independence was born. In fifteen years, namely in 1776, he grew up to manhood, and declared himself free." [20] So basic to liberty is the protection against governmental search and seizure, that every State in the Union has this as a constitutional safeguard.

This bleak recital of the past was living experience for Madison and his collaborators. They wrote that experience into the Fourth Amendment, not merely its words. Mention has been made of the doubt in the minds of English and Colonial libertarians whether searches and seizures could be sanctioned even by search warrants. It is significant that Madison deemed it necessary to put into the Fourth Amendment a qualifying permission for search and seizure by the judicial process of the search warrant — a search warrant exacting in its foundation and limited in scope. This qualification gives the key to what the framers had in mind by prohibiting "unreasonable" searches and seizures. The principle was that all seizures without judicial authority were deemed "unreasonable." If the purpose of its framers is to be respected, the meaning of the Fourth Amendment must be distilled from contemporaneous history.

16. 2 HALE, PLEAS OF THE CROWN 113–14, 149–51 (1678); 2 GABBETT, CRIMINAL LAW 156 *et seq.* (1843); 1 CHITTY, CRIMINAL LAW 64 *et seq.* (5th ed. 1847); BARBOUR, CRIMINAL LAW 499 *et seq.* (2d ed. 1852); 1 ARCHIBALD, CRIMINAL PROCEDURE 141 (7th ed. 1860). [F.F.]

17. *Ibid.*; see also 2 HAWKINS, PLEAS OF THE CROWN 130, 133 (1716). [F.F.]

18. 19 Howell's State Trials 1029 (1765). [F.F.]

19. Paxton's Case, Quincy (Mass.) 51 (1761). [F.F.]

20. 10 ADAMS, WORKS 247–49 (C. F. Adams ed. 1856). (For a description of Otis's speech in *Paxton's Case*, see 2 *id.* 523.) [F.F.]

The intention of the Amendment was accurately elucidated in an early Massachusetts case. The court there had before it the terms of the Massachusetts Constitution, on which, with like provisions in other State Constitutions, the Fourth Amendment was based:

"With the fresh recollection of those stirring discussions [respecting writs of assistance], and of the revolution which followed them, the article in the Bill of Rights, respecting searches and seizures, was framed and adopted. This article does not prohibit all searches and seizures of a man's person, his papers, and possessions; but such only as are 'unreasonable,' and the foundation of which is 'not previously supported by oath or affirmation.' The legislature were not deprived of the power to authorize search warrants for probable causes, supported by oath or affirmation, and for the punishment or suppression of any violation of law. The law, therefore, authorizing search warrants in certain cases, is in no respect inconsistent with the declaration of rights." [21]

Such was the contemporaneous construction of the Fourth Amendment by the Congress. It gave specific authorization whenever it wished to permit searches and seizures. Beginning with the first Congress down to 1917, Congress authorized search by warrant not as a generally available resource in aid of criminal prosecution but in the most restricted way, observing with a jealous eye the recurrence of evils with which our early statesmen were intimately familiar. For each concrete situation Congress deemed it necessary to pass a separate act. An incomplete examination finds scores of such *ad hoc* enactments scattered through the Statutes at Large. Not until 1917, and then only after repeated demands by the Attorney General, did Congress pass the present statute authorizing the issue of search warrants for generalized situations.[22] Even then the situations were restricted and the scope of the authority was strictly defined. In the case before us no attempt was made to get a search warrant because none could have been got. Congress did not authorize one either on the charges on which Davis was originally arrested or on which he was ultimately tried. And even since the 1917 Act Congress has emphasized the importance of basing the compulsory demand for evidence upon judicial process rather than the zeal of arresting officers. The habit of continual watchfulness against the dangers of police abuses has been reflected in that Congress has continued to authorize search warrants for particular situations by specific legislation or by reference to the 1917 Act. . . .

21. Commonwealth v. Dana, 2 Met. (Mass.) 329, 336 (1841). [F.F.]
22. 40 Stat. 217, 228, 18 U.S.C. §§ 611 *et seq.*

In the course of its decisions, with a deviation promptly retraced, this Court has likewise reflected the broad purpose of the Fourth Amendment. The historic reach of the Amendment and the duty to observe it was expounded for the Court by Mr. Justice Bradley in *Boyd* v. *United States*,[23] "a case that will be remembered as long as civil liberty lives in the United States."[24] The Amendment has not been read in a niggardly spirit or with the outlook of a narrow-minded lawyer. . . .

It is too often felt, though not always avowed, that what is called nice observance of these constitutional safeguards makes apprehension and conviction of violators too difficult. Want of alertness and enterprise on the part of the law enforcers too often is the real obstruction to law enforcements. The present case affords a good instance. . . .

. . . Stern enforcement of the criminal law is the hallmark of a healthy and self-confident society. But in our democracy such enforcement presupposes a moral atmosphere and a reliance upon intelligence whereby the effective administration of justice can be achieved with due regard for those civilized standards in the use of the criminal law which are formulated in our Bill of Rights. If great principles sometimes appear as finicky obstructions in bringing a criminal to heel, this admonition of a wise judge gives the final answer: "Such constitutional limitations arise from grievances, real or fancied, which their makers have suffered, and should go pari passu with the supposed evil. They withstand the winds of logic by the depth and toughness of their roots in the past. Nor should we forget that what seems fair enough against a squalid huckster of bad liquor may take on a very different face, if used by a government determined to suppress political opposition under the guise of sedition."[25]

In the more contemporary context of electronic devices used to invade the privacy of citizens, Frankfurter was equally vehement in his stated objections. In *On Lee v. United States*[26] he wrote:[27]

The law of this Court ought not to be open to the just charge of having been dictated by the "odious doctrine," as Mr. Justice Brandeis

23. 116 U.S. 616 (1856). [F.F.]

24. Brandeis, J., in Olmstead v. United States, 277 U.S. 438, 471, 474 (1928). [F.F.]

25. Learned Hand, J., in United States v. Kirschenblatt, 16 F.2d 202, 203 (2d Cir. 1926). [F.F.]

26. 343 U.S. 747 (1952).

27. *Id.* at 758–62.

called it, that the end justifies reprehensible means. To approve legally what we disapprove morally, on the ground of practical convenience, is to yield to a short-sighted view of practicality. It derives from a preoccupation with what is episodic and a disregard of long-run consequences. The method by which the state chiefly exerts an influence upon the conduct of its citizens, it was wisely said by Archbishop William Temple, is "the moral qualities which it exhibits in its own conduct."

Loose talk about war against crime too easily infuses the administration of justice with the psychology and morals of war. It is hardly conducive to the soundest employment of the judicial process. Nor are the needs of an effective penal code seen in the truest perspective by talk about a criminal prosecution's not being a game in which the Government loses because its officers have not played according to rule. Of course criminal prosecution is more than a game. But in any event it should not be deemed to be a dirty game in which "the dirty business" of criminals is outwitted by "the dirty business" of law officers. The contrast between morality professed by society and immorality practiced on its behalf makes for contempt of law. Respect for law cannot be turned off and on as though it were a hot-water faucet.

It is a quarter century since this Court, by the narrowest margin, refused to put wiretapping beyond the constitutional pale where a fair construction of the Fourth Amendment should properly place it. Since then, instead of going from strength to strength in combatting crime, we have gone from inefficiency to inefficiency, from corruption to corruption. The moral insight of Mr. Justice Brandeis unerringly foresaw this inevitability. "The progress of science in furnishing the Government with means of espionage is not likely to stop with wire-tapping. Ways may some day be developed by which the Government, without removing papers from secret drawers, can reproduce them in court, and by which it will be enabled to expose to a jury the most intimate occurrences of the home. Advances in the psychic and related sciences may bring means of exploring unexpressed beliefs, thoughts and emotions."[28] The circumstances of the present case show how the rapid advances of science are made available for that police intrusion into our private lives against which the Fourth Amendment of the Constitution was set on guard.

It is noteworthy that, although this Court deemed wiretapping not outlawed by the Constitution, Congress outlawed it legislatively by the Communications Act of 1934.[29] What is perhaps even more

28. Olmstead v. United States, 277 U.S. 438, 471, 474 (1928). [F.F.]

29. 48 Stat. 1064, 1103, 47 U.S.C. § 605; Nardone v. United States, 302 U.S. 379 (1937); 308 U.S. 338 (1939). [F.F.]

noteworthy is its pervasive disregard in practice by those who as law officers owe special obedience to law. What is true of the federal Act against wiretapping and its violations is widely true of related state legislation and its disobedience.[30] Few sociological generalizations are more valid than that lawlessness begets lawlessness.

The members of this Court who so vigorously urged that wiretapping is within the clear scope of the prohibition of the Fourth Amendment were no sentimentalists about crime or criminals. Mr. Justice Holmes, Mr. Justice Brandeis, Mr. Justice Butler and Mr. Chief Justice Stone were no softies. In all matters of social policy we have to choose, and it was the hardy philosophy of life that his years in the Army of the Potomac taught him that led Mr. Justice Holmes to deem it "a less evil that some criminals should escape than that the Government should play an ignoble part."[31]

Suppose it be true that through "dirty business" it is easier for prosecutors and police to bring an occasional criminal to heel. It is most uncritical to assume that unless the Government is allowed to practice "dirty business" crime would become rampant or would go unpunished.

In the first place, the social phenomena of crime are imbedded in the texture of our society. Equally deep-seated are the causes of all that is sordid and ineffective in the administration of our criminal law. These are outcroppings, certainly in considerable part, of modern industrialism and of the prevalent standards of the community, related to the inadequacy in our day of early American methods and machinery for law enforcement and to the small pursuit of scientific inquiry into the causes and treatment of crime.

Of course we cannot wait on the slow progress of the sociological sciences in illuminating so much that is still dark. Nor should we relax for a moment vigorous enforcement of the criminal law until society, by its advanced civilized nature, will beget an atmosphere and environment in which crime will shrink to relative insignificance. My deepest feeling against giving legal sanction to such "dirty business" as the record in this case discloses is that it makes for lazy and not alert law enforcement. It puts a premium on force and fraud, not on imagination and enterprise and professional training. The third degree, search without warrant, wiretapping and the like, were not tolerated in what was probably the most successful administration in our time of the busiest United States Attorney's office. This experience under Henry L. Stimson in the Southern District of New York, compared with happenings elsewhere, doubtless

30. See Westin, *The Wire-Tapping Problem*, 52 Colum. L. Rev. 165 (1952). [F.F.]

31. Olmstead v. United States, note 28 *supra*, at 470. [F.F.]

planted in me a deep conviction that these short-cuts in the detection and prosecution of crime are as self-defeating as they are immoral.

Sir James Fitzjames Stephen brings significant testimony on this point: [32]

"During the discussions which took place on the Indian Code of Criminal Procedure in 1872 some observations were made on the reasons which occasionally lead native police officers to apply torture to prisoners. An experienced civil officer observed, 'There is a great deal of laziness in it. It is far pleasanter to sit comfortably in the shade rubbing red pepper into a poor devil's eyes than to go about in the sun hunting up evidence.' This was a new view to me, but I have no doubt of its truth."

And Fitzjames Stephen, who acted on this experience in drawing the Indian Evidence Act, was no softie, either before he became a judge or on the bench.

Accordingly I adhere to the views expressed in *Goldman* v. *United States*,[33] that the *Olmstead* case should be overruled for the reasons set forth in the dissenting opinions in that case. These views have been strongly underlined by the steady increase of lawlessness on the part of law officers, even after Congress has forbidden what the dissenters in *Olmstead* found the Constitution to forbid.

Even on the basis of the prior decisions of this Court, however, I feel bound to dissent. The Court seems not content with calling a halt at the place it had reached on what I deem to be the wrong road. As my brother BURTON shows, the Court now pushes beyond the lines of legality heretofore drawn. Such encouragement to lazy, immoral conduct by the police does not bode well for effective law enforcement. Nor will crime be checked by such means.

Frankfurter's zeal on behalf of the rights of privacy under the Fourth Amendment was not matched in his approach to problems of self-crimination under the Fifth Amendment. His views were expounded in his opinion for the Court in *Ullmann* v. *United States*,[34] where the question presented was the validity of a federal statute compelling incrimination in exchange for a grant of immunity. He made it clear that he regarded the self-crimination clause as indeed conferring a "privilege" and not a "right": [35]

32. 1 STEPHEN, A HISTORY OF THE CRIMINAL LAW OF ENGLAND 442 n. (1883); *cf.* §§ 25 and 26 of the Indian Evidence Act (1872). [F.F.]

33. 316 U.S. 129, 136 (1942). [F.F.]

34. 350 U.S. 422 (1956).

35. *Id.* at 426–31, 438–39.

It is relevant to define explicitly the spirit in which the Fifth Amendment's privilege against self-incrimination should be approached. This command of the Fifth Amendment ("nor shall any person . . . be compelled in any criminal case to be a witness against himself . . . .") registers an important advance in the development of our liberty — "one of the great landmarks in man's struggle to make himself civilized." Time has not shown that protection from the evils against which this safeguard was directed is needless or unwarranted. This constitutional protection must not be interpreted in a hostile or niggardly spirit. Too many, even those who should be better advised, view this privilege as a shelter for wrongdoers. They too readily assume that those who invoke it are either guilty of crime or commit perjury in claiming the privilege. Such a view does scant honor to the patriots who sponsored the Bill of Rights as a condition to acceptance of the Constitution by the ratifying States. The Founders of the Nation were not naive or disregardful of the interests of justice. The difference between them and those who deem the privilege an obstruction to due inquiry has been appropriately indicated by Chief Judge Magruder:[36]

"Our forefathers, when they wrote this provision into the Fifth Amendment of the Constitution, had in mind a lot of history which has been largely forgotten to-day. See VIII Wigmore on Evidence (3d ed. 1940) § 2250 *et seq.*; Morgan, The Privilege Against Self-Incrimination, 34 Minn. L. Rev. 1 (1949). They made a judgment and expressed it in our fundamental law, that it were better for an occasional crime to go unpunished than that the prosecution should be free to build up a criminal case, in whole or in part, with the assistance of enforced disclosures by the accused. The privilege against self-incrimination serves as a protection to the innocent as well as to the guilty, and we have been admonished that it should be given a liberal application. Hoffman v. United States, . . . 341 U.S. 479, 486. . . . If it be thought that the privilege is outmoded in the conditions of this modern age, then the thing to do is to take it out of the Constitution, not to whittle it down by the subtle encroachments of judicial opinion."

Nothing new can be put into the Constitution except through the amendatory process. Nothing old can be taken out without the same process.

No doubt the constitutional privilege may, on occasion, save a guilty man from his just deserts. It was aimed at a more far-reaching

36. Maffie v. United States, 209 F.2d 225, 227 (1st Cir. 1954). [F.F.]

evil — a recurrence of the Inquisition and the Star Chamber, even if not in their stark brutality. Prevention of the greater evil was deemed of more importance than occurrence of the lesser evil. Having had much experience with a tendency in human nature to abuse power, the Founders sought to close the doors against like future abuses by law-enforcing agencies.

As no constitutional guarantee enjoys preference, so none should suffer subordination or deletion. It is appropriate to read the conviction expressed in a memorable address by Senator Albert J. Beveridge to the American Bar Association in 1920, a time when there was also manifested impatience with some of the restrictions of the Constitution in the presumed interest of security. His appeal was to the Constitution — to the whole Constitution, not to a mutilating selection of those parts only which for the moment find favor. To view a particular provision of the Bill of Rights with disfavor inevitably results in a constricted application of it. This is to disrespect the Constitution.

It is in this spirit of strict, not lax, observance of the constitutional protection of the individual that we approach the claims made by petitioner in this case. The attack on the Immunity Act as violating the Fifth Amendment is not a new one. Sixty years ago this Court considered [37] the constitutionality of a similar Act.[38] In that case, Brown, auditor for a railroad company, had been subpoenaed to testify before a grand jury which was investigating charges that officers and agents of the company had violated the Interstate Commerce Act. Invoking the privilege against self-incrimination, he refused to answer certain questions concerning the operations and the rebate policy of the railroad. On an order to show cause before the United States District Court for the Western District of Pennsylvania, he was adjudged in contempt. His petition for a writ of habeas corpus to the Circuit Court for the Western District of Pennsylvania was dismissed. Petitioner appealed to this Court, urging that the 1893 immunity statute was unconstitutional.

The Court considered and rejected petitioner's arguments, holding that a statute which compelled testimony but secured the witness against a criminal prosecution which might be aided directly or indirectly by his disclosures did not violate the Fifth Amendment's privilege against self-incrimination and that the 1893 statute did provide such immunity. "While the constitutional provision in question is justly regarded as one of the most valuable prerogatives of the citizen, its object is fully accomplished by the statutory immunity,

37. Brown v. Walker, 161 U.S. 591 (1896). [F.F.]
38. Act of 11 February 1893, 27 Stat. 443. [F.F.]

and we are, therefore, of the opinion that the witness was compellable to answer. . . ."[39]

Petitioner, however, attempts to distinguish *Brown* v. *Walker*. He argues that this case is different from *Brown* v. *Walker* because the impact of the disabilities imposed by federal and state authorities and the public in general — such as loss of job, expulsion from labor unions, state registration and investigation statutes, passport eligibility, and general public opprobrium — is so oppressive that the statute does not give him true immunity. This, he alleges, is significantly different from the impact of testifying on the auditor in *Brown* v. *Walker*, who could the next day resume his job with reputation unaffected. But, as this Court has often held, the immunity granted need only remove those sanctions which generate the fear justifying the invocation of the privilege: "The interdiction of the Fifth Amendment operates only where a witness is asked to incriminate himself — in other words, to give testimony which may possibly expose him to a criminal charge. But if the criminality has already been taken away, the Amendment ceases to apply."[40] Here, since the Immunity Act protects a witness who is compelled to answer to the extent of his constitutional immunity, he has of course, when a particular sanction is sought to be imposed against him, the right to claim that it is criminal in nature. . . .

We are not dealing here with one of the vague, undefinable, admonitory provisions of the Constitution whose scope is inevitably addressed to changing circumstances. The privilege against self-incrimination is a specific provision of which it is peculiarly true that "a page of history is worth a volume of logic."[41] For the history of the privilege establishes not only that it is not to be interpreted literally, but also that its sole concern is, as its name indicates, with the danger to a witness forced to give testimony leading to the infliction of "penalties affixed to the criminal acts. . . ."[42] We leave *Boyd* v. *United States* unqualified, as it was left unqualified in *Brown* v. *Walker*. Immunity displaces the danger. Once the reason for the privilege ceases, the privilege ceases. We reaffirm *Brown* v. *Walker*, and in so doing we need not repeat the answers given by that case to the other points raised by petitioner.

Earlier, joined by Mr. Justice Douglas, Frankfurter had dissented in *United States* v. *Monia*[43] from a ruling that immunity had been

39. 161 U.S. at 610 [F.F.]

40. Hale v. Henkel, 201 U.S. 43, 67 (1906). [F.F.]

41. New York Trust Co. v. Eisner, 256 U.S. 345, 349 (1921). [F.F.]

42. Boyd v. United States, 116 U.S. 616, 634 (1856). [F.F.]

43. 317 U.S. 424, 431 (1943).

conferred by a federal statute to a person who had made no claim
of the privilege. The opinion is noteworthy as an exploration of problems of statutory construction as well as of constitutional doctrine: [44]

This question cannot be answered by closing our eyes to everything
except the naked words of the Act of June 30, 1906. The notion that
because the words of a statute are plain, its meaning is also plain,
is merely pernicious oversimplification. It is a wooden English
doctrine of rather recent vintage [45] to which lip service has on occasion
been given here, but which since the days of Marshall this Court
has rejected, especially in practice.[46] A statute, like other living
organisms, derives significance and sustenance from its environment,
from which it cannot be severed without being mutilated. Especially
is this true where the statute, like the one before us, is part of a
legislative process having a history and purpose. The meaning of such
a statute cannot be gained by confining inquiry within its four
corners. Only the historic process of which such legislation is an
incomplete fragment — that to which it gave rise as well as that which
gave rise to it — can yield its true meaning. And so we must turn to
the history of federal immunity provisions. . . .

Duty, not privilege, lies at the core of this problem — the duty to
testify, and not the privilege that relieves of such duty. In the classic
phrase of Lord Chancellor Hardwicke, "the public has a right to
every man's evidence." The duty to give testimony was qualified at
common law by the privilege against self-incrimination. And the
Fifth Amendment has embodied this privilege in our fundamental law.
But the privilege is a privilege to withhold answers and not a privilege
to limit the range of public inquiry. The Constitution does not forbid
the asking of criminative questions. It provides only that a witness
cannot be compelled to answer such questions unless "a full substitute"
for the constitutional privilege is given.[47] The compulsion which the
privilege entitles a witness to resist is the compulsion to answer
questions which he justifiably claims would tend to incriminate him.
But the Constitution does not protect a refusal to obey a process. A
subpoena is, of course, such a process, merely a summons to appear.[48]

44. *Id.* at 431–34, 441–42, 446–47.

45. See PLUCKNETT, A CONCISE HISTORY OF THE COMMON LAW 294–300 (2d
ed. 1936); Amos, *The Interpretation of Statutes,* 5 CAMB. L.J. 163 (1934);
Davies, *The Interpretation of Statutes,* 35 COLUM. L. REV. 519 (1935). [F.F.]

46. *E.g.,* United States v. Fisher, 2 Cranch 358, 385–86 (1805); Boston Sand
Co. v. United States, 278 U.S. 41, 48 (1928); United States v. American Truck-
ing Ass'ns, 310 U.S. 534, 542–44 (1940). [F.F.]

47. Counselman v. Hitchcock, 142 U.S. 547, 586 (1892). [F.F.]

48. 8 WIGMORE ON EVIDENCE § 2199, p. 106 (3d ed. 1940). [F.F.]

There never has been a privilege to disregard the duty to which a subpoena calls. And when Congress turned to the device of immunity legislation, therefore, it did not provide a "substitute" for the performance of the universal duty to appear as a witness — it did not undertake to give something for nothing. It was the refusal to give incriminating testimony for which Congress bargained, and not the refusal to give any testimony. And it was only in exchange for self-incriminating testimony which "otherwise could not be got"[49] because of the witness's invocation of his constitutional rights that Congress conferred immunity against the use of such testimony.

Instead of giving more than the constitutional equivalent for the privilege against self-incrimination, Congress for a long time did not give enough.[50] In order to remove the gap between what this Act gave and what the Constitution was construed to require, Congress promptly passed the Act of February 11, 1893,[51] in order not to interrupt the effective enforcement of the Interstate Commerce Act. As the debates reveal, Congress acted on its understanding of what this Court in the *Counselman* decision indicated was an adequate legislative alternative.[52] The 1893 Act followed the language of the Act of the January 24, 1857, by providing that "no person shall be *excused from attending and testifying* or from producing books. . . ."[53] And in 1896, this Court,[54] found that the 1893 Act "sufficiently satisfies the constitutional guarantee of protection." There was no indication of any belief that Congress had given anything more than it had to give — and, indeed, only a bare majority of the Court thought that the statute had given as much as the Constitution required. . . .

Once the confusion is avoided between an act of amnesty and an act which gives immunity in order "to make evidence available and compulsory that otherwise could not be got" because it could be withheld upon a claim of constitutional privilege, it becomes clear that a witness is not "entrapped" by requiring him to claim his constitutional privilege before affording him a substitute. A witness is no more entrapped by the requirement that he must stand upon his constitutional rights, if he desires their protection, when there is an immunity statute than he is where there is none at all. It is one thing

49. Heike v. United States, 227 U.S. 131, 142 (1913). [F.F.]

50. See Counselman v. Hitchcock, 142 U.S. 547 (1892), invalidating the Act of 25 February 1886, 15 Stat. 37, Rev. Stat. § 860. [F.F.]

51. 27 Stat. 443. [F.F.]

52. See remarks of Senator Cullum, 18 July 1892, 23 CONG. REC. 6333 [F.F.]

53. 27 Stat. 443 (italics added). [F.F.]

54. Brown v. Walker, 161 U.S. 591, 595 (1896). [F.F.]

to find that incriminating answers given by a witness were given because in the setting of the particular circumstances he would not have been allowed to withhold them. It is quite another to suggest that one who appears as a witness should, merely because his appearance is in response to a subpoena, thereby obtain immunity "on account of any transaction, matter or thing concerning which he may testify," even though the incrimination may relate to a transaction wholly foreign to the inquiry in which the testimony is given and even though the most alert and conscientious prosecutor would not have the slightest inkling that the testimony led to a trail of self-crimination. Such a construction makes of the immunity statute not what its history clearly reveals it to be, namely, a carefully devised instrument for the achievement of criminal justice, but a measure for the gratuitous relief of criminals. The statute reflects the judgment of Congress that "the public has a right to every man's evidence." It is not for us to relax the demands of society upon its citizens to appear in proceedings to enforce laws enacted for the public good. . . .

I am therefore of opinion that an appearance in response to a subpoena does not of itself confer immunity from prosecution for anything that a witness so responding may testify. There must be conscious surrender of the privilege of silence in the course of a testimonial inquiry. Of course no form of words is necessary to claim one's privilege. Circumstances may establish such a claim. But there must be some manifestation of surrender of the privilege. The prosecutor's insistence upon disclosure which, but for immunity from prosecution, could be withheld is that for which alone the immunity is given. History and reason alike reject the notion that immunity from prosecution is to be squandered by giving it gratuitously for responding to the duty, owed by everyone, to appear when summoned as a witness.

An expansive reading of the double jeopardy provision also held no appeal for the Justice, in either the federal or state realm. He dissented on behalf of a four-man minority in *Green v. United States*[55] from a decision that found double jeopardy in the ordinary processes of ordering a new trial:[56]

Since the prohibition in the Constitution against double jeopardy is derived from history, its significance and scope must be determined, "not simply by taking the words and a dictionary, but by considering [its] . . . origin and the line of [its] . . . growth."[57]

55. 355 U.S. 184 (1957).

56. *Id.* at 199–205, 215–19.

57. Gompers v. United States, 233 U.S. 604, 610 (1914). [F.F.]

The origin of this constitutional protection is found in the common-law pleas of *autrefois acquit* and *autrefois convict*. In *Vaux's Case*,[58] it was accepted as established that "the life of a man shall not be twice put in jeopardy for one and the same offence, and that is the reason and cause that *autrefois* acquitted or convicted of the same offence is a good plea. . . ." Likewise Blackstone stated that "the plea of *autrefoits acquit*, or a former acquittal, is grounded on this universal maxim of the common law of England, that no man is to be brought into jeopardy of his life, more than once, for the same offence. And hence it is allowed as a consequence, that when a man is once fairly found not guilty upon any indictment, or other prosecution, before any court having competent jurisdiction of the offence, he may plead such acquittal in bar of any subsequent accusation for the same crime."[59] To try again one who had been previously convicted or acquitted of the same offense was "abhorrent to the law of England."[60]

A principle so deeply rooted in the law of England, as an indispensable requirement of a civilized criminal procedure, was inevitably part of the legal tradition of the English Colonists in America. The Massachusetts Body of Liberties of 1641, an early compilation of principles drawn from the statutes and common law of England, declared that, "No man shall be twise sentenced by Civil Justice for one and the same Crime, offence, or Trespasse," and that "Everie Action betweene partie and partie, and proceedings against delinquents in Criminal causes shall be briefly and destinctly entered on the Rolles of every Court by the Recorder thereof. That such actions be not afterwards brought againe to the vexation of any man."[61]

Thus the First Congress, which proposed the Bill of Rights, came to its task with a tradition against double jeopardy founded both on ancient precedents in the English law and on legislation that had grown out of colonial experience and necessities. The need for the principle's general protection was undisputed, though its scope was not clearly defined. Fear of the power of the newly established Federal Government required "an explicit avowal in [the Constitution] . . . of some of the plainest and best established principles in relation to the rights of the citizens, and the rules of the common law."[62] Although many States in ratifying the Constitution had

58. 4 Co. Rep. 44a, 45a (1591). [F.F.]

59. 4 BLACKSTONE'S COMMENTARIES ON THE LAWS OF ENGLAND 335. [F.F.]

60. Regina v. Tancock, 13 Cox. C.C. 217, 220 (1876); see The King v. Emden, 9 East 437, 445–47 (1808). [F.F.]

61. Colonial Laws of Massachusetts 43, 47. [F.F.]

62. People v. Goodwin, 18 Johns. (N.Y.) 187, 202 (1820). [F.F.]

proposed amendments considered indispensable to secure the rights of the citizen against the Federal Government, New York alone proposed a prohibition against double jeopardy. This is not surprising in view of the fact that only in New Hampshire had the common-law principle been embodied in a constitutional provision.[63] The bill of rights adopted by the New York convention, and transmitted to Congress with its ratification of the Constitution, included a declaration that, "no Person ought to be put twice in Jeopardy of Life or Limb for one and the same Offence, nor, unless in the case of impeachment, be punished more than once for the same Offence."[64] This declaration was doubtless before Madison when he drafted the constitutional amendments to be proposed to the States.

The terms in which Madison introduced into the House what became the specific provision that is our present concern were these: "No person shall be subject, except in cases of impeachment, to more than one punishment or one trial for the same offence. . . ."[65] Debate on this provision in the Committee of the whole evidenced a concern that the language should express what the members understood to be established common-law principle. There was fear that, as proposed by Madison, it might be taken to prohibit a second trial even when sought by a defendant who had been convicted. Representative Benson of New York objected to the provision because he presumed it was meant to express the established principle "that no man's life should be more than once put in jeopardy for the same offence; yet it was well known, that they were entitled to more than one trial."[66] Others who spoke agreed that although of course there could be no second trial following an acquittal, the prohibition should not extend to a second trial when a conviction had been set aside. The provision as amended by the Senate,[67] and eventually ratified as part of the Fifth Amendment to the Constitution, was substantially in the language used by Representative Benson to express his understanding of the common law.

The question that had concerned the House in debating Madison's proposal, the relation between the prohibition against double jeopardy and the power to order a new trial following conviction, was

63. 2 Poore, Federal and State Constitutions, Colonial Charters and Other Organic Laws 1282 (2d ed. 1878). [F.F.]

64. Documents Illustrative of the Formation of the Union, H.R. Doc. No. 398, 1035, 69th Cong., 1st Sess. (1927). [F.F.]

65. 1 Annals of Congress 451 (1789). [F.F.]

66. *Id.* at 753 [F.F.]

67. Sen. Journal, 1st Cong., 1st Sess. 77 (1789). [F.F.]

considered at length by Mr. Justice Story, on circuit.[68] The defendants in that case had been found guilty of robbery on the high seas, a capital offense, and moved for a new trial. Mr. Justice Story, after full consideration of the English and American authorities, concluded that the court had no power to grant a new trial when the first trial had been duly had on a valid indictment before a court of competent jurisdiction. According to his view, the prohibition against double jeopardy applied equally whether the defendant had been acquitted or convicted, and there was no exception for a case where the new trial was sought by the defendant for his own benefit. Earlier, Mr. Justice Story had himself taken a non-literal view of the constitutional provision in *United States* v. *Perez*,[69] where, writing for the Court, he found that discharge of a jury that had failed to agree was no bar to a second trial.[70]

Story's conclusion that English law prohibited, except in rare instances, granting a new trial after conviction of a felony was undoubtedly correct,[71] and on occasion this result has been expressly made to depend on the maxim prohibiting double jeopardy.[72] To this day the Court of Criminal Appeals has ordinarily no power to order a new trial even after quashing a conviction on appeal by the defendant,[73] and repeated efforts to secure this power for the court have met with the argument that a new trial would, at least in spirit, offend the principle that a defendant may not be put twice in jeopardy for the same offense.[74]

The old practice of the English courts, and the position taken by Mr. Justice Story, however, was generally rejected in the United States. The power to grant a new trial in the most serious cases appears to have been exercised by many American courts from an early date in spite of provisions against double jeopardy.[75] In *United States* v.

68. United States v. Gibert, 25 Fed. Cas. 1287, 1294–1303 (1834). [F.F.]

69. 9 Wheat. 579 (1824). [F.F.]

70. See also 3 STORY, COMMENTARIES ON THE CONSTITUTION 659–60 (1833). [F.F.]

71. See The King v. Mawbey, 6 T.R. 619, 638 (1796). [F.F.]

72. The Queen v. Murphy, 2 L.R.P.C. 535, 547–48 (1869); see The Attorney General v. Bertrand, 1 L.R.P.C. 520, 531–34 (1867); but see The Queen v. Scaife, 17 Q.B. 238 (1851). [F.F.]

73. Criminal Appeal Act, 7 Edw. VII, c. 23, § 4(2) (1907). [F.F.]

74. See 176 H.L. Deb. 759–62 (5th ser. 1952). [F.F.] England has since made provision for new trials by appellate order.

75. United States v. Fries, 3 Dall. 515 (1799) (treason); see People v. Morrison, 1 Parker's Crim. Rep. (N.Y.) 625, 626–43 (1854) (rape). [F.F.]

Keen,[76] a decision rendered only five years after *United States* v. *Gibert*, Mr. Justice McLean, on circuit, vigorously rejected the view that the constitutional provision prohibited a new trial on the defendant's motion after a conviction, or that it "guarantees to him the right of being hung, to protect him from the danger of a second trial."[77] Other federal courts that had occasion to consider the question also rejected Mr. Justice Story's position,[78] and statements by this Court cast serious doubt on its validity.[79] In *Hopt* v. *Utah*,[80] the defendant was in fact retried three times following reversals of his convictions.

Finally, *United States* v. *Ball*,[81] expressly rejected the view that the double jeopardy provision prevented a second trial when a conviction had been set aside. Two of the defendants in the case had been convicted of murder, and on writ of error the judgments were reversed with directions to quash the indictment. The same defendants were then convicted on a new indictment. In affirming these convictions the Court said, "it is quite clear that a defendant, who procures a judgment against him upon an indictment to be set aside, may be tried anew upon the same indictment, or upon another indictment, for the same offence of which he had been convicted."[82] On a literal reading of the constitutional provision, with an eye exclusively to the interests of the defendants, they had been "once in jeopardy," and were entitled to the benefit of a reversal of their convictions without the hazard of a new trial. The Court recognized, however, that such a wooden interpretation would distort the purposes of the constitutional provision to the prejudice of society's legitimate interest in convicting the guilty as much as, in *United States* v. *Gibert*, they had been distorted to the prejudice of defendants.[83] . . .

We should not be so unmindful, even when constitutional questions are involved, of the principle of *stare decisis*, by whose circumspect

76. 26 Fed Cas. 686, 687–90 (1839). [F.F.]

77. *Id.* at 690. [F.F.]

78. See United States v. Williams, 28 Fed. Cas. 636, 641 (1858); United States v. Harding, 26 Fed. Cas. 131, 136–38 (1846). [F.F.]

79. *Ex parte* Lange, 18 Wall. 163, 173–74 (1874); and Mr. Justice Clifford, dissenting, *id.* at 201–04. [F.F.]

80. 104 U.S. 631 (1881); 110 U.S. 574 (1884); 114 U.S. 488 (1885); 120 U.S. 430 (1887). [F.F.]

81. 163 U.S. 662, 662–71 (1896). [F.F.]

82. *Id.* at 672 [F.F.]

83. See also Murphy v. Massachusetts, 177 U.S. 155, 158–60 (1900). [F.F.]

observance the wisdom of this Court as an institution transcending the moment can alone be brought to bear on the difficult problems that confront us. The question in the present case is effectively indistinguishable from that in *Trono*.[84] Furthermore, we are not here called upon to weigh considerations generated by changing concepts as to minimum standards of fairness, which interpretation of the Due Process Clause inevitably requires. Instead, the defense of double jeopardy is involved, whose contours are the product of history. In this situation the passage of time is not enough, and the conviction borne to the mind of the rightness of an overturning decision must surely be of a highly compelling quality to justify overruling a well-established precedent when we are presented with no considerations fairly deemed to have been wanting to those who preceded us. Whatever might have been the allowable result if the question of retrying a defendant for the greater offense were here for the first time, to fashion a policy *in favorem vitae*, it is foreclosed by the decision in *Trono* v. *United States*.

Even if the question were here for the first time, we would not be justified in erecting the holding of the present case as a constitutional rule. Yet the opinion of the Court treats the question, not as one within our supervisory jurisdiction over federal criminal procedure, but as a question answered by the Fifth Amendment itself, and which therefore even Congress cannot undertake to affect.

Such an approach misconceives the purposes of the double jeopardy provision, and without warrant from the Constitution makes an absolute of the interests of the accused in disregard of the interests of society. In *Palko* v. *Connecticut*,[85] we held that a State could permit the prosecution to appeal a conviction of second degree murder and on retrial secure a conviction of first degree murder without violating any "fundamental principles of liberty and justice." Since the State's interest in obtaining a trial "free from the corrosion of substantial legal error" was sufficient to sustain the conviction of the greater offense after an appeal by the State, it would of course sustain such a conviction if the defendant had himself appealed. Although this case defined conduct permissible under the Due Process Clause of the Fourteenth Amendment, it cannot wisely be ignored in tracing the constitutional limits imposed on the Federal Government. Nor should we ignore the fact that a substantial body of opinion in the States permits what today the Court condemns as violative of a "vital safeguard in our society." The Court restricts Congress within limits that in the experience of many jurisdictions

84. Trono v. United States, 199 U.S. 521 (1905). [F.F.]

85. 302 U.S. 319 (1937). [F.F.]

are not a part of the protection against double jeopardy or required by its underlying purpose, and have not been imposed upon the States in the exercise of their governmental powers.

Undeniably the framers of the Bill of Rights were concerned to protect defendants from oppression and from efforts to secure, through the callousness of repeated prosecutions, convictions for whose justice no man could vouch. On the other hand, they were also aware of the countervailing interest in the vindication of criminal justice, which sets outer limits to the protections for those accused of crimes. Thus if a defendant appeals his conviction and obtains a reversal, all agree, certainly in this country, that he may be retried for the same offense. The reason is, obviously, not that the defendant has consented to the second trial — he would much prefer that the conviction be set aside and no further proceedings be had — but that the continuation of the proceedings by an appeal, together with the reversal of the conviction, are sufficient to permit a re-examination of the issue of the defendant's guilt without doing violence to the purposes behind the Double Jeopardy Clause. The balance represented by that clause leaves free another appeal to law. Since the propriety of the original proceedings has been called in question by the defendant, a complete re-examination of the issues in dispute is appropriate and not unjust. In the circumstances of the present case, likewise, the reversal of petitioner's conviction was a sufficient reason to justify a complete new trial in order that both parties might have one free from errors claimed to be prejudicial. As Mr. Justice Peckham pointed out in *Trono*, "the constitutional provision was really never intended to, and, properly construed, does not cover, the case of a judgment under these circumstances, which has been annulled by the court at the request of the accused. . . ." [86]

Nor would Frankfurter extend the double jeopardy concept to protect against multiple crimes growing out of a single set of operative facts. This time he spoke for the majority of the Court, again divided five to four, in *Gore v. United States*: [87]

Finally, we have had pressed upon us that the *Blockburger* [88] doctrine offends the constitutional prohibition against double jeopardy. If there is anything to this claim it surely has long been disregarded in decisions of this Court, participated in by judges especially sensitive to the application of the historic safeguard of double

86. See note 84 *supra*.

87. 357 U.S. 386, 392–93 (1958).

88. Blockburger v. United States, 284 U.S. 299 (1932).

jeopardy. In applying a provision like that of double jeopardy, which is rooted in history and is not an evolving concept like that of due process, a long course of adjudication in this Court carries impressive authority. Certainly if punishment for each of separate offenses as those for which the petitioner here has been sentenced, and not merely different descriptions of the same offense, is constitutionally beyond the power of Congress to impose, not only *Blockburger* but at least [seven other] cases would also have to overruled.[89]

Suppose Congress, instead of enacting the three provisions before us, had passed an enactment substantially in this form: "Anyone who sells drugs except from the original stamped package and who sells such drugs not in pursuance of a written order of the person to whom the drug is sold, and who does so by way of facilitating the concealment and sale of drugs knowing the same to have been unlawfully imported, shall be sentenced to not less than fifteen years' imprisonment: *Provided, however,* That if he makes such sale in pursuance of a written order of the person to whom the drug is sold he shall be sentenced to only ten years' imprisonment: *Provided further,* That if he sells such drugs in the original stamped package he shall also be sentenced to only ten years' imprisonment: *And provided further,* That if he sells such drugs in pursuance of a written order and from a stamped package, he shall be sentenced to only five years' imprisonment." Is it conceivable that such a statute would not be within the power of Congress? And is it rational to find such a statute constitutional but to strike down the *Blockburger* doctrine as violative of the double jeopardy clause?

In effect, we are asked to enter the domain of penology, and more particularly that tantalizing aspect of it, the proper apportionment of punishment. Whatever views may be entertained regarding severity of punishment, whether one believes in its efficacy or its futility,[90] these are peculiarly questions of legislative policy. Equally so are the much mooted problems relating to the power of the judiciary to review sentences. First the English and then the Scottish Courts of Criminal Appeal were given power to revise sentences, the power to increase as well as the power to reduce them.[91] This Court has no such power.

89. Carter v. McClaughry, 183 U.S. 436 (1902); Morgan v. Devine, 237 U.S. 632 (1915); Albrecht v. United States, 273 U.S. 1 (1927); Pinkerton v. United States, 328 U.S. 640 (1946); American Tobacco Co. v. United States, 328 U.S. 781 (1946); United States v. Michener, 331 U.S. 789 (1947); Pereira v. United States, 347 U.S. 1 (1954). [F.F.]

90. See RADZINOWICZ, A HISTORY OF ENGLISH CRIMINAL LAW: THE MOVEMENT FOR REFORM, 1750–1883 (1948). [F.F.]

91. See 7 Edw. VII, c. 23 §4(3) (1907); 16 & 17 Geo. V. c. 15, § 2(4) (1926). [F.F.]

His views of the proper reading of the Fifth Amendment have since been rejected by the Court. Frankfurter was no "softie," to use his own expression, in reviewing judgments in criminal cases. On the other hand, the new cult of "law and order" would not appreciate his attitude. For it was exactly in the area of impropriety of police conduct, especially that of federal officals, that he strongly insisted on the reversal of criminal convictions.

10

Criminal Justice:
State Courts

Perhaps the most abrasive — if not the most difficult — of the cases presented to the Supreme Court during Frankfurter's time were those involving the propriety of state criminal procedures when measured against the amorphous demands of the Due Process Clause of the Fourteenth Amendment. He fought unsuccessfully for the notion that "the Fourteenth Amendment is not to be applied so as to turn this Court into a tribunal for revision of criminal convictions in the State courts. I have on more than one occasion expressed my strong belief that the requirements of due process do not hamper the States, beyond the narrow limits of imposing upon them standards of decency deeply felt and widely recognized in Anglo-American jurisdictions, either in penalizing conduct or in defining procedures appropriate for securing obedience to penal laws. Nor is this substantial autonomy of the States to be curtailed in capital cases."[1] Since his time, the Court has undertaken to write a code of criminal procedure for the states and to act under that code as "a tribunal for revision of criminal convictions in State courts."

Rejecting such a role for the Court, Frankfurter was faced with the awesome task of stating his notions of the proper content of the Due Process Clause. For some, like Mr. Justice Black, the answers were made easier by the assumption that the Due Process Clause incorporated the provisions of the Bill of Rights and no more. But ease of decision, even so, could come only if these provisions themselves were clear in their commands. Needless to say, they are not. For others on the Court, conclusions were easily reached by the formulation of blanket rules so broad as to preclude, at least in theory, the possibility of undue imposition on a defendant. This required a disregard, in large part, of any countervailing interests that the state might have in the enforcement of its criminal laws.

Characteristically, for Frankfurter, these cases presented enormous difficulties. For he could not satisfy himself that the more simplistic approaches of his brethren afforded appropriate resolution of the complex problems that exist in the area of law enforcement.

1. Stein v. New York, 346 U.S. 156, 199 (1953).

Many cases involved the use by a state of confessions of defendants. Certainly a case-by-case review imposed a terrible burden on the Supreme Court. But the alternatives, for Frankfurter, were equally unpalatable. The problem was defined by the Justice many times. His opinion in *Haley v. Ohio*,[2] in which he joined in upsetting the conviction, may be taken as typical:[3]

The doubts and difficulties derive from the very nature of the problem before us. They arise frequently when this Court is obliged to give definiteness to "the vague contours" of Due Process or, to change the figure, to spin judgment upon the State action out of that gossamer concept. Subtle and even elusive as its criteria are, we cannot escape that duty of judicial review. The nature of the duty, however, makes it especially important to be humble in exercising it. Humility in this context means an alert self-scrutiny so as to avoid infusing into the vagueness of a Constitutional command one's merely private notions. Like other mortals, judges, though unaware, may be in the grip of prepossessions. The only way to relax such a grip, the only way to avoid finding in the Constitution the personal bias one has placed in it, is to explore the influences that have shaped one's unanalyzed views in order to lay bare prepossessions.

A lifetime's preoccupation with criminal justice, as prosecutor, defender of civil liberties, and scientific student, naturally leaves one with views. Thus, I disbelieve in capital punishment. But as a judge I could not impose the views of the very few States who through bitter experience have abolished capital punishment upon all the other States, by finding that "due process" proscribes it. Again, I do not believe that even capital offenses by boys of fifteen should be dealt with according to the conventional criminal procedure. It would, however, be bald judicial usurpation to hold that States violate the Constitution in subjecting minors like Haley to such a procedure. If a State, consistently with the Fourteenth Amendment, may try a boy of fifteen charged with murder by the ordinary criminal procedure, I cannot say that such a youth is never capable of that free choice of action which, in the eyes of the law, makes a confession "voluntary." Again, it would hardly be a justifiable exercise of judicial power to dispose of this case by finding in the Due Process Clause Constitutional outlawry of the admissibility of all private statements made by an accused to a police officer, however much legislation to that effect might seem to me wise.[4]

2. 332 U.S. 596 (1948).

3. *Id.* at 602–07.

4. See The Indian Evidence Act of 1872, § 25; *cf.* § 26. [F.F.]

But whether a confession of a lad of fifteen is "voluntary" and as such admissible, or "coerced" and thus wanting in due process, is not a matter of mathematical determination. Essentially it invites psychological judgment — a psychological judgment that reflects deep, even if inarticulate, feelings of our society. Judges must divine that feeling as best they can from all the relevant evidence and light which they can bring to bear for a confident judgment of such an issue, and with every endeavor to detach themselves from their merely private views.[5]

While the issue thus formulated appears vague and impalpable, it cannot be too often repeated that the limitations which the Due Process Clause of the Fourteenth Amendment placed upon the methods by which the States may prosecute for crime cannot be more narrowly conceived. This Court must give the freest possible scope to States in the choice of their methods of criminal procedure. But these procedures cannot include methods that may fairly be deemed to be in conflict with deeply rooted feelings of the community.[6] Of course this is a most difficult test to apply, but apply it we must, warily, and from case to case. . . .

The answer, as has already been intimated, depends on an evaluation of psychological factors, or, more accurately stated, upon the pervasive feeling of society regarding such psychological factors. Unfortunately, we cannot draw upon any formulated expression of the existence of such feeling. Nor are there available experts on such matters to guide the judicial judgment. Our Constitutional system makes it the Court's duty to interpret those feelings of society to which the Due Process Clause gives legal protection. Because of their inherent vagueness the tests by which we are to be guided are most unsatisfactory, but such as they are we must apply them.

The Ohio courts have in effect denied that the very nature of the circumstances of the boy's confession precludes a finding that it was voluntary. Their denial carries great weight, of course. It requires much to be overborne. But it does not end the matter. Against it we have the judgment that comes from judicial experience with the conduct of criminal trials as they pass in review before this Court. An impressive series of cases in this and other courts admonishes of the temptations to abuse of police endeavors to secure confessions

5. It is noteworthy that while American experience has been drawn upon in the framing of constitutions for other democratic countries, the Due Process Clause has not been copied. See, also, the illuminating debate on the proposal to amend the Irish Home Rule Bill by incorporating our Due Process Clause. 42 H.C. Deb. 2082–91, 2215–67 (5th ser., 22, 23 October 1912). [F.F.]

6. See concurring opinions in Malinski v. New York, 324 U.S. 401, 412 (1945); and Louisiana *ex rel.* Francis v. Resweber, 329 U.S. 459, 466 (1947). [F.F.]

from suspects, through protracted questioning, carried on in secrecy, with the inevitable disquietude and fears police interrogations naturally engender in individuals questioned while held incommunicado, without the aid of counsel and unprotected by the safeguards of a judicial inquiry. Disinterested zeal for the public good does not assure either wisdom or right in the methods it pursues. A report of President Hoover's National Commission on Law Observance and Enforcement gave proof of the fact, unfortunately, that these potentialities of abuse were not the imaginings of mawkish sentimentality, nor their tolerance desirable or necessary for a stern policy against crime. Legislation throughout the country reflects a similar belief that detention for purposes of eliciting confessions through secret, persistent, long-continued interrogation violates sentiments deeply embedded in the feelings of our people.[7]

It is suggested that Haley's guilt could easily have been established without the confessions elicited by the sweating process of the night's secret interrogation. But this only affords one more proof that in guarding against misuse of the law enforcement process the effective detection of crime and the prosecution of criminals are furthered and not hampered. Such constitutional restraints of decency derive from reliance upon the resources of intelligence in dealing with crime and discourage the too easy temptations of unimaginative crude force, even when such force is not brutally employed.

It would disregard standards that we cherish as part of our faith in the strength and well-being of a rational, civilized society to hold that a confession is "voluntary" simply because the confession is the product of a sentient choice. "Conduct under duress involves a choice," [8] and conduct devoid of physical pressure but not leaving a free exercise of choice is the product of duress as much so as choice reflecting physical constraint.

Unhappily we have neither physical nor intellectual weights and measures by which judicial judgment can determine when pressures in securing a confession reach the coercive intensity that calls for the exclusion of a statement so secured. Of course, the police meant to exercise pressures upon Haley to make him talk. That was the very purpose of their procedure. In concluding that a statement is not voluntary which results from pressures such as were exerted in this case to make a lad of fifteen talk when the Constitution gave him the right to keep silent and when the situation was so contrived that appreciation of his rights and thereby the means of asserting them were effectively withheld from him by the police, I do not believe I

7. See McNabb v. United States, 318 U.S. 332, 342–43 (1943). [F.F.]

8. Union Pacific R.R. v. Public Service Commission, 248 U.S. 67, 70 (1918). [F.F.]

express a merely personal bias against such a procedure. Such a finding, I believe, reflects those fundamental notions of fairness and justice in the determination of guilt or innocence which lie embedded in the feelings of the American people and are enshrined in the Due Process Clause of the Fourteenth Amendment. To remove the inducement to resort to such methods this Court has repeatedly denied use of the fruits of illicit methods.

Accordingly, I think Haley's confession should have been excluded and the conviction based upon it should not stand.

Mr. Justice Frankfurter spoke also to the problems that resulted, after his tenure, in the decisions in *Escobedo v. Illinois*[9] and *Miranda v. Arizona*,[10] five-to-four judgments that became a focal issue in the growing conflict between the Court and Congress, decisions that have certainly contributed much to the public's loss of faith in the Court as an institution. In 1961, when *Culombe v. Connecticut*[11] was decided, the Court itself was so badly divided on these issues that Frankfurter's opinion announcing the judgment of the Court garnered only Mr. Justice Stewart's support. The sixty-eight-page opinion was itself the subject of violent attack, even by those who joined in its conclusion: [12]

Once again the Court is confronted with the painful duty of sitting in judgment on a State's conviction for murder, after a jury's verdict was found flawless by the State's highest court, in order to determine whether the defendant's confessions, decisive for the conviction, were admitted into evidence in accordance with the standards for admissibility demanded by the Due Process Clause of the Fourteenth Amendment. This recurring problem touching the administration of criminal justice by the States presents in an aggravated form in this case the anxious task of reconciling the responsibility of the police for ferreting out crime with the right of the criminal defendant, however guilty, to be tried according to constitutional requirements.

On December 15, 1956, the dead bodies of two men were found in Kurp's Gasoline Station in New Britain, Connecticut. Edward J. Kurpiewski, the proprietor, was found in the boiler room with a bullet in his head. Daniel J. Janowski, a customer, was found in the men's toilet room shot twice in the head. Parked at the pumps in front of the station was Janowski's car. In it was Janowski's daughter,

9. 378 U.S. 478 (1964).

10. 384 U.S. 436 (1966).

11. 367 U.S. 568 (1961).

12. *Id.* at 568–77, 587–88, 601–02, 631–33, 635.

physically unharmed. She was the only surviving eyewitness of what had happened at the station. She was eighteen months old.

The Kurp's affair was one in a series of holdups and holdup killings that terrified the operators of gasoline stations, package stores and small shops throughout the environing Connecticut area. Newspapers and radio and television broadcasters reported each fresh depredation of the "mad killers." At Hartford, the State Police were at work investigating the crimes, apparently with little evidence to go on. At the scene of the killings of Kurpiewski and Janowski no physical clues were discovered. The bullet slugs removed from the brains of the two victims were split and damaged.

In the last week of February 1957, for reasons which do not appear in this record, suspicion in connection with at least two of the holdups under investigation, holdups of a country store in Coventry and of a package store in Rocky Hill, focused on two friends, Arthur Culombe and Joseph Taborsky. On the afternoon of February 23, the two were accosted by teams of officers and asked to come to State Police Headquarters. They were never again out of police custody. In the Headquarters' interrogation room and elsewhere, they were questioned about the Coventry and Rocky Hill holdups, Kurp's, and other matters. Within ten days Culombe had five times confessed orally to participation in the Kurp's Gasoline Station affair — once re-enacting the holdup for the police — and had signed three typed statements incriminating himself and Taborsky in the Kurp's killings. Taborsky also confessed.

The two were indicted and tried jointly for murder in the first degree before a jury in the Superior Court at Hartford. Certain of their oral and written statements were permitted to go to the jury over their timely objections that these had been extracted from them by police methods which made the confessions inadmissible consistently with the Fourteenth Amendment. Both men were convicted of first-degree murder and their convictions affirmed by the Supreme Court of Errors.[13] Only Culombe sought review by this Court. Because his petition for certiorari presented serious questions concerning the limitations imposed by the Federal Due Process Clause upon the investigative activities of state criminal law enforcement officials, we issued the writ.

The occasion which in December 1956 confronted the Connecticut State Police with two corpses and an infant as their sole informants to a crime of community-disturbing violence is not a rare one. Despite modern advances in the technology of crime detection, offenses frequently occur about which things cannot be made to

13. 147 Conn. 194, 158 A.2d 239 (1960), *cert. granted*, 363 U.S. 826 (1960). [F.F.]

speak. And where there cannot be found innocent human witnesses to such offenses, nothing remains — if police investigation is not to be balked before it has fairly begun — but to seek out possibly guilty witnesses and ask them questions, witnesses, that is, who are suspected of knowing something about the offense precisely because they are suspected of implication in it.

The questions which these suspected witnesses are asked may serve to clear them. They may serve, directly or indirectly, to lead the police to other suspects than the persons questioned. Or they may become the means by which the persons questioned are themselves made to furnish proofs which will eventually send them to prison or death. In any event, whatever its outcome, such questioning is often indispensable to crime detection. Its compelling necessity has been judicially recognized as its sufficient justification, even in a society which, like ours, stands strongly and constitutionally committed to the principle that persons accused of crime cannot be made to convict themselves out of their own mouths.

But persons who are suspected of crime will not always be unreluctant to answer questions put by the police. Since under the procedures of Anglo-American criminal justice they cannot be constrained by legal process to give answers which incriminate them, the police have resorted to other means to unbend their reluctance, lest criminal investigation founder. Kindness, cajolery, entreaty, deception, persistent cross-questioning, even physical brutality have been used to this end. In the United States, "interrogation" has become a police technique, and detention for the purposes of interrogation a common, although generally unlawful, practice. Crime detection officials, finding that if their suspects are kept under tight police control during questioning they are less likely to be distracted, less likely to be recalcitrant and, of course, less likely to make off and escape entirely, not infrequently take such suspects into custody for "investigation."

This practice has its manifest evils and dangers. Persons subjected to it are torn from the reliances of their daily existence and held at the mercy of those whose job it is — if such persons have committed crimes, as it is supposed they have — to prosecute them. They are deprived of freedom without a proper judicial tribunal having found them guilty, without a proper judicial tribunal having found even that there is probable cause to believe that they may be guilty. What actually happens to them behind the closed door of the interrogation room is difficult if not impossible to ascertain. Certainly, if through excess of zeal or aggressive impatience or flaring up of temper in the face of obstinate silence a prisoner is abused, he is faced with the task of overcoming, by his lone testimony, solemn official denials. The prisoner knows this — knows that no friendly or disinterested witness is present — and the knowledge may itself induce fear. But, in any case, the risk is great that the police will accomplish behind their closed door precisely what the demands of our legal order forbid: make a suspect the unwilling collaborator in establishing his guilt. This they may accomplish not only with ropes and a rubber hose, not only by relay questioning persistently, insistently subjugating a tired mind, but by subtler devices.

In the police station a prisoner is surrounded by known hostile forces. He is disoriented from the world he knows and in which he finds support. He is subject to coercing impingements, undermining even if not obvious pressures of every variety. In such an atmosphere, questioning that is long continued — even if it is only repeated at intervals, never protracted to the point of physical exhaustion — inevitably suggests that the questioner has a right to, and expects, an answer. This is so, certainly, when the prisoner has never been told that he need not answer and when, because his commitment to custody seems to be at the will of his questioners, he has every reason to believe that he will be held and interrogated until he speaks.

However, a confession made by a person in custody is not always the result of an overborne will. The police may be midwife to a declaration naturally born of remorse, or relief, or desperation, or calculation. If that is so, if the "suction process" has not been at the prisoner and drained his capacity for freedom of choice, does not the awful responsibility of the police for maintaining the peaceful order of society justify the means which they have employed? It will not do to forget, as Sir Patrick (Now Lord Justice) Devlin has put it, that "The least criticism of police methods of interrogation deserves to be most carefully weighed because the evidence which such interrogation produces is often decisive; the high degree of proof which the English law requires — proof beyond reasonable doubt — often could not be achieved by the prosecution without the assistance of the accused's own statement." Yet even if one cannot adopt "an undiscriminating hostility to mere interrogation . . . without unduly fettering the States in protecting society from the criminal," there remain the questions: When, applied to what practices, is a judgment of impermissibility drawn from the fundamental conceptions of Anglo-American accusatorial process "undiscriminating"? What are the characteristics of the "mere interrogation" which is allowable consistently with those conceptions? . . .

The dilemma posed by police interrogation of suspects in custody and the judicial use of interrogated confessions to convict their makers cannot be resolved simply by wholly subordinating one set of opposing considerations to the other. The argument that without such interrogation it is often impossible to close the hiatus between suspicion and proof, especially in cases involving professional criminals, is often pressed in quarters responsible and not unfeeling. It is the same argument that was once invoked to support the lash and the rack. Where it has been put to this Court in its extreme form, as justifying the all-night grilling of prisoners under circumstances of sustained, week-long terror, we have rejected it.[14] "The Constitution proscribes such lawless means irrespective of the end." . . .

In light of our past opinions and in light of the wide divergence of views which men may reasonably maintain concerning the propriety of various police investigative procedures not involving the employment of obvious brutality, this much seems certain: It is impossible for this Court, in enforcing the Fourteenth Amendment, to attempt precisely to delimit, or to surround with specific, all-inclusive restrictions, the power of interrogation allowed to state law enforcement officers in obtaining confessions. No single litmus-paper test for constitutionally impermissible interrogation has been evolved: neither extensive cross-questioning — deprecated by the English judges; nor undue delay in arraignment — proscribed by *McNabb*; nor failure to caution a prisoner — enjoined by the Judge's Rules; nor refusal to permit communication with friends and legal counsel at stages in the proceeding when the prisoner is still only a suspect — prohibited by several state statutes.[15]

Each of these factors, in company with all of the surrounding circumstances — the duration and conditions of detention (if the confessor has been detained), the manifest attitude of the police toward him, his physical and mental state, the diverse pressures which sap or sustain his powers of resistance and self-control — is relevant. The ultimate test remains that which has been the only clearly established test in Anglo-American courts for two hundred years: the test of voluntariness. Is the confession the product of an essentially free and unconstrained choice by its maker? If it is, if he has willed to confess, it may be used against him. If it is not, if his will has been overborne and his capacity for self-determination critically impaired, the use of his confession offends due process.[16] The line of distinction is that at which governing self-direction is lost and compulsion, of whatever nature or however infused, propels or helps to propel the confession. . . .

What appears in this case, then, is this. Culombe was taken by

14. Chambers v. Florida, 309 U.S. 227, 240–41 (1940). [F.F.]

15. See Lisenba v. California, 314 U.S. 219 (1941); Crooker v. California, 357 U.S. 433 (1958); Ashdown v. Utah, 357 U.S. 426 (1958). [F.F.]

16. Rogers v. Richmond, 365 U.S. 534 (1961). [F.F.]

the police and held in the carefully controlled environment of police custody for more than four days before he confessed. During that time he was questioned — questioned every day about the Kurp's affair — and with the avowed intention, not merely to check his story to ascertain whether there was cause to charge him, but to obtain a confession if a confession was obtainable.

All means found fit were employed to this end. Culombe was not told that he had a right to remain silent. Although he said that he wanted a lawyer, the police made no attempt to give him the help he needed to get one. Instead of bringing him before a magistrate with reasonable promptness, as Connecticut law requires, to be duly presented for the grave crimes of which he was in fact suspected (and for which he had been arrested under the felony-arrest statute), he was taken before the New Britain Police Court on the palpable ruse of a breach-of-the-peace charge concocted to give the police time to pursue their investigation. This device is admitted. It had a two-fold effect. First, it kept Culombe in police hands without any of the protections that a proper magistrate's hearing would have assured him. Certainly, had he been brought before it charged with murder instead of an insignificant misdemeanor, no court would have failed to warn Culombe of his rights and arrange for appointment of counsel. Second, every circumstance of the Police Court's procedure was, in itself, potentially intimidating. Culombe had been told that morning that he would be presented in a court of law and would be able to consult counsel. Instead, he was led into a crowded room, penned in a corner, and, without ever being brought before the bench or given a chance to participate in any way, his case was disposed of. Culombe had been convicted of crimes before and presumably was not ignorant of the way in which justice is regularly done. It would deny the impact of experience to believe that the impression which even his limited mind drew from his appearance before a court which did not even hear him, a court which may well have appeared a mere tool in the hands of the police, was not intimidating. . . .

Regardful as one must be of the problems of crime-detection confronting the States, one does not reach the result here as an easy decision. In the case of such unwitnessed crimes as the Kurp's killings, the trails of detection challenge the most imaginative capacities of law enforcement officers. Often there is little else the police can do than interrogate suspects as an indispensable part of criminal investigation. But when interrogation of a prisoner is so long continued, with such a purpose, and under such circumstances, as to make the whole proceeding an effective instrument for extorting an unwilling admission of guilt, due process precludes the use of the confession thus obtained. Under our accusatorial system, such an exploitation of interrogation, whatever its usefulness, is not a permissible substitute for judicial trial.

On the major issue of the right to counsel, Frankfurter also would have proceeded on a case-by-case basis rather than imposing the general rule that has since begun to emerge that the right to counsel means the right to have counsel assigned in all criminal cases before trial, during trial, and after trial. The breakthrough for the Court came in *Gideon v. Wainwright*.[17] Frankfurter's views were expressed earlier in *Carter v. Illinois*:[18]

> In a series of cases of which *Moore* v. *Dempsey*,[19] was the first, and *Ashcraft* v. *Tennessee*,[20] the latest, we have sustained an appeal to the Due Process Clause of the Fourteenth Amendment for a fair ascertainment of guilt or innocence. Inherent in the notion of fairness is ample opportunity to meet an accusation. Under pertinent circumstances, the opportunity is ample only when an accused has the assistance of counsel for his defense. And the need for such assistance may exist at every stage of the prosecution, from arraignment to sentencing. This does not, however, mean that the accused may not make his own defense; nor does it prevent him from acknowledging guilt when fully advised of all its implications and capable of understanding them. Neither the historic conception of Due Process nor the vitality it derives from progressive standards of justice denies a person the right to defend himself or to confess guilt. Under appropriate circumstances the Constitution requires that counsel be tendered; it does not require that under all circumstances counsel be forced upon a defendant.[21]

Frankfurter's most renowned exchange with Mr. Justice Black over the proper reach of the Fourteenth Amendment's Due Process Clause, especially in the area of criminal procedure, occurred in *Adamson v. California*,[22] where the Court was asked to overrule, as it later did in *Griffin v. California*,[23] the decision in *Twining v. New Jersey*[24] that

17. 372 U.S. 335 (1963).

18. 329 U.S. 173, 174–75 (1946).

19. 261 U.S. 86 (1923). [F.F.]

20. 327 U.S. 274 (1944). [F.F.]

21. United States *ex rel.* McCann v. Adams, 320 U.S. 220 (1943). [F.F.]

22. 332 U.S. 46 (1947).

23. 380 U.S. 609 (1965).

24. 211 U.S. 78 (1908).

the Fourteenth Amendment did not preclude comment by court and prosecutor on the failure of the defendant to take the witness stand: [25]

For historical reasons a limited immunity from the common duty to testify was written into the Federal Bill of Rights, and I am prepared to agree that, as part of that immunity, comment on the failure of an accused to take the witness stand is forbidden in federal prosecutions. It is so, of course, by explicit act of Congress.[26] But to suggest that such a limitation can be drawn out of "due process" in its protection of ultimate decency in a civilized society is to suggest that the Due Process Clause fastened fetters of unreason upon the States. . . .

Between the incorporation of the Fourteenth Amendment into the Constitution and the beginning of the present membership of the Court — a period of seventy years — the scope of that Amendment was passed upon by forty-three judges. Of all these judges, only one, who may respectfully be called an eccentric exception, ever indicated the belief that the Fourteenth Amendment was a shorthand summary of the first eight Amendments theretofore limiting only the Federal Government, and that due process incorporated those eight Amendments as restrictions upon the powers of the States. Among these judges were not only those who would have to be included among the greatest in the history of the Court, but — it is especially relevant to note — they included those whose services in the cause of human rights and the spirit of freedom are the most conspicuous in our history. It is not invidious to single out Miller, Davis, Bradley, Waite, Matthews, Gray, Fuller, Holmes, Brandeis, Stone and Cardozo (to speak only of the dead) as judges who were alert in safeguarding and promoting the interests of liberty and human dignity through law. But they were also judges mindful of the relation of our federal system to a progressively democratic society and therefore duly regardful of the scope of authority that was left to the States even after the Civil War. And so they did not find that the Fourteenth Amendment, concerned as it was with matters fundamental to the pursuit of justice, fastened upon the States procedural arrangements which, in the language of Mr. Justice Cardozo, only those who are "narrow or provincial" would deem essential to "a fair and enlightened system of justice." [27] To suggest that it is inconsistent with a truly free society to begin prosecutions without an indictment, to try petty civil cases without the paraphernalia of a common law jury, to take into consideration that one who has full opportunity to make

25. 332 U.S. at 61–68.

26. 20 Stat. 30; see Bruno v. United States, 308 U.S. 987 (1939). [F.F.]

27. Palko v. Connecticut, 302 U.S. 319, 325 (1937). [F.F.]

a defense remains silent is, in de Tocqueville's phrase, to confound the familiar with the necessary.

The short answer to the suggestion that the provision of the Fourteenth Amendment, which ordains "nor shall any State deprive any person of life, liberty, or property, without due process of law," was a way of saying that every State must thereafter initiate prosecutions through indictment by a grand jury, must have a trial by a jury of twelve in criminal cases, and must have trial by such a jury in common law suits where the amount in controversy exceeds twenty dollars, is that it is a strange way of saying it. It would be extraordinarily strange for a Constitution to convey such specific commands in such a round-about and inexplicit way. After all, an amendment to the Constitution should be read in a " 'sense most obvious to the common understanding at the time of its adoption.' . . . For it was for public adoption that it was proposed." [28] Those reading the English language with the meaning which it ordinarily conveys, those conversant with the political and legal history of the concept of due process, those sensitive to the relations of the States to the central government as well as the relation of some of the provisions of the Bill of Rights to the process of justice, would hardly recognize the Fourteenth Amendment as a cover for the various explicit provisions of the first eight Amendments. Some of these are enduring reflections of experience with human nature, while some express the restricted views of Eighteenth Century England regarding the best methods for the ascertainment of facts. The notion that the Fourteenth Amendment was a covert way of imposing upon the States all the rules which it seemed important to Eighteenth Century statesmen to write into the Federal Amendments, was rejected by judges who were themselves witnesses of the process by which the Fourteenth Amendment became part of the Constitution. Arguments that may now be adduced to prove that the first eight Amendments were concealed within the historic phrasing of the Fourteenth Amendment were not unknown at the time of its adoption. A surer estimate of their bearing was possible for judges at the time than distorting distance is likely to vouchsafe. Any evidence of design or purpose not contemporaneously known could hardly have influenced those who ratified the Amendment. Remarks of a particular proponent of the Amendment, no matter how influential, are not to be deemed part of the Amendment. What was submitted for ratification was his proposal, not his speech. Thus, at the time of the ratification of the Fourteenth Amendment the constitutions of nearly half of the ratifying States did not have the rigorous requirements of the Fifth

28. See Mr. Justice Holmes, in Eisner v. Macomber, 252 U.S. 189, 220 (1920). [F.F.]

Amendment for instituting criminal proceedings through a grand jury. It could hardly have occurred to these States that by ratifying the Amendment they uprooted their established methods for prosecuting crime and fastened upon themselves a new prosecutorial system.

Indeed, the suggestion that the Fourteenth Amendment incorporates the first eight Amendments as such is not unambiguously urged. Even the boldest innovator would shrink from suggesting to more than half the States that they may no longer initiate prosecutions without indictment by grand jury, or that thereafter all the States of the Union must furnish a jury of twelve for every case involving a claim above twenty dollars. There is suggested merely a selective incorporation of the first eight Amendments into the Fourteenth Amendment. Some are in and some are out, but we are left in the dark as to which are in and which are out. Nor are we given the calculus for determining which go in and which stay out. If the basis of selection is merely that those provisions of the first eight Amendments are incorporated which commend themselves to individual justices as indispensable to the dignity and happiness of a free man, we are thrown back to a merely subjective test. The protection against unreasonable search and seizure might have primacy for one judge, while trial by a jury of twelve for every claim above twenty dollars might appear to another as an ultimate need in a free society. In the history of thought "natural law" has a much longer and much better founded meaning and justification than such subjective selection of the first eight Amendments for incorporation into the Fourteenth. If all that is meant is that due process contains within itself certain minimal standards which are "of the very essence of a scheme of ordered liberty," [29] putting upon this Court the duty of applying these standards from time to time, then we have merely arrived at the insight which our predecessors long ago expressed. We are called upon to apply to the difficult issues of our own day the wisdom afforded by the great opinions in this field.[30] This guidance bids us to be duly mindful of the heritage of the past, with its great lessons of how liberties are won and how they are lost. As judges charged with the delicate task of subjecting the government of a continent to the Rule of Law we must be particularly mindful that it is "a *constitution* we are expounding," so that it should not

29. 302 U.S. at 325. [F.F.]

30. *E.g.*, Davidson v. New Orleans, 96 U.S. 97 (1878); Missouri v. Lewis, 101 U.S. 22 (1880); Hurtado v. California, 110 U.S. 516 (1884); Holden v. Hardy, 169 U.S. 366 (1898); Twining v. New Jersey, 211 U.S. 78 (1908); Palko v. Connecticut, 302 U.S. 319 (1937). [F.F.]

be imprisoned in what are merely legal forms even though they have the sanction of the Eighteenth Century.

It may not be amiss to restate the pervasive function of the Fourteenth Amendment in exacting from the States observance of basic liberties.[31] The Amendment neither comprehends the specific provisions by which the founders deemed it appropriate to restrict the federal government nor is it confined to them. The Due Process Clause of the Fourteenth Amendment has an independent potency, precisely as does the Due Process Clause of the Fifth Amendment in relation to the Federal Government. It ought not to require argument to reject the notion that due process of law meant one thing in the Fifth Amendment and another in the Fourteenth. The Fifth Amendment specifically prohibits prosecution of an "infamous crime" except upon indictment; it forbids double jeopardy; it bars compelling a person to be a witness against himself in any criminal case; it precludes deprivation of "life, liberty, or property, without due process of law. . . ." Are Madison and his contemporaries in the framing of the Bill of Rights to be charged with writing into it a meaningless clause? To consider "due process of law" as merely a shorthand statement of other specific clauses in the same amendment is to attribute to the authors and proponents of this Amendment ignorance of, or indifference to, a historic conception which was one of the great instruments in the arsenal of constitutional freedom which the Bill of Rights was to protect and strengthen.

A construction which gives to due process no independent function but turns it into a summary of the specific provisions of the Bill of Rights would, as has been noted, tear up by the roots much of the fabric of law in the several States, and would deprive the States of opportunity for reforms in legal process designed for extending the area of freedom. It would assume that no other abuses would reveal themselves in the course of time than those which had become manifest in 1791. Such a view not only disregards the historic meaning of "due process." It leads inevitably to a warped construction of specific provisions of the Bill of Rights to bring within their scope conduct clearly condemned by due process but not easily fitting into the pigeon-holes of the specific provisions. It seems pretty late in the day to suggest that a phrase so laden with historic meaning should be given an improvised content consisting of some but not all of the provisions of the first eight Amendments, selected on an undefined basis, with improvisation of content for the provisions so selected.

And so, when, as in a case like the present, a conviction in a State

31. See Malinski v. New York, 324 U.S. 401, 412 *et seq.* (1945); Louisiana *ex rel.* Francis v. Resweber, 329 U.S. 459, 466 *et seq.* (1947). [F.F.]

court is here for review under a claim that a right protected by the Due Process Clause of the Fourteenth Amendment has been denied, the issue is not whether an infraction of one of the specific provisions of the first eight Amendments is disclosed by the record. The relevant question is whether the criminal proceedings which resulted in conviction deprived the accused of the due process of law to which the United States Constitution entitled him. Judicial review of that guaranty of the Fourteenth Amendment inescapably imposes upon this Court an exercise of judgment upon the whole course of the proceedings in order to ascertain whether they offend those canons of decency and fairness which express the notions of justice of English-speaking peoples even toward those charged with the most heinous offenses. These standards of justice are not authoritatively formulated anywhere as though they were prescriptions in a pharmacopoeia. But neither does the application of the Due Process Clause imply that judges are wholly at large. The judicial judgment in applying the Due Process Clause must move within the limits of accepted notions of justice and is not to be based upon the idiosyncrasies of a merely personal judgment. The fact that judges among themselves may differ whether in a particular case a trial offends accepted notions of justice is not disproof that general rather than idiosyncratic standards are applied. An important safeguard against such merely individual judgment is an alert deference to the judgment of the State court under review.

Frankfurter's position on this issue — perhaps the most fundamental conception in his Supreme Court jurisprudence — was better stated in *Rochin v. California*,[32] where his opinion for the Court upset the state conviction. Unlike some of his brethren, Frankfurter's reasoning was not result oriented. The case involved the propriety of a conviction for illegal possession of narcotics. The police entering defendant's bedroom saw him put capsules into his mouth. Unable to extract the capsules from his mouth before they were swallowed, they forced an emetic down his throat. Thereupon he vomited the capsules which proved to contain morphine:[33]

In our federal system the administration of criminal justice is predominantly committed to the care of the States. The power to define crimes belongs to Congress only as an appropriate means of carrying into execution its limited grant of legislative powers. U.S. Const., Art. I, § 8, cl. 18. Broadly speaking, crimes in the United States are what the laws of the individual States make them,

32. 342 U.S. 165 (1952).

33. *Id.* at 168–74.

subject to the limitations of Art. I, § 10, cl. 1, in the original
Constitution, prohibiting bills of attainder and *ex post facto* laws,
and of the Thirteenth and Fourteenth Amendments.

These limitations, in the main, concern not restrictions upon the
powers of the States to define crime, except in the restricted area
where federal authority has pre-empted the field, but restrictions
upon the manner in which the States may enforce their penal codes.
Accordingly, in reviewing a State criminal conviction under a claim
of right guaranteed by the Due Process Clause of the Fourteenth
Amendment, from which is derived the most far-reaching and most
frequent federal basis of challenging State criminal justice, "we
must be deeply mindful of the responsibilities of the States for the
enforcement of criminal laws, and exercise with due humility our
merely negative function in subjecting convictions from state courts
to the very narrow scrutiny which the Due Process Clause of the
Fourteenth Amendment authorizes." [34] Due process of law, "itself a
historical product," [35] is not to be turned into a destructive dogma
against the States in the administration of their systems of criminal
justice.

However, this Court too has its responsibility. Regard for the
requirements of the Due Process Clause "inescapably imposes upon
this Court an exercise of judgment upon the whole course of the
proceedings [resulting in a conviction] in order to ascertain whether
they offend those canons of decency and fairness which express
the notions of justice of English-speaking peoples even toward those
charged with the most heinous offenses." [36] These standards of justice
are not authoritatively formulated anywhere as though they were
specifics. Due process of law is a summarized constitutional
guarantee of respect for those personal immunities which, as Mr. Justice Cardozo twice wrote for the Court, are "so rooted in the
traditions and conscience of our people as to be ranked as fundamental," [37] or are "implicit in the concept of ordered liberty." [38]

The Court's function in the observance of this settled conception
of the Due Process Clause does not leave us without adequate guides
in subjecting State criminal procedures to constitutional judgment.
In dealing not with the machinery of government but with human
rights, the absence of formal exactitude, or want of fixity of meaning,
is not an unusual way or even regrettable attribute of constitutional

34. Malinski v. New York, 324 U.S. 401, 412, 418 (1945). [F.F.]

35. Jackman v. Rosenbaum Co., 260 U.S. 22, 31 (1922). [F.F.]

36. 324 U.S. at 416–17. [F.F.]

37. Snyder v. Massachusetts, 291 U.S. 97, 105 (1934). [F.F.]

38. Palko v. Connecticut, 302 U.S. 319, 325 (1937). [F.F.]

provisions. Words being symbols do not speak without a gloss. On the one hand the gloss may be the deposit of history, whereby a term gains technical content. Thus the requirements of the Sixth and Seventh Amendments for trial by jury in the federal courts have a rigid meaning. No changes or chances can alter the content of the verbal symbol of "jury" — a body of twelve men who must reach a unanimous conclusion if the verdict is to go against the defendant. On the other hand, the gloss of some of the verbal symbols of the Constitution does not give them a fixed technical content. It exacts a continuing process of application.

When the gloss has thus not been fixed but is a function of the process of judgment, the judgment is bound to fall differently at different times and differently at the same time through different judges. Even more specific provisions, such as the guaranty of freedom of speech and the detailed protection against unreasonable searches and seizures, have inevitably evoked as sharp divisions in this Court as the least specific and most comprehensive protection of liberties, the Due Process Clause.

The vague contours of the Due Process Clause do not leave judges at large. We may not draw on our merely personal and private notions and disregard the limits that bind judges in their judicial function. Even though the concept of due process of law is not final and fixed, these limits are derived from considerations that are fused in the whole nature of our judicial process.[39] These are considerations deeply rooted and in the compelling traditions of the legal profession. The Due Process Clause places upon this Court the duty of exercising a judgment, within the narrow confines of judicial power in reviewing State convictions, upon interests of society pushing in opposite directions.

Due process of law thus conceived is not to be derided as resort to a revival of "natural law." To believe that this judicial exercise of judgment could be avoided by freezing "due process of law" at some fixed stage of time or thought is to suggest that the most important aspect of constitutional adjudication is a function for inanimate machines and not for judges, for whom the independence safeguarded by Article III of the Constitution was designed and who are presumably guided by established standards of judicial behavior. Even cybernetics has not yet made that haughty claim. To practice the requisite detachment and to achieve sufficient objectivity no doubt demands of judges the habit of self-discipline and self-criticism, incertitude that one's own views are incontestable and alert tolerance toward views not shared. But these are precisely the

39. See CARDOZO, THE NATURE OF THE JUDICIAL PROCESS (1921); THE GROWTH OF THE LAW (1924); THE PARADOXES OF LEGAL SCIENCE (1928). [F.F.]

presuppositions of our judicial process. They are precisely the qualities society has a right to expect from those entrusted with ultimate judicial power.

Restraints on our jurisdiction are self-imposed only in the sense that there is from our decisions no immediate appeal short of impeachment or constitutional amendment. But that does not make due process of law a matter of judicial caprice. The faculties of the Due Process Clause may be indefinite and vague, but the mode of their ascertainment is not self-willed. In each case "due process of law" requires an evaluation based on a disinterested inquiry pursued in the spirit of science, on a balanced order of facts exactly and fairly stated, on the detached consideration of conflicting claims,[40] on a judgment not *ad hoc* and episodic but duly mindful of reconciling the needs both of continuity and of change in a progressive society.

Applying these general considerations to the circumstances of the present case, we are compelled to conclude that the proceedings by which this conviction was obtained do more than offend some fastidious squeamishness or private sentimentalism about combatting crime too energetically. This is conduct that shocks the conscience. Illegally breaking into the privacy of the petitioner, the struggle to open his mouth and remove what was there, the forcible extraction of his stomach's contents — this course of proceeding by agents of government to obtain evidence is bound to offend even hardened sensibilities. They are methods too close to the rack and the screw to permit of constitutional differentiation.

It has long since ceased to be true that due process of law is heedless of the means by which otherwise relevant and credible evidence is obtained. This was not true even before the series of recent cases enforced the constitutional principle that the States may not base convictions upon confessions, however much verified, obtained by coercion. These decisions are not arbitrary exceptions to the comprehensive right of States to fashion their own rules of evidence for criminal trials. They are not sports in our constitutional law but applications of a general principle. They are only instances of the general requirement that States in their prosecutions respect certain decencies of civilized conduct. Due process of law, as a historic and generative principle, precludes defining, and thereby confining, these standards of conduct more precisely than to say that convictions cannot be brought about by methods that offend "a sense of justice."[41] It would be a stultification of the responsibility

40. See Hudson County Water Co. v. McCarter, 209 U.S. 349, 355 (1908). [F.F.]

41. See Mr. Chief Justice Hughes, speaking for a unanimous Court in Brown v. Mississippi, 297 U.S. 278, 285–86 (1936). [F.F.]

which the course of constitutional history has cast upon this Court
to hold that in order to convict a man the police cannot extract
by force what is in his mind but can extract what is in his stomach.

To attempt in this case to distinguish what lawyers call "real
evidence" from the verbal evidence is to ignore the reasons for excluding
coerced confessions. Use of involuntary verbal confessions in State
criminal trials is constitutionally obnoxious not only because of their
unreliability. They are inadmissible under the Due Process Clause
even though statements contained in them may be independently
established as true. Coerced confessions offend the community's sense
of fair play and decency. So here, to sanction the brutal conduct which
naturally enough was condemned by the court whose judgment is
before us, would be to afford brutality the cloak of law. Nothing
would be more calculated to discredit and thereby to brutalize the
temper of society.

A good example of Frankfurter's approach to a recurrent problem
under the Due Process Clause is to be found in a series of cases involving insane or allegedly insane defendants. That a person insane at
the time of his commission of a homicide could not be punished for
murder was clearly, for Frankfurter, a mandate of the Due Process
Clause, a precept of a civilized society. It necessarily followed that the
procedure for determining the fact of insanity must meet the requirements for a fair hearing. Dissenting in *United States* ex rel *Smith v.
Baldi*,[42] he wrote: [43]

Ever since our ancestral common law emerged out of the darkness
of its early barbaric days, it has been a postulate of Western civilization
that the taking of life by the hand of an insane person is not murder.
But the nature and operation of the mind are so elusive to the grasp
of the understanding that the basis for formulating standards of
criminal responsibility and the means for determining whether those
standards are satisfied in a particular case have greatly troubled
law and medicine for more than a century. . . .

The law of Pennsylvania in the abstract on this controversial
subject is clear and unassailable. "It is a principle embedded in the
common law — and we administer the common law in Pennsylvania —
that no insane person can be tried, sentenced or executed." [44] In
view of the fallibilities of human judgment regarding the same body
of evidence, it is inevitable that one may be doubtful, and even more

42. 344 U.S. 561 (1953).

43. *Id.* at 570–72.

44. Commonwealth *ex rel.* Smith v. Ashe, 364 Pa. 93, 116, 71 A.2d 107, 118
(1950). [F.F.]

than doubtful, whether in a particular case a plea of insanity was properly rejected. It is not for this Court to find a want of due process in a conviction for murder sustained by the highest court of the the State merely because a finding that the defendant is sane may raise the gravest doubts. But it is our duty under the Fourteenth Amendment to scrutinize the procedure by which the plea for insanity failed and defendant's life became forfeit. A denial of adequate opportunity to sustain the plea of insanity is a denial of the safeguard of due process in its historical procedural sense which is within the incontrovertible scope of the Due Process Clause of the Fourteenth Amendment.

One has only to read the opinions both of the four Judges who constituted the majority of the Court of Appeals and of the three dissenters to appreciate the tangled skein of procedural complexities in which the defendant in this case was hopelessly caught.[45] And I cannot read the opinion of Chief Judge Biggs,[46] without being left with such an unrelievable feeling of disquietude as amounts to a conviction that the accused in this case was deprived of a fair opportunity to establish his insanity. And this not the less so because the deprivation resulted from the tangled web that was woven for the defendant, even if unwittingly, by the courts of Pennsylvania.

Certainly, Frankfurter asserted, it was not consonant with the demands of due process for a state to impose on a defendant the burden of proving insanity beyond a reasonable doubt. Thus, in *Leland v. Oregon*,[47] he said:[48]

However much conditions may have improved since 1905, when William H. (later Mr. Chief Justice) Taft expressed his disturbing conviction "that the administration of the criminal law in all the states in the Union (there may be one or two exceptions) is a disgrace to our civilization,"[49] no informed person can be other than unhappy about the serious defects of present-day American criminal justice. It is not unthinkable that failure to bring the guilty to book for a heinous crime which deeply stirs popular sentiment may lead the legislature of a State, in one of those emotional storms which on occasion sweep over our people, to enact that thereafter an indictment for murder, following attempted rape, should be presumptive proof of guilt and cast upon the defendant the burden of proving beyond

45. 192 F.2d 540 (3d Cir. 1951). [F.F.]

46. *Id.* at 549. [F.F.]

47. 343 U.S. 790 (1952).

48. *Id.* at 802–07.

49. Taft, *The Administration of Criminal Law*, 15 YALE L.J. 1, 11 (1905). [F.F.]

a reasonable doubt that he did not do the killing. Can there be any doubt that such a statute would go beyond the freedom of the States, under the Due Process Clause of the Fourteenth Amendment, to fashion their own penal codes and their own procedures for enforcing them? Why is that so? Because from the time that the law which we have inherited has emerged from dark and barbaric times, the conception of justice which has dominated our criminal law has refused to put an accused at the hazard of punishment if he fails to remove every reasonable doubt of his innocence in the minds of jurors. It is the duty of the Government to establish his guilt beyond a reasonable doubt. This notion — basic in our law and rightly one of the boasts of a free society — is a requirement and a safeguard of due process of law in the historic, procedural content of "due process." Accordingly there can be no doubt, I repeat, that a State cannot cast upon an accused the duty of establishing beyond a reasonable doubt that his was not the act which caused the death of another.

But a muscular contraction resulting in a homicide does not constitute murder. Even though a person be the immediate occasion of another's death, he is not a deodand to be forfeited like a thing in the medieval law. Behind a muscular contraction resulting in another's death there must be culpability to turn homicide into murder.

The tests by which such culpability may be determined are varying and conflicting. One does not have to echo the scepticism uttered by Brian, C.J., in the fifteenth century, that "the devil himself knoweth not the mind of men" to appreciate how vast a darkness still envelopes man's understanding of man's mind. Sanity and insanity are concepts of incertitude. They are given varying and conflicting content at the same time and from time to time by specialists in the field. Naturally there has always been conflict between the psychological views absorbed by law and the contradictory views of students of mental health at a particular time. At this stage of scientific knowledge it would be indefensible to impose upon the States, through the due process of law which they must accord before depriving a person of life or liberty, one test rather than another for determining criminal culpability, and thereby to displace a State's own choice of such a test, no matter how backward it may be in the light of the best scientific canons. Inevitably, the legal tests for determining the mental state on which criminal culpability is to be based are in strong conflict in our forty-eight States. But when a State has chosen its theory for testing culpability, it is a deprivation of life without due process to send a man to his doom if he cannot prove beyond a reasonable doubt that the physical events of homicide did not constitute murder because under the State's theory he was incapable of acting culpably.

This does not preclude States from utilizing common sense regarding mental irresponsibility for acts resulting in homicide — from taking for granted that most men are sane and responsible for their acts. That a man's act is not his, because he is devoid of that mental state which begets culpability, is so exceptional a situation that the law has a right to devise an exceptional procedure regarding it. Accordingly, States may provide various ways for dealing with this exceptional situation by requiring, for instance, that the defense of "insanity" be specially pleaded, or that he on whose behalf the claim of insanity is made should have the burden of showing enough to overcome the assumption and presumption that normally a man knows what he is about and is therefore responsible for what he does, or that the issue be separately tried, or that a standing disinterested expert agency advise court and jury, or that these and other devices be used in the satisfaction of a jury beyond a reasonable doubt. . . .

The laws of the forty-eight States present the greatest diversity in relieving the prosecution from proving affirmatively that a man is sane in the way it must prove affirmatively that the defendant is the man who pulled the trigger or struck the blow. Such legislation makes no inroad upon the basic principle that the State must prove guilt, not the defendant innocence, and prove it to the satisfaction of a jury beyond a reasonable doubt.

Whatever tentative and intermediate steps experience makes permissible for aiding the State in establishing the ultimate issues in a prosecution for crime, the State cannot be relieved, on a final showdown, from proving its accusation. To prove the accusation it must prove each of the items which in combination constitute the offense. And it must make such proof beyond a reasonable doubt. This duty of the State of establishing every fact of the equation which adds up to a crime, and of establishing it to the satisfaction of a jury beyond a reasonable doubt is the decisive difference between criminal culpability and civil liability. The only exception is that very limited class of cases variously characterized as *mala prohibita* or public torts or enforcement of regulatory measures.[50] Murder is not a *malum prohibitum* or a public tort or the object of regulatory legislation. To suggest that the legal oddity by which Oregon imposes upon the accused the burden of proving beyond reasonable doubt that he had not the mind capable of committing murder is a mere difference in the measure of proof, is to obliterate the distinction between civil and criminal law. . . .

To repeat the extreme reluctance with which I find a constitutional barrier to any legislation is not to mouth a threadbare phrase. Especially is deference due to the policy of a State when it deals with

50. See United States v. Dotterwich, 320 U.S. 277 (1943); Morissette v. United States, 342 U.S. 246 (1952). [F.F.]

local crime, its repression and punishment. There is a gulf, however narrow, between deference to local legislation and complete disregard of the duty of judicial review which has fallen to this Court by virtue of the limits placed by the Fourteenth Amendment upon State action. This duty is not to be escaped, whatever I may think of investing judges with the power which the enforcement of that Amendment involves.

So, too, a person who became insane after conviction for murder could not, consistently with the Due Process Clause, be put to death while insane. Therefore, said Frankfurter, appropriate procedures must be afforded for the ascertainment of the fact of insanity, no less after conviction than when the insanity preceded the crime. These views were expressed in dissent both in *Solesbee v. Balkcom*[51] and again in *Caritativo v. California*.[52] In *Solesbee*, he wrote:[53]

That it offends our historic heritage to kill a man who has become insane while awaiting sentence cannot be gainsaid. This limitation on the power of the State to take life has been part of our law for centuries, recognized during periods of English history when feelings were more barbarous and men recoiled less from brutal action than we like to think is true of our time. . . .

However quaint some of these ancient authorities of our law may sound to our ears, the Twentieth Century has not so far progressed as to outmode their reasoning. We should not be less humane than were Englishmen in the centuries that preceded this Republic. And the practical considerations are not less relevant today than they were when urged by Sir John Hawles and Hale and Hawkins and Blackstone in writings which nurtured so many founders of the Republic. If a man has gone insane, is he still himself? Is he still the man who was convicted? In any event "were he of sound memory, he might allege somewhat" to save himself from doom. It is not an idle fancy that one under sentence of death ought not, by becoming *non compos*, be denied the means to "allege somewhat" that might free him. Such an opportunity may save life, as the last minute applications to this Court from time to time and not always without success amply attest.

The short of it is that American law is not more brutal than what is revealed as the unbroken command of English law for centuries preceding the separation of the Colonies. The Court puts out of sight, as it were, what is basic to a disposition of this case, namely,

---

51. 339 U.S. 9 (1950).

52. 357 U.S. 549 (1958).

53. 339 U.S. at 16–17, 19–21, 24–25.

that not a State in the Union supports the notion that an insane man under sentence of death would legally be executed. If respect is to be given to claims so deeply rooted in our common heritage as this limitation upon State power, the Fourteenth Amendment stands on guard to enforce it.

Unless this restriction on State power is fully recognized and its implications are duly respected, the crucial questions presented by this case are avoided. We are here not dealing with the Crown's prerogative of mercy continued through the pardoning power in this country as an exercise of grace.[54] Nor are we dealing with the range of discretion vested in judges by penal laws carrying flexible instead of fixed penalties.[55] We are dealing with a restriction upon the States against taking life if a certain fact is established, to-wit, insanity, like unto other restrictions upon the State in taking liberty or property. In view of the Due Process Clause it is not for the State to say: "I choose not to take life if a man under sentence becomes insane." The Due Process Clause says to a State: "Thou shalt not." . . .

Since it does not go to the question of guilt but to its consequences, the determination of the issue of insanity after sentence does not require the safeguards of a judicial proceeding.[56] Nor need the proceeding be open; it may be *in camera*. But precisely because the inquiry need not be open and may be made *in camera*, it must be fair in relation to the issue for determination. In the present state of the tentative and dubious knowledge as to mental diseases and the great strife of schools in regard to them, it surely operates unfairly to make such determinations not only behind closed doors but without any opportunity for the submission of relevant considerations on the part of the man whose life hangs in the balance.

To say that an inquiry so conducted is unfair because of the treacherous uncertainties in the present state of psychiatric knowledge is not to impugn the good faith of Governors or boards in excluding what is sought to be put before them on behalf of a putative insane person. The fact that a conclusion is reached in good conscience is no proof of its reliability. The validity of a conclusion depends largely on the mode by which it was reached. A Governor might not want to have it on his conscience to have sent a man to death after hearing conflicting views, equally persuasive, regarding the man's sanity. Claims obviously frivolous need of course not be heard, even as this Court does not listen to claims that raise no substantial

---

54. See *Ex parte* Grossman, 267 U.S. 87 (1925). [F.F.]

55. See Williams v. New York, 337 U.S. 241 (1949). [F.F.]

56. See Ng Fung Ho v. White, 256 U.S. 276, 284–85 (1922). [F.F.]

question. It is not suggested that petitioner's claim of insanity was baseless.

It is a groundless fear to assume that it would obstruct the rigorous administration of criminal justice to allow the case to be put for a claim of insanity, however informal and expeditious the procedure for dealing with the claim. The time needed for such a fair procedure would not unreasonably delay the execution of the sentence unless in all fairness and with due respect for a basic principle in our law the execution should be delayed. The risk of an undue delay is hardly comparable to the grim risk of the barbarous execution of an insane man because of a hurried, one-sided, untested determination of the question of insanity, the answers to which are as yet so wrapped in confusion and conflict and so dependent on elucidation by more than one-sided partisanship.

In *Caritativo v. California*, he added to his argument: [57]

Surely the right of an insane man not to be executed, a right based on moral principles deeply embedded in the traditions and feelings of our people and itself protected by the Due Process Clause of the Fourteenth Amendment, merits the procedural protection that that Amendment safeguards. What kind of a constitutional right is it, especially if life is at stake, the vindication of which rests wholly in the hands of an administrative official whose actions cannot be inquired into, and who need not consider the claims of the person most vitally affected, the person in whom the constitutional right is said to inhere? In *Solesbee* v. *Balkcom* the Court found that a State had not offended due process in constituting its governor an "apt and special tribunal" for determining, in *ex parte* proceedings, the sanity of a condemned man at the time of execution. The Court relied particularly on "the solemn responsibility of a state's highest executive." [58] It analogized the function given the governor to the power to pardon and reprieve, powers traditionally confided to the chief executive of the State. It did not appear in that case whether, in exercising this function, the governor had declined to hear statements on the defendant's behalf. In the present case, however, the determination is not to be made on the "solemn responsibility of a state's highest executive," but by a prison warden. There is no apparent reason why this awesome power, surely without parallel under our law in the freedom of its exercise and the seriousness of its consequences, should not after today's decision be entrusted to still lower administrative officials. It is no reflection on the qualities

57. 357 U.S. at 557–59.
58. 339 U.S. at 13. [F.F.]

of wardens and similar officials to point out that when wielded by them in *ex parte* proceedings this power can scarcely be assimilated to the chief executive's traditional power to pardon or reprieve. Finally, in these cases, it does appear that the warden did in fact refuse to consider evidence tendered on the prisoners' behalf, and refused to allow an examination by independent psychiatrists. He expressly rested his determination on the untested conclusions of his own staff.

Audi alteram partem — hear the other side! — a demand made insistently through the centuries, is now a command, spoken with the voice of the Due Process Clause of the Fourteenth Amendment, against state governments, and every branch of them — executive, legislative, and judicial — whenever any individual, however lowly and unfortunate, asserts a legal claim. It is beside the point that the claim may turn out not to be meritorious. It is beside the point that delay in the enforcement of the law may be entailed. The protection of a constitutional right to life ought not be subordinated to the fear that some lawyers will be wanting in the observance of their professional responsibilities. The right to be heard somehow by someone before a claim is denied, particularly if life hangs in the balance, is far greater in importance to society, in the light of the sad history of its denial, than inconvenience in the execution of the law. If this is true when mere property interests are at stake,[59] how much more so when the difference is between life and death. As Mr. Justice Holmes said, happily speaking for the Court,[60] "It cannot be that the safeguards of the person, so often and so rightly mentioned with solemn reverence, are less than those that protect from a liability in debt."

It may well be that if the warden of a California prison cannot act on his arbitrary judgment — for it is inherently arbitrary if the condemned man or those who speak for him are not allowed to be heard — in deciding whether there is good reason to believe that a person about to be executed is insane, that unworthy claims will be put to the warden and perchance add to delays in the execution of the law. But far better such minor inconveniences, and an effective penal administration ought to find no difficulty in making them minor, than that the State of California should have on its conscience a single execution that would be barbaric because the victim was in fact, though he had no opportunity to show it, mentally unfit to meet his destiny.

59. See Walker v. City of Hutchinson, 352 U.S. 112 (1956); Covey v. Town of Somers, 351 U.S. 141 (1956); Mullane v. Central Hanover Bank & Trust Co., 339 U.S. 306 (1950). [F.F.]

60. United States v. Oppenheimer, 242 U.S. 85, 87 (1916). [F.F.]

If Frankfurter would require that state post-conviction remedies afford real means for convicted defendants to demonstrate constitutional infirmities in their convictions, he did not ask that they assure defendants that they would be released. So long as the state courts afforded appropriate process and exercised judgment based on reason, it was not, to Frankfurter's way of thinking, for the Supreme Court to reject a state court's conclusions. And so he wrote for the Court in *Hysler v. Florida*: [61]

After the Supreme Court of Florida had affirmed his conviction for murder, the petitioner applied to that court for leave to ask the trial court to review the judgment of conviction. The basis of his application was the claim that the testimony of two witnesses implicating him was perjured, and that they had testified falsely against him because they were "coerced, intimidated, beaten, threatened with violence and otherwise abused and mistreated" by the police and were "promised immunity from the electric chair" by the district attorney. After twice considering the matter, the Supreme Court of Florida denied the application. [62] We brought the case here, [63] in view of our solicitude, especially where life is at stake, for those liberties which are guaranteed by the Due Process Clause of the Fourteenth Amendment.

The guides for decision are clear. If a state, whether by the active conduct or the connivance of the prosecution, obtains a conviction through the use of perjured testimony, it violates civilized standards for the trial of guilt or innocence and thereby deprives an accused of liberty without due process of law. [64] Equally offensive to the Constitutional guarantees of liberty are confessions wrung from an accused by overpowering his will, whether through physical violence or the more subtle forms of coercion commonly known as "the third degree." [65] In this collateral attack upon the judgment of conviction, the petitioner bases his claim on the recantation of one of the witnesses against him. He cannot, of course, contend that mere recantation of testimony is in itself ground for invoking the Due Process Clause against a conviction. However, if Florida through her responsible officials knowingly used false testimony which was extorted from a witness "by violence and torture," one convicted may

61. 315 U.S. 411, 412–13, 421–22 (1942).

62. 146 Fla. 593, 1 So.2d 628 (1941). [F.F.]

63. 313 U.S. 557 (1941). [F.F.]

64. Mooney v. Holohan, 294 U.S. 103 (1935). [F.F.]

65. Brown v. Mississippi, 297 U.S. 278 (1936); Chambers v. Florida, 309 U.S. 227 (1940); Lisenba v. California, 314 U.S. 219 (1941). [F.F.]

claim the protection of the Due Process Clause against a conviction based upon such testimony. . . .

The essence of Hysler's claim before the Supreme Court of Florida was that his conviction was secured by unconstitutional means, that Baker was coerced to testify falsely by responsible state officials. The Court had to judge the substantiality of this claim on the basis of all that was before it, namely, the petition with its accompanying affidavits and the records of prior cases arising out of the same crime. The Court concluded that Hysler's proof did not make out a prima facie case for asking the trial court to reconsider its judgment of conviction. However ineptly the Florida Supreme Court may have formulated the grounds for denying the application, its action leaves no room for doubt that the Court deemed the petitioner's claim without substantial foundation. We construe its finding that the "petition" did not show the responsibility of the state officials for the alleged falsity of Baker's original testimony to mean that the petitioner had failed to make the showing of substantiality which, according to the local procedure of Florida, was necessary in order to obtain the extraordinary relief furnished by the writ of error *coram nobis*. And our independent examination of the affidavits upon which his claim was based leaves no doubt that the finding of insubstantiality was justified. It certainly precludes a holding that such a finding was not justified.

The State's security in the just administration of its criminal law must largely rest upon the competence of its trial courts. But that does not bar the state Supreme Court from exercising the vigilance of a hardheaded consideration of appeals to it for upsetting a conviction. That in the course of four years witnesses die or disappear, that memories fade, that a sense of responsibility may became attenuated, that repudiations and new incriminations like Baker's on the eve of execution are not unfamiliar as a means of relieving others or as an irrational hope for self — these of course are not valid considerations for relaxing the protection of Constitutional rights. But they are relevant in exercising a hardy judgment in order to determine whether such a belated disclosure springs from the impulse for truth-telling or is the product of self-delusion or artifice prompted by the instinct of self-preservation.

Our ultimate inquiry is whether the State of Florida has denied to the petitioner the protection of the Due Process Clause. The record does not permit the conclusion that Florida has deprived him of his Constitutional rights.

Frankfurter's concern for the protection of privacy afforded by the Fourth Amendment in federal cases also surfaced in Fourteenth

Amendment cases coming from the state courts. His dissent in *Irvine
v. California* [66] revealed his usual approach to such problems. Here
again was a rejection of absolutes and of fictions that purported to
define one set of amorphous rules in terms of another, equally
amorphous: [67]

Mere failure to have an appropriate warrant for arrest or search,
without aggravating circumstances of misconduct in obtaining
evidence, invalidates a federal conviction helped by such an unreasonable search and seizure. Such was the construction placed upon the
Fourth Amendment by *Weeks* v. *United States.* [68] But *Wolf* v.
Colorado [69] held that the rule of the *Weeks* case was not to be deemed
part of the Due Process Clause of the Fourteenth Amendment and
hence was not binding upon the States. Still more recently, however, in
Rochin v. *California*, [70] the Court held that "stomach pumping" to
obtain morphine capsules, later used as evidence in a trial, was
offensive to prevailing notions of fairness in the conduct of a prosecution and therefore invalidated a resulting conviction as contrary
to the Due Process Clause.

The comprehending principle of these two cases is at the heart
of "due process." The judicial enforcement of the Due Process Clause
is the very antithesis of a Procrustean rule. In its first full-dress
discussion of the Due Process Clause of the Fourteenth Amendment,
the Court defined the nature of the problem as a "gradual process of
judicial inclusion and exclusion, as the cases presented for decision
shall require, with the reasoning on which such decisions may be
founded." [71] The series of cases whereby, in the light of this attitude,
the scope of the Due Process Clause has been unfolded is the most
striking, because the liveliest, manifestation of the wide and deep
areas of law in which adjudication "depends upon differences of degree.
The whole law does so as soon as it is civilized." [72] It is especially
true of the concept of due process that between the differences of
degree which that inherently undefinable concept entails "and the

66. 347 U.S. 128 (1954).

67. *Id* at 142–45.

68. 232 U.S. 383 (1914). [F.F.]

69. 338 U.S. 25 (1949). [F.F.]

70. 342 U.S. 165 (1952). [F.F.]

71. Davidson v. New Orleans, 96 U.S. 97, 104 (1878). [F.F.]

72. Holmes, J., concurring, in LeRoy Fibre Co. v. Chicago, M. & St. P. Ry.,
232 U.S. 340, 354 (1914). [F.F.]

simple universality of the rules in the Twelve Tables or the Leges Barbarorum, there lies the culture of two thousand years."[73]

In the *Wolf* case, the Court rejected one absolute. In *Rochin*, it rejected another.

In holding that not all conduct which by federal law is an unreasonable search and seizure vitiates a conviction in connection with which it transpires, *Wolf* did not and could not decide that as long as relevant evidence adequately supports a conviction, it is immaterial how such evidence was acquired. For the exact holding of that case is defined by the question to which the opinion addressed itself: "Does a conviction by a State court for a State offense deny the 'due process of law' required by the Fourteenth Amendment, solely because evidence that was admitted at the trial was obtained under circumstances which would have rendered it inadmissible in a prosecution for violation of a federal law in a court of the United States because there deemed to be an infraction of the Fourth Amendment as applied in *Weeks* v. *United States*, 232 U.S. 383?" Thus, *Wolf* did not change prior applications of the requirements of due process, whereby this Court considered the whole course of events by which a conviction was obtained and was not restricted to consideration of the trustworthiness of the evidence.

Rochin decided that the Due Process Clause of the Fourteenth Amendment does not leave States free in their prosecutions for crime. The Clause puts limits on the wide discretion of a State in the process of enforcing its criminal law. The holding of the case is that a State cannot resort to methods that offend civilized standards of decency and fairness. The conviction in the *Rochin* case was found to offend due process not because evidence had been obtained through an unauthorized search and seizure or was the fruit of compulsory self-incrimination. Neither of these concepts, relevant to federal prosecutions, was invoked by the Court in *Rochin*, so of course the *Wolf* case was not mentioned. While there is in the case before us, as there was in *Rochin*, an element of unreasonable search and seizure, what is decisive here, as in *Rochin*, is additional aggravating conduct which the Court finds repulsive.

Perhaps it should be noted that *Wolf* was later overruled in *Mapp v. Ohio*[74] so that the exclusionary rule did become applicable to the states.

So, too, Frankfurter's reluctance to expand the concept of double jeopardy in federal prosecutions was matched by a similar reluctance

73. *Ibid.* [F.F.]
74. 367 U.S. 643 (1961).

to allow either the state or federal government to preempt the other from prosecution where each had a claim to do so because of the violation of its own laws. Frankfurter wrote the opinion for the Court in *Bartkus v. Illinois*[75] where a state court conviction for bank robbery followed an acquittal in the federal courts where the same charge had been leveled:[76]

The state and federal prosecutions were separately conducted. It is true that the agent of the Federal Bureau of Investigation who had conducted the investigation on behalf of the Federal Government turned over to the Illinois prosecuting officials all the evidence he had gathered against the petitioner. Concededly, some of that evidence had been gathered after acquittal in the federal court. The only other connection between the two trials is to be found in a suggestion that the federal sentencing of the accomplices who testified against petitioner in both trials was purposely continued by the federal court until after they testified in the state trial. The record establishes that the prosecution was undertaken by state prosecuting officials within their discretionary responsibility and on the basis of evidence that conduct contrary to the penal code of Illinois had occurred within their jurisdiction. It establishes also that federal officials acted in cooperation with state authorities, as is the conventional practice between the two sets of prosecutors throughout the country. It does not support the claim that the State of Illinois in bringing its prosecution was merely a tool of the federal authorities, who thereby avoided the prohibition of the Fifth Amendment against a retrial of a federal prosecution after an acquittal. It does not sustain a conclusion that the state prosecution was a sham and a cover for a federal prosecution, and thereby in essential fact another federal prosecution.

Since the new prosecution was by Illinois, and not by the Federal Government, the claim of unconstitutionality must rest upon the Due Process Clause of the Fourteenth Amendment. Prior cases in this Court relating to successive state and federal prosecutions have been concerned with the Fifth Amendment, and the scope of its proscription of second prosecutions by the Federal Government, not with the Fourteenth Amendment's effect on state action. We are now called upon to draw on the considerations which have guided the Court in applying the limitations of the Fourteenth Amendment on state powers. . . .

Constitutional challenge to successive state and federal prosecutions

75. 359 U.S. 121 (1959).
76. *Id.* at 122–24, 128–29, 132–39.

based upon the same transaction or conduct is not a new question before the Court though it has now been presented with conspicuous ability. The Fifth Amendment's proscription of double jeopardy has been invoked and rejected in over twenty cases of real or hypothetical successive state and federal prosecution cases before this Court. While *United States* v. *Lanza*[77] was the first case in which we squarely held valid a federal prosecution arising out of the same facts which had been the basis of a state conviction, the validity of such a prosecution by the Federal Government has not been questioned by this Court since the opinion in *Fox* v. *Ohio*,[78] more than one hundred years ago. . . .

In a dozen cases decided by this Court between *Moore* v. *Illinois*[79] and *United States* v. *Lanza* this Court had occasion to reaffirm the principle first enunciated in *Fox* v. *Ohio*. Since *Lanza* the Court has five times repeated the rule that successive state and federal prosecutions are not in violation of the Fifth Amendment. Indeed Mr. Justice Holmes once wrote of this rule that it "is too plain to need more than statement." One of the post-Lanza cases, *Jerome* v. *United States*,[80] involved the same federal statute under which Bartkus was indicted and in *Jerome* this Court recognized that successive state and federal prosecutions were thereby made possible because all States had general robbery statutes. Nonetheless, a unanimous Court, as recently as 1943, accepted as unquestioned constitutional law that such successive prosecutions would not violate the proscription of double jeopardy included in the Fifth Amendment.[81] . . .

The experience of state courts in dealing with successive prosecutions by different governments is obviously also relevant in considering whether or not the Illinois prosecution of Bartkus violated due process of law. Of the twenty-eight States which have considered the validity of successive state and federal prosecutions as against a challenge of violation of either a state constitutional double-jeopardy provision or a common-law evidentiary rule of *autrefois acquit* and *autrefois convict*, twenty-seven have refused to rule that the second prosecution was or would be barred. These States were not bound to follow this Court and its interpretation of the Fifth Amendment. The rules, constitutional, statutory, or common law which bound

77. 260 U.S. 377 (1922). [F.F.]

78. 5 How. 410 (1847). [F.F.]

79. 14 How. 13 (1853). [F.F.]

80. 318 U.S. 101 (1943). [F.F.]

81. *Id.* at 105. [F.F.]

them, drew upon the same experience as did the Fifth Amendment, but were and are of separate and independent authority. . . .

With this body of precedent as irrefutable evidence that state and federal courts have for years refused to bar a second trial even though there had been a prior trial by another government for a similar offense, it would be disregard of a long, unbroken, unquestioned course of impressive adjudication for the Court now to rule that due process compels such a bar. A practical justification for rejecting such a reading of due process also commends itself in aid of this interpretation of the Fourteenth Amendment. In *Screws* v. *United States*,[82] defendants were tried and convicted in a federal court under federal statutes with maximum sentences of a year and two years respectively. But the state crime there involved was a capital offense. Were the federal prosecution of a comparatively minor offense to prevent state prosecution of so grave an infraction of state law, the result would be a shocking and untoward deprivation of the historic right and obligation of the States to maintain peace and order within their confines. It would be in derogation of our federal system to displace the reserved power of States over state offenses by reason of prosecution of minor federal offenses by federal authorities beyond the control of the States.

Some recent suggestions that the Constitution was in reality a deft device for establishing a centralized government are not only without factual justification but fly in the face of history. It has more accurately been shown that the men who wrote the Constitution as well as the citizens of the member States of the Confederation were fearful of the power of centralized government and sought to limit its power. Mr. Justice Brandeis has written that separation of powers was adopted in the Constitution "not to promote efficiency but to preclude the exercise of arbitrary power."[83] Time has not lessened the concern of the Founders in devising a federal system which would likewise be a safeguard against arbitrary government. The greatest self-restraint is necessary when that federal system yields results with which a court is in little sympathy.

The entire history of litigation and contention over the question of the imposition of a bar to a second prosecution by a government other than the one first prosecuting is a manifestation of the evolutionary unfolding of law. Today a number of States have statutes which bar a second prosecution if the defendant has been once tried by another government for a similar offense. A study of the cases under the New York statute, which is typical of these laws, demon-

82. 325 U.S. 91 (1945). [F.F.]

83. Myers v. United States, 272 U.S. 52, 240, 293 (1926) (dissenting opinion). [F.F.]

strates that the task of determining when the federal and state statutes are so much alike that a prosecution under the former bars a prosecution under the latter is a difficult one. The proper solution of that problem frequently depends upon a judgment of the gravamen of the state statute. It depends also upon an understanding of the scope of that bar that has been historically granted in the State to prevent successive state prosecutions. Both these problems are ones with which the States are obviously more competent to deal than is this Court. Furthermore, the rules resulting will intimately affect the efforts of a State to develop a rational and just body of criminal law in the protection of its citizens. We ought not to utilize the Fourteenth Amendment to interfere with this development. Finally, experience such as that of New York may give aid to Congress in its consideration of adoption of similar provisions in individual federal criminal statutes or in the federal criminal code.

The problems created by federalism for those in jeopardy under both state and national laws were again revealed in *Knapp v. Schweitzer*.[84] The question there was whether a state could compel testimony from a witness although that testimony would allegedly incriminate him under national law. Frankfurter's temporary answer, for the Court has since changed its position,[85] was in favor of state power: [86]

Petitioner does not claim that his conviction of contempt for refusal to answer questions put to him in a state proceeding deprived him of liberty or property without due process of law in violation of the Fourteenth Amendment; that such a claim is without merit was settled in *Twining* v. *New Jersey*.[87] His contention is, rather, that, because the Congress of the United States has in the exercise of its constitutional powers made certain conduct unlawful, the Fifth Amendment gives him the privilege, which he can assert against either a State or the National Government, against giving testimony that might tend to implicate him in a violation of the federal Act. Because of the momentum of adjudication whereby doctrine expands from case to case, such a claim carries dangerous implications. It may well lead to the contention that when Congress enacts a statute carrying criminal sanctions it has as a practical matter withdrawn from the States their traditional power to investigate in aid of

84. 357 U.S. 371 (1958).

85. Murphy v. N.Y. Waterfront Comm'n, 378 U.S. 52 (1964).

86. 357 U.S. at 374–81.

87. 211 U.S. 78 (1908). [F.F.]

prosecuting conventional state crimes, some facts of which may be entangled in a federal offense. To recognize such a claim would disregard the historic distribution of power as between Nation and States in our federal system.

The essence of a constitutionally formulated federalism is the division of political and legal powers between two systems of government constituting a single Nation. The crucial difference between federalisms is in a wide sweep of powers conferred upon the central government with a reservation of specific powers to the constituent units as against a particularization of powers granted to the federal government with the vast range of governmental powers left to the constituent units. The difference is strikingly illustrated by the British North America Act,[88] and the Commonwealth of Australia Constitution Act.[89] It is relevant to remind that our Constitution is one of particular powers given to the National Government with the powers not so delegated reserved to the States or, in the case of limitations upon both governments, to the people. Except insofar as penal remedies may be provided by Congress under the explicit authority to "make all Laws which shall be necessary and proper for carrying into Execution" the other powers granted by Art. I, § 8, the bulk of authority to legislate on what may be compendiously described as criminal justice, which in other nations belongs to the central government, is under our system the responsibility of the individual States.

The choice of this form of federal arrangement was the product of a jealous concern lest federal power encroach upon the proper domain of the States and upon the rights of the people. It was the same jealous concern that led to the restrictions on the National Government expressed by the first ten amendments, colloquially known as the Bill of Rights. These provisions are deeply concerned with procedural safeguards pertaining to criminal justice within the restricted area of federal jurisdiction. They are not restrictions upon the vast domain of the criminal law that belongs exclusively to the States. Needless to say, no statesman of his day cared more for safeguarding the liberties that were enshrined in the Bill of Rights than did James Madison. But it was his view that these liberties were already protected against federal action by the Constitution itself. "My own opinion," he wrote to Thomas Jefferson, "has always been in favor of a bill of rights; provided it be so framed as not to imply powers not meant to be included in the enumeration. At the same time I have never thought the omission of material defect, nor been

88. 30 Vict. c. 3 (1867). [F.F.]

89. 63 & 64 Vict. c. 12 (1900). [F.F.]

anxious to supply it even by subsequent amendment, for any other reason than that it is anxiously desired by others. I have favored it because I supposed it might be of use, and if properly executed could not be of disservice. I have not viewed it in an important light 1. Because I conceive that in a certain degree, though not in the extent argued by Mr. Wilson, the rights in question are reserved by the manner in which the federal powers are granted. . . ."[90] Plainly enough the limitations arising from the manner in which the federal powers were granted were limitations on the Federal Government, not on the States. The Bill of Rights that Madison sponsored because others anxiously desired that these limitations be made explicit patently was likewise limited to the Federal Government. If conclusive proof of this were needed, it is afforded by the fact that when Madison came to sponsor the Bills of Rights in the House of Representatives as safeguards against the Federal Government he proposed that like safeguards against the States be placed in the United States Constitution. Congress, however, rejected such limitations upon state power.

While the adoption of the Fourteenth Amendment in 1868 did not change the distribution of powers between the States and the Federal Government so as to withdraw the basic interests of criminal justice from the exclusive control of the States, it did impose restrictions upon the States in the making and in the enforcement of the criminal laws. It did this insofar as the "fundamental principles of liberty and justice which lie at the base of all our civil and political institutions"[91] are implied in the comprehensive concept of due process of law. But this concept does not blur the great division of powers between the Federal Government and the individual States in the enforcement of the criminal law.

Generalities though these observations be, they bear decisively on the issue that has been tendered in this case. To yield to the contention of the petitioner would not only disregard the uniform course of decision by this Court for over a hundred years in recognizing the legal autonomy of state and federal governments. In these days of the extensive sweep of such federal statutes as the income tax law and the criminal sanctions for their evasions, investigation under state law to discover corruption and misconduct, generally, in violation of state law could easily be thwarted if a State were deprived of its power to expose such wrongdoing with a view

90. Letter to Thomas Jefferson, 17 October 1788. 14 PAPERS OF THOMAS JEFFER- 16, 18 (Boyd ed. 1958). [F.F.]

91. Hebert v. Louisiana, 272 U.S. 312, 316 (1926); Palko v. Connecticut, 302 U.S. 319 (1937); Malinski v. New York, 324 U.S. 401, 412–16, 438 (1945). [F.F.]

to remedial legislation or prosecution. While corruption and generally low standards in local government may not today be as endemic as Lord Bryce reported them to be in The American Commonwealth (1888), not even the most cheerful view of the improvements that have since taken place can afford justification for blunting the power of States to ferret out, and thereby guard against, such corruption by restrictions that would reverse our whole constitutional history. To achieve these essential ends of state government the States may find it necessary, as did New York, to require full disclosure in exchange for immunity from prosecution. This cannot be denied on the claim that such state law of immunity may expose the potential witness to prosecution under federal law.[92] Every witness before a state grand jury investigation would feel free to block those vitally important proceedings.

In construing the Fifth Amendment and its privilege against self-incrimination, one must keep in mind its essential quality as a restraint upon compulsion of testimony by the newly organized Federal Government at which the Bill of Rights was directed, and not as a general declaration of policy against compelling testimony. It is plain that the amendment can no more be thought of as restricting action by the States than as restricting the conduct of private citizens. The sole — although deeply valuable — purpose of the Fifth Amendment privilege against self-incrimination is the security of the individual against the exertion of the power of the Federal Government to compel incriminating testimony with a view to enabling that same Government to convict a man out of his own mouth.

Of course the Federal Government may not take advantage of this recognition of the States' autonomy in order to evade the Bill of Rights. If a federal officer should be a party to the compulsion of testimony by state agencies, the protection of the Fifth Amendment would come into play. Such testimony is barred in a federal prosecution.[93] Whether, in a case of such collaboration between state and federal officers, the defendant could successfully assert his privilege in the state proceeding, we need not now decide, for the record before us is barren of the evidence that the State was used as an instrument of federal prosecution or investigation. Petitioner's assertion that a federal prosecuting attorney announced his intention of cooperating with state officials in the prosecution of cases in a general field of criminal law presents a situation devoid of legal significance as a joint state and federal endeavor.

92. See Jack v. Kansas, 199 U.S. 372 (1905). [F.F.]
93. See Byars v. United States, 372 U.S. 28 (1927). [F.F.]

This Court with all its shifting membership has repeatedly found occasion to say that whatever inconveniences and embarrassments may be involved, they are the price we pay for our federalism, for having our people amenable to — as well as served and protected by — two governments. If a person may, through immunized self-disclosure before a law-enforcing agency of the State, facilitate to some extent his amenability to federal process, or *vice versa*, this too is a price to be paid for our federalism. Against it must be put what would be a greater price, that of sterilizing the power of both governments by not recognizing the autonomy of each within its proper sphere.

In conclusion, it might be noted that the concept of substantive due process was no more palatable to Frankfurter in the area of criminal law than it was in economic matters. When the Court ruled in *Lambert v. California*,[94] that it was beyond the power of the state to make it a crime for a convicted felon to fail to register with the police in the absence of a showing of willingness, Frankfurter wrote the dissent:[95]

The present laws of the United States and of the forty-eight States are thick with provisions that command that some things not be done and others be done, although persons convicted under such provisions may have had no awareness of what the law required or that what they did was wrongdoing. The body of decisions sustaining such legislation, including innumerable registration laws, is almost as voluminous as the legislation itself. The matter is summarized in *United States* v. *Balint*.[96] "Many instances of this are to be found in regulatory measures in the exercise of what is called the police power where the emphasis of the statute is evidently upon achievement of some social betterment rather than the punishment of the crimes as in cases of *mala in se*."

Surely there can hardly be a difference as a matter of fairness, of hardship, or of justice, if one may invoke it, between the case of a person wholly innocent of wrongdoing, in the sense that he was not remotely conscious of violating any law, who is imprisoned for five years for conduct relating to narcotics, and the case of another person who is placed on probation for three years on condition that she pay $250, for failure, as a local resident, convicted under local law of a felony, to register under a law passed as an exercise of the State's "police power." Considerations of hardship often lead

94. 355 U.S. 225 (1957).

95. *Id*. at 230–32.

96. 258 U.S. 250, 252 (1922). [F.F.]

courts, naturally enough, to attribute to a statute the requirement of a certain mental element — some consciousness of wrongdoing and knowledge of the law's command — as a matter of statutory construction. Then, too, a cruelly disproportionate relation between what the law requires and the sanction for its disobedience may constitute a violation of the Eighth Amendment as a cruel and unusual punishment, and, in respect to the States, even offend the Due Process Clause of the Fourteenth Amendment.

But what the Court here does is to draw a constitutional line between a State's requirement of doing and not doing. What is that but a return to Year Book distinctions between feasance and non-feasance — a distinction that may have significance in the evolution of common-law notions of liability, but is inadmissible as a line between constitutionality and unconstitutionality. One can be confident that Mr. Justice Holmes would have been the last to draw such a line. What he wrote about "blameworthiness" is worth quoting in its context: [97]

"It is not intended to deny that criminal liability, as well as civil, is founded on blameworthiness. Such a denial would shock the moral sense of any civilized community; or, to put it another way, a law which punished conduct which would not be blameworthy in the average member of the community would be too severe for that community to bear."

If the generalization that underlies, and alone can justify, this decision were to be given its relevant scope, a whole volume of the United States Reports would be required to document in detail the legislation in this country that would fall or be impaired. I abstain from entering upon a consideration of such legislation, and adjudications upon it, because I feel confident that the present decision will turn out to be an isolated deviation from the strong current of precedents — a derelict on the waters of the law. Accordingly, I content myself with dissenting.

97. This passage must be read in the setting of the broader discussion of which it is an essential part. HOLMES, THE COMMON LAW 49–50 (1881). [F.F.]

11   Due Process
of Law

Due process of law, of course, is a requirement that extends beyond the realm of criminal procedure. Some understanding of the variety of problems arising under that rubric of constitutional law and of Mr. Justice Frankfurter's approach to them may be garnered by examination of a few examples in addition to those already noted.

In *Schware v. Board of Bar Examiners*,[1] the question was whether an applicant for admission to a state bar had been improperly excluded in violation of the Due Process Clause. Frankfurter engaged in his usual balancing act before concluding in his concurring opinion that the scales were weighted on the side of the applicant:[2]

Certainly since the time of Edward I, through all the vicissitudes of seven centuries of Anglo-American history, the legal profession has played a role all its own. The bar has not enjoyed prerogatives; it has been entrusted with anxious responsibilities. One does not have to inhale the self-adulatory bombast of after-dinner speeches to affirm that all the interests of man that are comprised under the constitutional guarantees given to "life, liberty and property" are in the professional keeping of lawyers. It is a fair characterization of the lawyer's responsibility in our society that he stands "as a shield," to quote Devlin, J., in defense of right and to ward off wrong. From a profession charged with such responsibilities there must be extracted those qualities of truth-speaking, of a high sense of honor, of granite discretion, of the strictest observance of fiduciary responsibility, that have, throughout the centuries, been compendiously described as "moral character."

From the thirteenth century to this day, in England the profession itself has determined who should enter it. In the United States the courts exercise ultimate control. But while we have nothing comparable to the Inns of Court, with us too the profession itself, through appropriate committees, has long had a vital interest, as a sifting agency, in determining the fitness, and above all the moral fitness, of those who are certified to be entrusted with the fate of clients. With us too the requisite "moral character" has been the historic unquestioned

1. 353 U.S. 232 (1957).

2. *Id.* at 247–49, 251.

182

prerequisite of fitness. Admission to practice in a State and before its courts necessarily belongs to that State. Of course, legislation laying down general conditions, like other legislation, falls afoul of the Fourteenth Amendment.[3] A very different question is presented when this Court is asked to review the exercise of judgment in refusing admission to the bar in an individual case, such as we have here.

It is beyond this Court's function to act as overseer of a particular result of the procedure established by a particular State for admission to its bar. No doubt satisfaction of the requirement of moral character involves an exercise of delicate judgment on the part of those who reach a conclusion, having heard and seen the applicant for admission, a judgment of which it may be said as it was of "many honest and sensible judgments" in a different context that it expresses "an intuition of experience which outruns analysis and sums up many unnamed and tangled impressions; impressions which may lie beneath consciousness without losing their worth."[4] Especially in this realm it is not our business to substitute our judgment for the State's judgment — for it is the State in all the panoply of its powers that is under review when the action of its Supreme Court is under review.

Nor is the division of power between this Court and that of the States in such matters altered by the fact that the judgment here challenged involves the application of a conception like that of "moral character," which has shadowy rather than precise bounds. It cannot be that that conception — moral character — has now been found to be so indefinite, because necessarily implicating what are called subjective factors, that the States may no longer exact it from those who are to carry on "the public profession of the law."[5] To a wide and deep extent, the law depends upon the disciplined standards of the profession and belief in the integrity of the courts. We cannot fail to accord such confidence to the state process, and we must attribute to its courts the exercise of a fair and not a biased judgment in passing upon the applications of those seeking entry into the profession. . . .

This brings me to the inference that the court drew from petitioner's early, pre-1940 affiliations. To hold, as the court did, that Communist affiliation for six to seven years up to 1940, fifteen years prior to the court's assessment of it, in and of itself made the petitioner "a person of questionable character" is so dogmatic an inference as to be wholly unwarranted. History overwhelmingly establishes that

3. See Cummings v. Missouri, 4 Wall. 277 (1867). [F.F.]

4. Chicago, B. & Q. Ry. v. Babcock, 204 U.S. 585, 598 (1907). [F.F.]

5. Root, *The Public Profession of the Law*, 2 A.B.A.J. 736 (1916). [F.F.]

many youths like the petitioner were drawn by the mirage of communism during the depression era, only to have their eyes later opened to reality. Such experiences no doubt may disclose a wooly mind or naive notions regarding the problems of society. But facts of history that we would be arbitrary in rejecting bar the presumption, let alone an irrebuttable presumption, that response to foolish, baseless hopes regarding the betterment of society made those who had entertained them but who later undoubtedly came to their senses and their sense of responsibility "questionable characters." Since the Supreme Court of New Mexico as a matter of law took a contrary view of such a situation in denying petitioner's application, it denied him due process of law.

Galvan v. Press[6] presented an analogous problem in which, for Frankfurter, the scales came down on the other side. There the question was whether an alien could be deported because of his affiliation with the Communist Party. Frankfurter's opinion for the Court held that he could be deprived of his privilege of residence in this country in keeping with the commands of the Due Process Clause of the Fifth Amendment:[7]

The power of Congress over the admission of aliens and their right to remain is necessarily very broad, touching as it does basic aspects of national sovereignty, more particularly our foreign relations and the national security. Nevertheless, considering what it means to deport an alien who legally became part of the American community, and the extent to which, since he is a "person," an alien has the same protection for his life, liberty and property under the Due Process Clause as is afforded to a citizen, deportation without permitting the alien to prove that he was unaware of the Communist Party's advocacy of violence strikes one with a sense of harsh incongruity. If due process bars Congress from enactments that shock the sense of fair play — which is the essence of due process — one is entitled to ask whether it is not beyond the power of Congress to deport an alien who was duped into joining the Communist Party, particularly when his conduct antedated the enactment of the legislation under which his deportation is sought. And this because deportation may, as this Court has said in *Ng Fung Ho* v. *White*,[8] deprive a man "of all that makes life worth living"; and, as it has

6. 347 U.S. 522 (1954).

7. *Id.* at 530–32.

8. 259 U.S. 276, 284 (1922). [F.F.]

said in *Fong Haw Tan* v. *Phalen*,[9] "deportation is a drastic measure and at times the equivalent of banishment or exile."

In light of the expansion of the concept of substantive due process as a limitation upon all powers of Congress, even the war power,[10] much could be said for the view, were we writing on a clean slate, that the Due Process Clause qualifies the scope of political discretion heretofore recognized as belonging to Congress in regulating the entry and deportation of aliens. And since the intrinsic consequences of deportation are so close to punishment for crime, it might fairly be said also that the *ex post facto* Clause, even though applicable only to punitive legislation, should be applied to deportation.

But the slate is not clean. As to the extent of the power of Congress under review, there is not merely "a page of history,"[11] but a whole volume. Policies pertaining to the entry of aliens and their right to remain here are peculiarly concerned with the political conduct of government. In the enforcement of these policies, the Executive Branch of the Government must respect the procedural safeguards of due process.[12] But that the formulation of these policies is entrusted exclusively to Congress has become about as firmly imbedded in the legislative and judicial tissues of our body politic as any aspect of our government. And whatever might have been said at an earlier date for applying the *ex post facto* Clause, it has been the unbroken rule of this Court that it has no application to deportation.

We are not prepared to deem ourselves wiser or more sensitive to human rights than our predecessors, especially those who have been most zealous in protecting civil liberties under the Constitution, and must therefore under our constitutional system recognize congressional power in dealing with aliens, on the basis of which we are unable to find the Act of 1950 unconstitutional.[13]

Hannah v. Larche[14] presented the Court with the issue of the propriety of the procedures of the Commission on Civil Rights, procedures which did not afford those accused of racial discrimination the right to be apprised of the charges against them, or of the identity

9. 333 U.S. 6, 10 (1948). [F.F.]

10. See Hamilton v. Kentucky Distilleries Co., 251 U.S. 146, 155 (1919). [F.F.]

11. New York Trust Co. v. Eisner, 256 U.S. 345, 349 (1921). [F.F.]

12. The Japanese Immigrant Case, 189 U.S. 86, 101 (1903); Wong Yang Sung v. McGrath, 339 U.S. 33, 49 (1950). [F.F.]

13. See Bugajewitz v. Adams, 228 U.S. 585 (1913); Ng Fung Ho v. White, 259 U.S. 276, 280 (1922). [F.F.]

14. 363 U.S. 420 (1960).

of the accusers, or of the rights of confrontation and cross-examination. Such procedures would be highly suspect if indulged by some less worthy bodies for less worthy ends. But the Court sustained the propriety of the commission's actions and Frankfurter concurred in an opinion of his own: [15]

To conduct the Shreveport hearing on the basis of sworn allegations of wrongdoings by the plaintiffs, without submitting to them these allegations and disclosing the identities of the affiants, would, it is claimed, violate the Constitution. The issue thus raised turns exclusively on the application of the Due Process Clause of the Fifth Amendment. The Commission's hearings are not proceedings requiring a person to answer for an "infamous crime," which must be based on an indictment of a grand jury (Amendment V), nor are they "criminal prosecutions" giving an accused the rights defined by Amendment VI. Since due process is the constitutional axis on which decision must turn, our concern is not with absolutes, either of governmental power or of safeguards protecting individuals. Inquiry must be directed to the validity of the adjustment between these clashing interests — that of Government and of the individual, respectively — in the procedural scheme devised by the Congress and the Commission. Whether the scheme satisfies those strivings for justice which due process guarantees, must be judged in the light of reason drawn from the considerations of fairness that reflect our traditions of legal and political thought, duly related to the public interest Congress sought to meet by this legislation as against the hazards or hardship to the individual that the Commission procedure would entail.

Barring rare lapses, this Court has not unduly confined those who have the responsibility of governing within a doctrinaire conception of "due process." The Court has been mindful of the manifold variety and perplexity of the tasks which the Constitution has vested in the legislative and executive branches of the Government by recognizing that what is unfair in one situation may be fair in another.[16] Whether the procedure now questioned offends "the rudiments of fair play"[17] is not to be tested by loose generalities or sentiments abstractly appealing. The precise nature of the interest alleged to be adversely affected or of the freedom of action claimed to be curtailed, the manner in which this is to be done and the reasons

15. *Id.* at 486–93.

16. *Compare*, for instance, Murray's Lessee v. Hoboken Land & Improvement Co., 18 How. 272 (1856), *with* Ng Fung Ho v. White, 259 U.S. 276 (1922), and see F.C.C. v. WJR, 337 U.S. 265, 275 (1949). [F.F.]

17. Chicago, M. & St. P. Ry. v. Polt, 232 U.S. 165, 168 (1914). [F.F.]

for doing it, the balance of individual hurt and the justifying public good — these and such like are the considerations, avowed or implicit, that determine the judicial judgment when appeal is made to "due process."

The proposed Shreveport hearing creates risks of harm to the plaintiffs. It is likewise true that, were the plaintiffs afforded the procedural rights they seek, they would have a greater opportunity to reduce these risks than will be theirs under the questioned rules of the Commission. Some charges touching the plaintiffs might be withdrawn or modified, if those making them knew that their identities and the content of their charges were to be revealed. By the safeguards they seek the plaintiffs might use the hearing as a forum for subjecting the charges against them to a scrutiny that might disprove them or, at least, establish that they are not incompatible with innocent conduct.

Were the Commission exercising an accusatory function, were its duty to find that named individuals were responsible for wrongful deprivation of voting rights and to advertise such finding or to serve as part of the process of criminal prosecution, the rigorous protections relevant to criminal prosecutions might well be the controlling starting point for assessing the protection which the Commission's procedure provides. The objectives of the Commission on Civil Rights, the purpose of its creation, and its true functioning are quite otherwise. It is not charged with official judgment on individuals nor are its inquiries so directed. The purpose of its investigations is to develop facts upon which legislation may be based. As such, its investigations are directed to those concerns that are the normal impulse to legislation and the basis for it. To impose upon the Commission's investigations the safeguards appropriate to inquiries into individual blameworthiness would be to divert and frustrate its purpose. Its investigation would be turned into a forum for the litigation of individual culpability — matters which are not within the keeping of the Commission, with which it is not effectively equipped to deal, and which would deflect it from the purpose for which it was within its limited life established.

We would be shutting our eyes to actualities to be unmindful of the fact that it would dissuade sources of vitally relevant information from making that information known to the Commission, if the Commission were required to reveal its sources and subject them to cross-examination. This would not be a valid consideration for secrecy were the Commission charged with passing official incriminatory or even defamatory judgment on individuals. Since the Commission is merely an investigatorial arm of Congress, the narrow risk of unintended harm to the individual is outweighed by the legislative justification for permitting the Commission to be the critic and protector of the information given it. It would be wrong not to assume that the Commission will responsibly scrutinize the reliability of sworn allegations that are to serve as the basis for further investigation and that it will be rigorously vigilant to protect the fair name of those brought into question.

In appraising the constitutionally permissive investigative procedure claimed to subject individuals to incrimination or defamation without adequate opportunity for defense, a relevant distinction is between those proceedings which are preliminaries to official judgments on individuals and those, like the investigation of this Commission, charged with responsibility to gather information as a solid foundation for legislative action. Judgments by the Commission condemning or stigmatizing individuals are not called for. When official pronouncements on individuals purport to rest on evidence and investigation, it is right to demand that those so accused be given a full opportunity for their defense in such investigation, excepting, of course, grand jury investigations. The functions of that institution and its constitutional prerogatives are rooted in long centuries of Anglo-American history. On the other hand, to require the introduction of adversary contests relevant to determination of individual guilt into what is in effect a legislative investigation is bound to thwart it by turning it into a serious digression from its purpose.

The cases in which this Court has recently considered claims to procedural rights in investigative inquiries alleged to deal unfairly with the reputation of individuals or to incriminate them, have made clear that the fairness of their procedures is to be judged in light of the purpose of the inquiry, and, more particularly, whether its essential objective is official judgment on individuals under scrutiny. Such a case was *Greene* v. *McElroy*.[18] There the inquiry was for the purpose of determining whether the security clearance of a particular person was to be revoked. A denial of clearance would shut him off from the opportunity of access to a wide field of employment. The Court concluded that serious constitutional questions were raised by denial of the rights to confront accusatory witnesses and to have access to unfavorable reports on the basis of which the very livelihood of an individual would be gravely jeopardized. Again, *Joint Anti-Fascist Refugee Committee* v. *McGrath*[19] presented a contrasting situation to the one before us. The Government there sought through the Attorney General to designate organizations as "Communist," thus furnishing grounds on which to discharge their members from

18. 360 U.S. 474 (1959). [F.F.]

19. 341 U.S. 123 (1951). [F.F.]

government employment. No notice was given of the charges against the organizations nor were they given an opportunity to establish the innocence of their aims and acts. It was well within the realities to say of what was under scrutiny in *Joint Anti-Fascist Refugee Committee* v. *McGrath* that "It would be blindness . . . not to recognize that in the conditions of our time such designation drastically restricts the organizations, if it does not proscribe them." [20] And the procedure which was found constitutionally wanting in that case could be fairly characterized as action "to maim or decapitate, on the mere say-so of the Attorney General, an organization to all outward-seeming engaged in lawful objectives. . . ." [21] Nothing like such characterization can remotely be made regarding the procedure for the proposed inquiry of the Commission on Civil Rights. . . .

Moreover, the limited, investigatorial scope of the challenged hearing is carefully hedged in with protections for the plaintiffs. They will have the right to be accompanied by counsel. The rules insure that they will be made aware of the subject of the hearings. They will have the right to appeal to the Commission's power to subpoena additional witnesses. The rules significantly direct the Commission to abstain from public exposure by taking in executive session any evidence or testimony tending "to defame, degrade, or incriminate any person." A person so affected is given the right to read such evidence and to reply to it. These detailed provisions are obviously designed as safeguards against injury to persons who appear in public hearings before the Commission. The provision for screening defamatory and incriminatory testimony in order to keep it from the public may well be contrasted with the procedure in the *Joint Anti-Fascist* case, where the very purpose of the inquiry was to make an official judgment that certain organizations were "Communist." Such condemnation of an organization would of course taint its members. The rules of the Commission manifest a sense of its responsibility in carrying out the limited investigatorial task confided to it. It is not a constitutional requirement that the Commission be argumentatively turned into a forum for trial of the truth of particular allegations of denial of voting rights in order thereby to invalidate its functioning. Such an inadmissible transformation of the Commission's function is in essence what is involved in the claims of the plaintiffs. Congress has entrusted the Commission with a very different role — that of investigating and appraising general conditions and reporting them to Congress so as to inform the legislative judgment. Resort to a legislative commission as a vehicle

20. *Id.* at 161 (concurring opinion). [F.F.]

21. *Ibid.* [F.F.]

for proposing well-founded legislation and recommending its passage to Congress has ample precedent.

Finally it should be noted that arguments directed either at the assumed novelty of employing the Commission in the area of legislative interest which led Congress to its establishment, or at the fact that the source of the Commission's procedures were those long used by Committees of Congress, are not particularly relevant. History may satisfy constitutionality, but constitutionality need not produce the title deeds of history. Mere age may establish due process, but due process does not preclude new ends of government or new means for achieving them. Since the Commission has, within its legislative framework, provided procedural safeguards appropriate to its proper function, claims of unfairness offending due process fall. The proposed Shreveport hearing fully comports with the Constitution and the law. Accordingly I join the judgment of the Court in reversing the District Court.

Economic due process always remained anathema to Frankfurter, even when it was invoked by those who had been its victims at an earlier stage of American constitutional history. *A. F. of L. v. American Sash & Door Co.*,[22] involving the validity of state statutes forbidding employers to restrict employment to union members — the converse of the yellow-dog statutes — brought forth a lengthy concurring opinion invoking the shades of many past battles, in some of which Frankfurter had been a contestant and not an umpire. He provided a synopsis of the rise and fall of substantive economic due process:[23]

Arizona, Nebraska, and North Carolina have passed laws forbidding agreements to employ only union members. The United States Constitution is invoked against these laws. Since the cases bring into question the judicial process in its application to the Due Process Clause, explicit avowal of individual attitudes towards that process may elucidate and thereby strengthen adjudication. Accordingly, I set forth the steps by which I have reached concurrence with my brethren on what I deem the only substantial issue here, on all other issues joining the Court's opinion.

The coming of the machine age tended to despoil human personality. It turned men and women into "hands." The industrial history of the early Nineteenth Century demonstrated the helplessness of the individual employee to achieve human dignity in a society so largely

22. 335 U.S. 538 (1949).

23. *Id.* at 542–57.

affected by technological advances. Hence the trade union made itself increasingly felt, not only as an indispensable weapon of self-defense on the part of workers but as an aid to the well-being of a society in which work is an expression of life and not merely the means of earning subsistence. But unionization encountered the shibboleths of a pre-machine age and these were reflected in juridical assumptions that survived the facts on which they were based. Adam Smith was treated as though his generalizations had been imparted to him on Sinai and not as a thinker who addressed himself to eliminations of restrictions which had become fetters upon initiative and enterprise in his day. Basic human rights expressed by the constitutional conception of "liberty" were equated with theories of *laissez faire*. The result was that economic views of confined validity were treated by lawyers and judges as though the Framers had enshrined them in the Constitution. This misapplication of the notions of the classic economists and resulting disregard of the perduring reach of the Constitution led to Mr. Justice Holmes' famous protest in the *Lochner* case against measuring the Fourteenth Amendment by Mr. Herbert Spencer's Social Statics.[24] Had not Mr. Justice Holmes' awareness of the impermanence of legislation as against the permanence of the Constitution gradually prevailed, there might indeed have been "hardly any limit but the sky" to the embodiment of "our economic or moral beliefs" in that Amendment's "prohibitions."[25]

The attitude which regarded any legislative encroachment upon the existing economic order as infected with unconstitutionality led to disrespect for legislative attempts to strengthen the wage-earner's bargaining power. With that attitude as a premise, *Adair* v. *United States*,[26] and *Coppage* v. *Kansas*,[27] followed logically enough; not even *Truax* v. *Corrigan*[28] could be considered unexpected. But when the tide turned, it was not merely because circumstances had changed and there had arisen a new order with new claims to divine origin. The opinion of Mr. Justice Brandeis in *Senn* v. *Tile Layers Union*,[29] shows the current running strongly in the new direction — the direction not of social dogma but of increased deference to the legislative judgment. "Whether it was wise," he said, now speaking for the Court and not in dissent, "for the State to permit the unions

24. Lochner v. New York, 198 U.S. 45, 75 (1905). [F.F.]

25. Baldwin v. Missouri, 281 U.S. 586, 595 (1930). [F.F.]

26. 208 U.S. 161 (1908). [F.F.]

27. 236 U.S. 1 (1915). [F.F.]

28. 257 U.S. 312 (1921). [F.F.]

29. 301 U.S. 468 (1937). [F.F.]

to [picket] is a question of its public policy — not our concern." [30]
Long before that, he had warned: [31]

"All rights are derived from the purposes of the society in which
they exist; above all rights rises duty to the community. The conditions
developed in industry may be such that those engaged in it cannot
continue their struggle without danger to the community. But it is
not for judges to determine whether such conditions exist, nor is it
their function to set the limits of permissible contest and to declare
the duties which the new situation demands. This is the function of
the legislature which, while limiting individual and group rights
of aggression and defense, may substitute processes of justice for
the more primitive method of trial by combat."

Unions are powers within the State. Like the power of industrial
and financial aggregations, the power of organized labor springs from
a group which is only a fraction of the whole that Mr. Justice Holmes
referred to as "the one club to which we all belong." The power of
the former is subject to control, though, of course, the particular
incidence of control may be brought to test at the bar of this Court.[32]
Neither can the latter claim constitutional exemption. Even the
Government — the organ of the whole people — is restricted by
the system of checks and balances established by our Constitution.
The designers of that system distributed authority among the three
branches "not to promote efficiency but to preclude the exercise
of arbitrary power." [33] Their concern for individual members of
society, for whose well-being government is instituted, gave urgency
to the fear that concentrated power would become arbitrary. It is
a fear that the history of such power, even when professedly employed
for democratic purposes, has hardly rendered unfounded.

If concern for the individual justifies incorporating in the Constitution itself devices to curb public authority, a legislative judgment
that his protection requires the regulation of the private power of
unions cannot be dismissed as insupportable. A union is no more
than a medium through which individuals are able to act together;
union power was begotten of individual helplessness. But that power
can come into being only when, and continue to exist only so long
as, individual aims are seen to be shared in common with the other

30. *Id.* at 481. [F.F.]

31. Duplex Printing Press Co. v. Deering, 254 U.S. 443, 488 (1921). [F.F.]

32. *E.g.*, Northern Securities Co. v. United States, 193 U.S. 197 (1904); North
American Co. v. S.E.C., 327 U.S. 686 (1946). [F.F.]

33. Mr. Justice Brandeis, dissenting, in Myers v. United States, 272 U.S. 52,
293 (1926). [F.F.]

members of the group. There is a natural emphasis, however, on what is shared and a resulting tendency to subordinate the inconsistent interests and impulses of individuals. From this, it is an easy transition to thinking of the union as an entity having rights and purposes of its own. An ardent supporter of trade unions who is also no less a disinterested student of society has pointed out that "As soon as we personify the idea, whether it is a country or a church, a trade union or an employer's association, we obscure individual responsibility by transferring emotional loyalties to a fictitious creation which then acts upon us psychologically as an obstruction, especially in times of crisis, to the critcal exercise of a reasoned judgment." [34]

The right of association, like any other right carried to its extreme, encounters limiting principles.[35] At the point where the mutual advantage of association demands too much individual disadvantage, a compromise must be struck.[36] When that point has been reached — where the intersection should fall — is plainly a question within the special province of the legislature. This Court has given effect to such a compromise in sustaining a legislative purpose to protect individual employees against the exclusionary practices of unions.[37] The rationale of the Arizona, Nebraska, and North Carolina legislation prohibiting union-security agreements is founded on a similar resolution of conflicting interests. Unless we are to treat as unconstitutional what goes against the grain because it offends what we may strongly believe to be socially desirable, that resolution must be given respect.

It is urged that the compromise which this legislation embodies is no compromise at all because fatal to the survival of organized labor. But it can be said that the legislators and the people of Arizona, Nebraska, and North Carolina could not in reason be sceptical of organized labor's insistence upon the necessity to its strength of power to compel rather than to persuade the allegiance of its reluctant members? In the past fifty years the total number of employed, counting salaried workers and the self-employed but not farmers or farm laborers, has not quite trebled, while total union membership has increased more than thirty-three times; at the time of the open-shop drive following the First World War, the ratio of

---

34. Laski, *Morris Cohen's Approach to Legal Philosophy*, 15 U. Chi. L. Rev. 575, 581 (1948). [F.F.]

35. See Hudson County Water Co. v. McCarter, 209 U.S. 349, 355 (1908). [F.F.]

36. See Dicey, Law and Public Opinion in England 465–55 (1904). [F.F.]

37. Steele v. Louisville & N. R.R., 323 U.S. 192 (1944); Wallace Corp. v. Labor Board, 323 U.S. 248 (1944); Railway Mail Ass'n v. Corsi, 326 U.S. 88 (1945); *cf.* Elgin, J. & E. Ry. v. Burley, 325 U.S. 711, 733–34 (1945). [F.F.]

organized to unorganized non-agricultural workers was about one to nine, and now it is almost one to three. However necessitous may have been the circumstances of unionism in 1898 or even in 1923, its status in 1948 precludes constitutional condemnation of a legislative judgment, whatever we may think of it, that the need of this type of regulation outweighs its detriments. It would be arbitrary for this Court to deny the States the right to experiment with such laws, especially in view of the fact that the Railroad Brotherhoods have held their own despite congressional prohibition of union security and in the light of the experience of countries advanced in industrial democracy, such as Great Britain and Sweden, where deeply rooted acceptance of the principles of collective bargaining is not reflected in uncompromising demands for contractually guaranteed security. Whether it is preferable in the public interest that trade unions should be subjected to State intervention or left to the free play of social forces, whether experience has disclosed "union unfair labor practices" and, if so, whether legislative correction is more appropriate than self-discipline and the pressure of public opinion — these are questions on which it is not for us to express views. The very limited function of this Court is discharged when we recognize that these issues are not so unrelated to the experience and feelings of the community as to render legislation addressing itself to them wilfully destructive of cherished rights. For these are not matters, like censorship of the press or separation of Church and State, on which history, through the Constitution, speaks so decisively as to forbid legislative experimentation.

But the policy which finds expression in the prohibtion of union-security agreements need not rest solely on a legislative conception of the public interest which includes but transcends the special claims of trade unions. The States are entitled to give weight to views combining opposition to the "closed shop" with long-range concern for the welfare of trade unions. Mr. Justice Brandeis, for example, before he came to this Court, had been a staunch promoter of unionism. . . . Yet at the same time he believed that "The objections, legal, economic, and social, against the closed shop are so strong, and the ideas of the closed shop so antagonistic to the American spirit, that the insistence upon it has been a serious obstacle to union progress." [38] . . . Mr. Brandeis on the long view deemed the preferential shop a more reliable form of security both for unions and for society than the closed shop; that he did so only serves to

---

38. Letter of 6 September 1910, to Lawrence F. Abbott of the *Outlook*. Copy obtained from the collection of Brandeis papers at the Law Library of the University of Louisville. [F.F.]

prove that these are pragmatic issues not appropriate for dogmatic solution.

Whatever one may think of Mr. Brandeis' views, they have been reinforced by the adoption of laws insuring against that undercutting of union standards which was one of the most serious effects of a dissident minority in a union shop. Under interpretations of the National Labor Relations Act undisturbed by the Taft-Hartley Act, and of the Railway Labor Act, the bargaining representative designated by a majority of employees has exclusive power to deal with the employer on matters of wages and working conditions. Individual contracts, whether on more or less favorable terms than those obtained by the union, are barred.[39] Under these laws, a non-union bidder for a job in a union shop cannot, if he would, undercut the union standards.

Even where the social undesirability of a law may be convincingly urged, invalidation of the law by a court debilitates popular democratic government. Most laws dealing with economic and social problems are matters of trial and error. That which before trial appears to be demonstrably bad may belie prophecy in actual operation. It may not prove good, but it may prove innocuous. But even if a law is found wanting on trial, it is better that its defects should be demonstrated and removed than that the law should be aborted by judicial fiat. Such an assertion of judicial power deflects responsibility from those on whom in a democratic society it ultimately rests — the people. If the proponents of union-security agreements have confidence in the arguments addressed to the Court in their "economic brief," they should address those arguments to the electorate. Its endorsement would be a vindication that the mandate of this Court could never give. That such vindication is not a vain hope has been recently demonstrated by the voters of Maine, Massachusetts, and New Mexico. And although several States in addition to those at bar now have such laws, the legislatures of as many other States have, sometimes repeatedly, rejected them. What one State can refuse to do, another can undo.

But there is reason for judicial restraint in matters of policy deeper than the value of experiment: it is founded on a recognition of the gulf of difference between sustaining and nullifying legislation. This difference is theoretical in that the function of legislating is for legislatures who have also taken oaths to support the Constitution, while the function of courts, when legislation is challenged, is

39. J. I. Case Co. v. Labor Board, 321 U.S. 332 (1944); Order of R.R. Telegraphers v. Railway Express Agency, 321 U.S. 342 (1944); Medo Photo Supply Corp. v. Labor Board, 321 U.S. 678 (1944); see Elgin, J. & E. Ry. v. Burley, 325 U.S. 711, 737 n.35 (1945) [F.F.]

merely to make sure that the legislature has exercised an allowable judgment, and not to exercise their own judgment, whether a policy is within or without "the vague contours" of due process. Theory is reinforced by the notorious fact that lawyers predominate in American legislatures. In practice also the difference is wide. In day-to-day working of our democracy it is vital that the power of the non-democratic organ of our Government be exercised with rigorous self-restraint. Because the powers exercised by this Court are inherently oligarchic, Jefferson all of his life thought of the Court as "an irresponsible body" and "independent of the nation itself." The Court is not saved from being oligarchic because it professes to act in the service of humane ends. As history amply proves, the judiciary is prone to misconceive the public good by confounding private notions with constitutional requirements, and such misconceptions are not subject to legitimate displacement by the will of the people except at too slow a pace. Judges appointed for life whose decisions run counter to prevailing opinion cannot be voted out of office and supplanted by men of views more consonant with it. They are even farther removed from democratic pressures by the fact that their deliberations are in secret and remain beyond disclosure either by periodic reports or by such a modern device for securing responsibility to the electorate as the "press conference." But a democracy need not rely on the courts to save it from its own unwisdom. If it is alert — and without alertness by the people there can be no enduring democracy — unwise or unfair legislation can readily be removed from the statute books. It is by such vigilance over its representatives that democracy proves itself.

Our right to pass on the validity of legislation is now too much part of our constitutional system to be brought into question. But the implications of that right and the conditions for its exercise must constantly be kept in mind and vigorously observed. Because the Court is without power to shape measures for dealing with the problems of society but has merely the power of negation over measures shaped by others, the indispensable judicial requisite is intellectual humility, and such humility presupposes complete disinterestedness. And so, in the end, it is right that the Court should be indifferent to public temper and popular wishes. Mr. Dooley's "th' Supreme Coort follows th' iliction returns" expressed the wit of cynicism, not the demand of principle. A court which yields to the popular will thereby licenses itself to practice despotism, for there can be no assurance that it will not on another occasion indulge its own will. Courts can fulfill their responsibility in a democratic society only to the extent that they succeed in shaping their judgments by rational standards, and rational standards are both impersonal and communicable. Matters of policy, however, are by definition matters which demand the resolution of conflicts of value, and the elements of conflicting values are largely imponderable. Assessment of their competing worth involves differences of feeling; it is also an exercise in prophecy. Obviously the proper forum for mediating a clash of feelings and rendering a prophetic judgment is the body chosen for those purposes by the people. Its functions can be assumed by this Court only in disregard of the historic limits of the Constitution.

This opinion reveals more than the basic philosophy of the Justice toward judicial review of economic legislation. The necessity for the repetition of the theme and the history suggests that, however moribund the concept of economic due process may presently be, it is not dead.[40] Or, to change the metaphor, this ghost will have to be exorcized over and over again.

Frankfurter was most impatient with attempts to hobble the states in their collection of taxes on the basis of the Due Process Clause of the Fourteenth Amendment. His attitude was revealed in *Newark Fire Ins. Co. v. State Board*,[41] where he was joined by Stone, Black, and Douglas: [42]

Wise tax policy is one thing; constitutional prohibition quite another. The task of devising means for distributing the burdens of taxation equitably has always challenged the wisdom of the wisest financial statesmen. Never has this been more true than today when wealth has so largely become the capitalization of expectancies derived from a complicated network of human relations. The adjustment of such relationships, with due regard to the promotion of enterprise and to the fiscal needs of different governments with which these relations are entwined, is peculiarly a phase of empirical legislation. It belongs to that range of experimental activities of government which should not be constrained by rigid and artificial legal concepts. Especially important is it to abstain from intervention within the autonomous area of the legislative taxing power where there is no claim of encroachment by the states upon powers granted to the National Government. It is not for us to sit in judgment on attempts by the states to evolve fair tax policies. When a tax appropriately challenged before us is not found to be in plain violation of the Constitution our task is ended.

40. See McCloskey, *Economic Due Process and the Supreme Court: An Exhumation and Reburial*, 1962 Supreme Court Review 34.

41. 307 U.S. 313 (1939).

42. *Id.* at 323–24.

Essentially then the problem of the validity of state taxation was a problem in judicial self-restraint when measured against the commands of the Due Process Clause of the Fourteenth Amendment. Thus, Frankfurter wrote in his concurring opinion in *State Tax Comm'n v. Aldrich*: [43]

"A good deal has to be read into the Fourteenth Amendment to give it any bearing upon this case." [44] We would have to read into that Amendment private notions as to tax policy. But whether a tax is wise or expedient is the business of the political branches of government, not ours. Considerations relevant to invalidation of a tax measure are wholly different from those that come into play in justifying disapproval of a tax on the score of political or financial unwisdom.

It may well be that the last word has not been said by the various devices now available — through uniform and reciprocal legislation, through action by the States under the Compact Clause, Art. I, § 10[3], or through whatever other means statesmen may devise — for distributing wisely the total national income for governmental purposes as between the States and the Nation. But even if it were possible to make the needed adjustments in the fiscal relations of the States to one another and to the Federal Government through the process of episodic litigation — which to me seems most ill-adapted for devising fiscal policies — it is enough that our Constitutional system denies such a function to this Court.

I agree, therefore, that *First National Bank* v. *Maine* [45] should be overruled and that the tax imposed by Utah in this case is valid. To refuse to nullify legislation the frailties of which we think we see, is to respect the bounds of our Constitutional authority and not to indulge in a fiction. [46] To allow laws to stand is to allow laws to be made by those whose task it is to legislate. The nullification of legislation on Constitutional grounds has been recognized from the beginning as a most "delicate" function, not to be indulged in by this Court simply because it has formal power to do so, but only when compelling considerations leave no other choice. To suggest that when this Court finds that a law is not offensive to the Constitution and that it must therefore stand, we make the same kind of judgment as when on rare occasions we find that a law is offensive to the

43. 316 U.S. 174, 184–85 (1942).

44. Holmes, J., dissenting, in Farmers Loan Co. v. Minnesota, 280 U.S. 204, 218 (1930). [F.F.]

45. 284 U.S. 313 (1932). [F.F.]

46. See Thayer, *The Origin and Scope of the American Doctrine of Constitutional Law*, 7 HARV. L. REV. 129 (1893). [F.F.]

Constitution and must therefore fall, is to disregard the rôle of this Court in our Constitutional system since its establishment in 1789.

Nor was this essential power of the state to be inhibited because of an inappropriate choice of label by the state legislature. Substance, not form, was to be controlling in disposing of these issues, as Frankfurter wrote for the Court in *Wisconsin v. J. C. Penney Co.*:[47]

The case thus reduces itself to the inquiry whether Wisconsin has transgressed its taxing power because its supreme court has described the practical result of the exertion of that power by one legal formula rather than another — has labeled it a tax on the privilege of declaring dividends rather than a supplementary income tax.

A tax is an exaction. Ascertainment of the scope of the exaction — what is included in it — is for the state court. But the descriptive pigeon-hole into which a state court puts a tax is of no moment in determining the constitutional significance of the exaction. "In whatever language a statute may be framed, its purpose must be determined by its natural and reasonable effect."[48] Such has been the repeated import of the cases which only recently were well summarized by the guiding formulation for adjudicating a tax measure, that "in passing on its constitutionality we are concerned only with its practical operation, not its definition or the precise form of descriptive words which may be applied to it."[49]

The Constitution is not a formulary. It does not demand of states strict observance of rigid categories nor precision of technical phrasing in their exercise of the most basic power of government, that of taxation. For constitutional purposes the decisive issue turns on the operating incidence of a challenged tax. A state is free to pursue its own fiscal policies, unembarrassed by the Constitution, if by the practical operation of a tax the state has exerted its power in relation to opportunities which it has given, to protection which it has afforded, to benefits which it has conferred by the fact of being an orderly, civilized society. . . .

. . . At best, the responsibility for devising just and productive sources of revenue challenges the wit of legislators. Nothing can be less helpful than for courts to go beyond the extremely limited restrictions that the Constitution places upon the states and to inject themselves in a merely negative way into the delicate processes of fiscal policy-making. We must be on guard against imprisoning the taxing power of the states within formulas that are not compelled

47. 311 U.S. 435, 443–45 (1940).

48. Henderson v. Mayor of New York, 92 U.S., 259, 268 (1876). [F.F.]

49. Lawrence v. State Tax Commission, 286 U.S. 276, 280 (1932). [F.F.]

by the Constitution but merely represent judicial generalizations exceeding the concrete circumstances which they profess to summarize.

It was after Frankfurter's retirement that so many of the Court's efforts were turned to the center of "substantive equal protection," *i.e.*, the invalidating of legislative classification essentially not because the differences in the categories were nonexistent but rather because the Court disliked the classifications that were made by the legislatures. It is clear that Frankfurter would have had no part of this new version of "a super-legislature."

12   Equal Protection of the Laws

Mr. Justice Frankfurter's role in the Court's attempt to destroy racial segregation has confounded many of those who make such easy classifications of judicial liberals and judicial conservatives. Some, like Professor A. A. Berle have been so confused as to suggest that Frankfurter urged the Court's abstention from decision in the school desegregation cases.[1] But the fact is that he set his hand early to that task of conforming governmental action to the commands of the Equal Protection Clause in the area of race relations. His part in bringing the school desegregation cases to fruition, recognizing the difficulties inherent in the social revolution for which it called, will one day be fully revealed. In one little-noted opinion, he forecast the approbation of state action that would seek to inhibit racial discrimination. In his concurring opinion in *Railway Mail Ass'n v. Corsi*,[2] a decade before *Brown v. Board of Education*,[3] he offered his view of state antidiscrimination laws in terms that may yet be used to approve commanded integration — not merely desegregation — in the public schools:[4]

Apart from other objections, which are too unsubstantial to require consideration, it is urged that the Due Process Clause of the Fourteenth Amendment precludes the State of New York from prohibiting racial and religious discrimination against those seeking employment. Elaborately to argue against this contention is to dignify a claim devoid of constitutional substance. Of course a State may leave abstention from such discriminations to the conscience of individuals. On the other hand, a State may choose to put its authority behind one of the cherished aims of American feeling by forbidding indulgence in racial or religious prejudice to another's hurt. To use the Fourteenth Amendment as a sword against such State power would stultify that Amendment. Certainly the insistence by individuals on

1. See BERLE, THE THREE FACES OF POWER 12 (1968).
2. 326 U.S. 88 (1945).
3. 347 U.S. 483 (1954).
4. 326 U.S. at 98.

their private prejudices as to race, color or creed, in relations like those now before us, ought not to have a higher constitutional sanction than the determination of a State to extend the area of non-discrimination beyond that which the Constitution itself exacts.

Nevertheless, the Equal Protection Clause of the Fourteenth Amendment did not hold the charm for him that it has lately held for the Court. Occasionally he chose to rest his decision on the Equal Protection Clause in preference to invoking the First Amendment grounds chosen by his brethren, as in *Niemotko v. Maryland*.[5] Where, however, the Court chose to apply to the national government through the Fifth Amendment the equal protection standards it had applied to the states through the Fourteenth, as in the case of restrictive covenants in the District of Columbia, Frankfurter found it sufficient to suggest that a court of equity had its own standards of conscience. In *Hurd v. Hodge*,[6] he wrote:[7]

In these cases, the plaintiffs ask equity to enjoin white property owners who are desirous of selling their houses to Negro buyers simply because the houses were subject to an original agreement not to have them pass into Negro ownership. Equity is rooted in conscience. An injunction is, as it always has been, "an extraordinary remedial process which is granted, not as a matter of right but in the exercise of a sound judicial discretion."[8] In good conscience it cannot be "the exercise of a sound judicial discretion" by a federal court to grant the relief here asked for when the authorization of such an injunction by the States of the Union violates the Constitution — and violates it, not for any narrow technical reason, but for considerations that touch rights so basic to our society that, after the Civil War, their protection against invasion by the States was safeguarded by the Constitution. This is to me a sufficient and conclusive ground for reaching the Court's result.

Frankfurter's general attitude toward the Equal Protection Clause reveals an unwillingness to derive from it the concepts of "substantive equal protection" that underlie so much of the Court's recent efforts. "Substantive equal protection," he believed, deserved the same short shrift that he gave to "substantive due process." This is underscored by two cases, one involving criminal procedure, the other economic

5. 340 U.S. 268 (1951).

6. 334 U.S. 24 (1948).

7. *Id.* at 36.

8. Morrison v. Work, 266 U.S. 481, 490 (1925). [F.F.]

regulation. In the first he found the Equal Protection Clause commanded relief; in the second he rejected the Court's use of that clause.

In *Griffin v. Illinois*,[9] Frankfurter expounded on the demands of the Equal Protection Clause in matters of criminal procedure. In this case he also made appeal for the use of a device that would gain support only later in the Court's history. That was the device of "prospective overruling," a concept that itself contains thorny problems of equal protection of the laws on which he did not elaborate:[10]

Nor does the equal protection of the laws deny a State the right to make classifications in law when such classifications are rooted in reason. "The equality at which the 'equal protection' clause aims is not a disembodied equality. The Fourteenth Amendment enjoins 'the equal protection of the laws,' and laws are not abstract propositions."[11] Since capital offenses are *sui generis*, a State may take account of the irrevocability of death by allowing appeals in capital cases and not in others. Again, "the right of appeal may be accorded by the State to the accused upon such terms as in its wisdom may be deemed proper."[12] The States have exercised this discriminating power. The different States and the same State from time to time have conditioned criminal appeals by fixing the time within which an appeal may be taken, by delimiting the scope of review, by shaping the mechanism by which alleged errors may be brought before the appellate tribunal, and so forth.

But neither the fact that a State may deny the right of appeal altogether nor the right of a State to make an appropriate classification, based on differences in crimes and their punishment, nor the right of a State to lay down conditions it deems appropriate for criminal appeals, sanctions differentiations by a State that have no relation to a rational policy of criminal appeal or authorizes the imposition of conditions that offend the deepest presuppositions of our society. Surely it would not need argument to conclude that a State could not, within its wide scope of discretion in these matters, allow an appeal for persons convicted of crimes punishable by imprisonment of a year or more, only on payment of a fee of $500. Illinois, of course, has done nothing so crude as that. But Illinois has said, in effect, that the Supreme Court of Illinois can consider alleged errors occurring in a criminal trial only if the basis for determining whether there were errors is brought before it by a bill of exceptions

9. 351 U.S. 12 (1956).

10. *Id.* at 21–26.

11. Tigner v. Texas, 310 U.S. 141, 147 (1940). [F.F.]

12. McKane v. Durston, 153 U.S. 684, 687–88 (1894). [F.F.]

and not otherwise. From this it follows that Illinois has decreed that only defendants who can afford to pay for the stenographic minutes of a trial may have trial errors reviewed on appeal by the Illinois Supreme Court.[13] It has thereby shut off means of appellate review for indigent defendants.

This Court would have to be willfully blind not to know that there have in the past been prejudicial trial errors which called for reversal of convictions of indigent defendants, and that the number of those who have not had the means for paying for the cost of a bill of exceptions is not so negligible as to invoke whatever truth there may be in the maxim *de minimis*.

Law addresses itself to actualities. It does not face actuality to suggest that Illinois affords every convicted person, financially competent or not, the opportunity to take an appeal, and that it is not Illinois that is responsible for disparity in material circumstances. Of course a State need not equalize economic conditions. A man of means may be able to afford the retention of an expensive, able counsel not within reach of a poor man's purse. Those are contingencies of life which are hardly within the power, let alone the duty, of a State to correct or cushion. But when a State deems it wise and just that convictions be susceptible to review by an appellate court, it cannot by force of its exactions draw a line which precludes convicted indigent persons, forsooth erroneously convicted, from securing such a review merely by disabling them from bringing to the notice of an appellate tribunal errors of the trial court which would upset the conviction were practical opportunity for review not foreclosed.

To sanction such a ruthless consequence, inevitably resulting from a money hurdle erected by a State, would justify a latter-day Anatole France to add one more item to his ironic comments on the "majestic equality" of law. "The law, in its majestic equality, forbids the rich as well as the poor to sleep under bridges, to beg in the streets, and to steal bread." [14]

The State is not free to produce such a squalid discrimination. If it has a general policy of allowing criminal appeals, it cannot make lack of means an effective bar to the exercise of this opportunity. The State cannot keep the word of promise to the ear of those illegally convicted and break it to their hope. But in order to avoid or minimize abuse and waste, a State may appropriately hedge about the opportunity to prove a conviction wrong. When a State not only

---

13. See People v. La Frana, 4 Ill.2d 261, 266, 122 N.E.2d 583, 585–86 (1954). [F.F.]

14. COURNOS, A MODERN PLUTARCH 27 (1928). [F.F.]

gives leave for appellate correction of trial errors but must pay for the cost of its exercise by the indigent, it may protect itself so that frivolous appeals are not subsidized and public moneys are not needlessly spent. The growing experience of reforms in appellate procedure and sensible, economic modes for securing review still to be devised, may be drawn upon to the end that the State will neither bolt the door to equal justice nor support a wasteful abuse of the appellate process. . . .

We must be mindful of the fact that there are undoubtedly convicts under confinement in Illinois prisons, in numbers unknown to us and under unappealed sentences imposed years ago, who will find justification in this opinion, unless properly qualified, for proceedings both in the state and the federal courts upon claims that they are under illegal detention in that they have been denied a right under the Federal Constitution. It would be an easy answer that a claim that was not duly asserted — as was the timely claim by these petitioners — cannot be asserted now. The answer is too easy. Candor compels acknowledgement that the decision rendered today is a new ruling. Candor compels the further acknowledgement that it would not be unreasonable for all indigent defendants, now incarcerated, who at the time were unable to pay for transcripts of proceedings in trial courts, to urge that they were justified in assuming that such a restriction upon criminal appeals in Illinois was presumably a valid exercise of the State's power at the time when they suffered its consequences. Therefore it could well be claimed that thereby any conscious waiver of a constitutional right is negatived.

The Court ought neither to rely on casuistic arguments in denying constitutional claims, nor deem itself imprisoned within a formal, abstract dilemma. The judicial choice is not limited to a new ruling necessarily retrospective, or to rejection of what the requirements of equal protection of the laws, as now perceived, require. For sound reasons, law generally speaks prospectively. More than hundred years ago, for instance, the Supreme Court of Ohio, confronted with a problem not unlike the one before us, found no difficulty in doing so when it concluded that legislative divorces were unconstitutional.[15] In arriving at a new principle, the judicial process is not impotent to define its scope and limits. Adjudication is not a mechanical exercise nor does it compel "either/or" determinations.

We should not indulge in the fiction that the law now announced has always been the law and, therefore, that those who did not avail themselves of it waived their rights. It is much more conducive to law's self-respect to recognize candidly the considerations that give

15. Bingham v. Miller, 17 Ohio 445 (1848). [F.F.]

prospective content to a new pronouncement of law. That this is consonant with the spirit of our law and justified by those considerations of reason which should dominate the law, has been luminously expounded by Mr. Justice Cardozo, shortly before he came here and in an opinion which he wrote for the Court.[16] Such a molding of law, by way of adjudication, is peculiarly applicable to the problem at hand. The rule of law announced this day should be delimited as indicated.

In *Morey v. Doud*[17] the attack was on legislation that distinguished between large and small issuers of money orders. Frankfurter rejected the utilization of the Equal Protection Clause to destroy this regulatory legislation:[18]

The sole question before the Court is whether the Fourteenth Amendment of the United States Constitution, in prohibiting a State from denying any person "the equal protection of the laws," has barred Illinois from formulating its domestic policy as it did, in an area concededly within the regulatory power of that State. As is usually true of questions arising under the Equal Protection Clause, the answer will turn on the way in which that clause is conceived. It is because of differences in judicial approach that the divisions in the Court in applying the clause have been frequent and marked. It is, I believe, accurate to summarize the matter by saying that the great divide in the decisions lies in the difference between emphasizing the actualities or the abstractions of legislation.

The more complicated society becomes, the greater the diversity of its problems and the more does legislation direct itself to the diversities. Statutes, that is, are directed to less than universal situations. Law reflects distinctions that exist in fact or at least appear to exist in the judgment of legislators — those who have the responsibility for making law fit fact. Legislation is essentially empiric. It addresses itself to the more or less crude outside world and not to the neat, logical models of the mind. Classification is inherent in legislation; the Equal Protection Clause has not forbidden it. To recognize marked differences that exist in fact is living law; to disregard practical differences and concentrate on some abstract identities is lifeless logic. . . .

" 'Legislation which regulates business may well make distinctions

16. See *Address of Chief Judge Cardozo*, 55 REP. N.Y. STATE BAR ASS'N 263, 294, *et seq.* (1932); Great Northern Ry. v. Sunburst Oil & Ref. Co., 287 U.S. 358, 363–66 (1933). [F.F.]

17. 354 U.S. 457 (1957).

18. *Id.* at 472, 475.

depend upon the degree of evil.' *Heath & Milligan Mfg. Co. v. Worst*, 207 U.S. 338, 355, 356. It is true, no doubt, that where size is not an index to an admitted evil the law cannot discriminate between the great and small. But in this case size is an index." [19] Neither the record nor our own judicial information affords any basis for concluding that Illinois may not put the United States Post Office, the Western Union Co., and the American Express Co. in one class and all the other money order issuers in another. Illinois may not the less relieve the American Express Co. from regulations to which multitudinous small issuers are subject because that company has its own reliabilities that may well be different from those of the United States Post Office and the Western Union Telegraph Co. The vital fact is that the American Express Co. is decisively different from those money order issuers that are within the regulatory scheme.

Sociologically one may think what one may of the State's recognition of the special financial position obviously enjoyed by the American Express Co. Whatever one may think is none of this Court's business. In applying the Equal Protection Clause, we must be fastidiously careful to observe the admonition of Mr. Justice Brandeis, Mr. Justice Stone, and Mr. Justice Cardozo that we do not "sit as a super-legislature." [20]

19. Engel v. O'Malley, 219 U.S. 128, 138 (1911). [F.F.]

20. See their dissenting opinion in the ill-fated case of Colgate v. Harvey, 296 U.S. 404, 411 (1935). See also Asbury Hospital v. Cass County, 326 U.S. 207, 214–15 (1945). [F.F.]

13 The Commerce Clause

The Commerce Clause has presented essentially three kinds of questions to the Supreme Court, although in a multitude of factual guises. The first tests the scope of authority granted by that clause to the national government. Whatever the boundaries might have been in earlier times when the efficiencies of transportation and communication had not reduced distance to such short intervals of time, during Frankfurter's tenure on the Court the limitations on national power over commercial transactions had to be found elsewhere in the Constitution. So far as the Commerce Clause was concerned, Congress was restrained only by its own inhibitions. There remained the necessity for burial of some authority that had lost its vitality when the Nine Old Men became the Roosevelt Court. Frankfurter played little part in the funeral ceremonies.

The second major area for consideration under the Commerce Clause is concerned with the sphere of state power even in the absence of congressional action. To what extent does the Commerce Clause by itself invalidate state action that affects interstate commerce? The last series of problems under the Commerce Clause involves the reconciliation of state and national interests when Congress has spoken on a subject. The second question is one of the negative inferences as to state power to be derived from the Commerce Clause. The third may be described as the problem of the negative inferences as to state power to be derived from national legislation.

Probably no set of problems has so plagued the Court without adequate doctrinal resolution as those arising from the "negative" implications of the Commerce Clause. When does state regulation or taxation so adversely affect free trade among the states as to be unconstitutional? At one time, Mr. Justice Black was pressing for an easy answer: unless specifically interdicted by congressional action, the states were free to impose their will on interstate commerce. Even he abandoned that proposition in *Morgan v. Virginia*.[1] Mr. Justice Frankfurter, too, sought legislative guidance by imploring Congress

1. 328 U.S. 373 (1946).

to act in this complicated area. He repeatedly urged that Congress had the tools to solve the problem that the Court lacked. Congress had not acted. We are left with Thomas Reed Powell's suggested Restatement of Constitutional Law: "Congress may regulate interstate commerce. The States may also regulate interstate commerce, but not too much. How much is too much is beyond the scope of this restatement."[2] No more than with the opinions of the Court as a whole can one find in Frankfurter's opinions a consistent pattern suggesting a rationale.

Perhaps in *Freeman v. Hewit*,[3] he came closer to expressing fully his approach to those problems than he did anywhere else. The issue was the validity of a state tax alleged to be a charge on interstate commerce:[4]

The history of this problem is spread over hundreds of volumes of our Reports. To attempt to harmonize all that has been said in the past would neither clarify what has gone before nor guide the future. Suffice it to say that especially in this field opinions must be read in the setting of the particular cases and as the product of preoccupation with their special facts.

Our starting point is clear. In two recent cases we applied the principle that the Commerce Clause was not merely an authorization to Congress to enact laws for the protection and encouragement of commerce among the States, but by its own force created an area of trade free from interference by the States. In short, the Commerce Clause even without implementing legislation by Congress is a limitation upon the power of the States.[5] In so doing we reaffirmed, upon fullest consideration, the course of adjudication unbroken through the Nation's history. This limitation on State power, as the *Morgan* case so well illustrates, does not merely forbid a State to single out interstate commerce for hostile action. A State is also precluded from taking any action which may fairly be deemed to have the effect of impeding the free flow of trade between States. It is immaterial that local commerce is subjected to a similar encumbrance. It may commend itself to a State to encourage a pastoral instead of industrial society. That is its concern and its privilege. But to compare a State's treatment of its local trade with the exertion

2. POWELL, VAGARIES AND VARIETIES IN CONSTITUTIONAL INTERPRETATION ix (1956).

3. 329 U.S. 249 (1946).

4. *Id.* at 252–59.

5. Southern Pacific Co. v. Arizona, 325 U.S. 761 (1945); Morgan v. Virginia, 328 U.S. 373 (1946). [F.F.]

of authority against commerce in the national domain is to compare incomparables.

These principles of limitation on State power apply to all State policy no matter what State interest gives rise to its legislation. A burden on interstate commerce is none the lighter and no less objectionable because it is imposed by a State under the taxing power rather than under manifestations of police power in the conventional sense. But, in the necessary accommodation between local needs and the overriding requirement of freedom for the national commerce, the incidence of a particular type of State action may throw the balance in support of the local need because interference with the national interest is remote or unsubstantial. A police regulation of local aspects of interstate commerce is a power often essential to a State in safeguarding vital local interests. At least until Congress chooses to enact a nation-wide rule, the power will not be denied to the State.[6] State taxation falling on interstate commerce, on the other hand, can only be justified as designed to make such commerce bear a fair share of the cost of the local government whose protection it enjoys. But revenue serves as well no matter what the source. To deny a State a particular source of income because it taxes the very process of interstate commerce does not impose a crippling limitation on a State's ability to carry on its local function. Moreover, the burden on interstate commerce involved in a direct tax upon it is inherently greater, certainly less uncertain in its consequences, than results from the usual police regulations. The power to tax is a dominant power over commerce. Because the greater or more threatening burden of a direct tax on commerce is coupled with the lesser need to a State of a particular source of revenue, attempts at such taxation have always been more carefully scrutinized and more consistently resisted than police power regulations of aspects of such commerce. The task of scrutinizing is a task of drawing lines. This is the historic duty of the Court so long as Congress does not undertake to make specific arrangements between the National Government and the States in regard to revenues from interstate commerce. . . . Considerations of proximity and degree are here, as so often in the law, decisive.

It has been suggested that such a tax is valid when a similar tax is placed on local trade, and a specious appearance of fairness is sought to be imparted by the argument that interstate commerce should not be favored at the expense of local trade. So to argue is to disregard the life of the Commerce Clause. Of course a State is not

---

6. The Minnesota Rate Case, 230 U.S. 352, 402 *et seq.* (1913); S.C. Hwy. Dept. v. Barnwell Bros., 303 U.S. 177 (1938); Union Brokerage Co. v. Jensen, 322 U.S. 202, 209–12 (1944). [F.F.]

required to give active advantage to interstate trade. But it cannot aim to control that trade even though it desires to control its own. It cannot justify what amounts to a levy upon the very process of commerce across States lines by pointing to a similar hobble on its local trade. It is true that the existence of a tax on its local commerce detracts from the deterrent effect of a tax on interstate commerce to the extent that it removes the temptation to sell the goods locally. But the fact of such a tax, in any event, puts impediments upon the currents of commerce across the State line, while the aim of the Commerce Clause was precisely to prevent States from exacting toll from those engaged in national commerce. The Commerce Clause does not involve an exercise in the logic of empty categories. It operates within the framework of our federal scheme and with due regard to the national experience reflected by the decisions of this Court, even though the terms in which these decisions have been cast may have varied. Language alters, and there is a fashion in judicial writing as in other things.

This case, like *Adams Mfg.* v. *Storen*,[7] involves a tax imposed by the State of the seller on the proceeds of interstate sales. To extract a fair tithe from interstate commerce for the local protection afforded to it, a seller State need not impose the kind of tax which Indiana here levied. As a practical matter, it can make such commerce pay its way, as the phrase runs, apart from taxing the very sale. Thus, it can tax local manufacturers even if the products are destined for other States. For some purposes, manufacturer and the shipment of its products beyond a State may be looked upon as an integral transaction. But when the accommodation must be made between state and national interests, manufacture within a State, though destined for shipment outside, is not a seamless web so as to prevent a State from giving the manufacturing part detached relevance for purposes of local taxation. . . . It can impose license taxes on domestic and foreign corporations who would do business in the State, . . . though it cannot, even under the guise of such excises, "hamper" interstate commerce. . . . It can tax the privilege of residence in the State and measure the privilege by net income, including that derived from interstate commerce. . . . And where, as in this case, the commodities subsequently sold interstate are securities, they can be reached by a property tax by the State of domicil of the owner. . . .

These illustrative instances show that a seller State has various means of obtaining legitimate contributions to the cost of its government, without imposing a direct tax on interstate sales. While these

7. 304 U.S. 307 (1938). [F.F.]

permitted taxes may, in an ultimate sense, come out of interstate commerce, they are not, as would be a tax on gross receipts, a direct imposition on that very freedom of commercial flow which for more than a hundred and fifty years has been the ward of the Commerce Clause.

It is suggested, however, that the validity of a gross sales tax should depend on whether another State has also sought to impose its burden on the transactions. If another State has taxed the same interstate transaction, the burdensome consequences to interstate trade are undeniable. But that, for the time being, only one State has taxed is irrelevant to the kind of freedom of trade which the Commerce Clause generated. The immunities implicit in the Commerce Clause and the potential taxing power of a State can hardly be made to depend, in the world of practical affairs, on the shifting incidence of the varying tax laws of the various States at a particular moment. Courts are not possessed of instruments of determination so delicate as to enable them to weigh the various factors in a complicated economic setting which, as to an isolated application of a State tax, might mitigate the obvious burden generally created by a direct tax on commerce. Nor is there any warrant in the constitutional principles heretofore applied by this Court to support the notion that a State may be allowed one single-tax-worth of direct interference with the free flow of commerce. An exaction by a State from interstate commerce falls not because of a proven increase in the cost of the product. What makes the tax invalid is in the fact that there is interference by a State with the freedom of interstate commerce. Such a tax by the seller State alone must be judged burdensome in the context of the circumstances in which the tax takes effect. Trade being a sensitive plant, a direct tax upon it to some extent at least deters trade even if its effect is not precisely calculable. . . .

There remains only the claim that an interstate sale of intangibles differs from an interstate sale of tangibles in respects material to the issues in this case. . . . Latin tags like *mobilia sequuntur personam* often do service for legal analysis, but they ought not to confound constitutional issues. What Mr. Justice Holmes said about that phrase is relevant here. "It is a fiction, the historical origin of which is familiar to scholars, and it is this fiction that gives whatever meaning it has to the saying *mobilia sequuntur personam*. But being a fiction it is not allowed to obscure the facts, when the facts become important." [8] Of course this is an interstate sale. And constitutionally it is commerce no less and no different because the subject was pieces of paper worth $65,214.20, rather than machines.

8. Blackstone v. Miller, 188 U.S. 189, 204 (1903). [F.F.]

On the question of preemption of the area by federal legislation, Frankfurter's dissenting opinion in *Bethlehem Steel Co. v. New York State Labor Relations Board* [9] may be taken as typical of his approach. The majority opinion was read by the Justice to mean "that, regardless of the consent of the National [Labor Relations] Board, New York is excluded from enforcing rights of collective bargaining in all industries within its borders as to which Congress has granted opportunity to invoke the authority of the National Board." [10] Frankfurter would sustain state authority whenever the National Board eschewed the exercise of its power. It is his general approach rather than the issues of the case itself that is relevant to our purposes: [11]

The inability of the National Board to exercise its dormant powers because of its lack of funds ought not to furnish a more persuasive reason for finding that concurrent state power may function than a deliberate exercise of judgment by the National Board that industrial relations having both national and state concern can most effectively be promoted by an appropriate division of administrative resources between the National and State Boards. This states abstractly a very practical situation. Based on the realization that as a practical matter the National Board could not effectuate the policies of the act committed to it over the whole range of its authority, an arrangement was worked out whereby the National Board leaves to the State Board jurisdiction over so-called local industries covered by the federal Act, while the State Board does not entertain matters over which the National Board has consistently taken jurisdiction. This practical Federal-State working arrangement, arrived at by those carrying the responsibility for breathing life into the bare bones of legislation, is so relevant to the solution of the legal issues arising out of State-Nation industrial relations, that I have set forth the agreement in full in an Appendix. Particularly when dealing with legal aspects of industrial relations is it important for courts not to isolate legal issues from their workaday context. I cannot join the Court's opinion because I read it to mean that it is beyond the power of the National Board to agree with State agencies enforcing laws like the Wagner Act to divide, with due regard to local interests, the domain over which Congress had given the National Board abstract discretion but which, practically, cannot be covered by it alone. If such cooperative agreements between State and

9. 330 U.S. 767 (1947).

10. *Id.* at 778.

11. *Id.* at 778–80, 782–84.

National Boards are barred because the power which Congress has granted the National Board ousted or superseded State authority, I am unable to see how State authority can revive because Congress has seen fit to put the Board on short rations.

Since we are dealing with aspects of commerce between the States that are not legally outside State action by virtue of the Commerce Clause itself, New York has authority to act so long as Congress has not interdicted her action. While what the State does she does on sufferance, in ascertaining whether Congress has allowed State action we are not to consider the matter as though Congress were conferring a mere bounty, the extent of which must be viewed with a thrifty eye. When construing federal legislation that deals with matters that also lie within the authority, because within the proper interests, of the States, we must be mindful that we are part of the delicate process of adjusting the interacting areas of National and State authority over commerce. The inevitable extension of federal authority over economic enterprise has absorbed the authority that was previously left to the States. But in legislating, Congress is not indulging in doctrinaire, hard-and-fast curtailment of the State powers reflecting special State interests. Federal legislation of this character must be construed with due regard to accommodation between the assertions of new federal authority and the functions of the individual States, as reflecting the historic and persistent concerns of our dual system of government. Since Congress can, if it chooses, entirely displace the States to the full extent of the far-reaching Commerce Clause, Congress needs no help from generous judicial implications to achieve the supersession of State authority. To construe federal legislation so as not needlessly to forbid preexisting State authority is to respect our federal system. Any indulgence in construction should be in favor of the States, because Congress can speak with drastic clarity whenever it chooses to assure full federal authority, completely displacing the States.

This is an old problem and considerations involved in its solution are commonplace. But results not always harmonious have from time to time been drawn from the same precepts. In law also the emphasis makes the song. It may make a decisive difference what view judges have of the place of the States in our national life when they come to apply the governing principle that for an Act of Congress completely to displace a State law "the repugnance or conflict should be direct and positive, so that the two acts could not be reconciled or consistently stand together." [12] Congress can speak so unequivocally as to leave no doubt. But real controversies arise only when Congress has left the matter in doubt, and then the result

12. Sinnott v. Davenport, 22 How. 227, 243 (1860). [F.F.]

depends on whether we require that actual conflict between State and federal action be shown, or whether argumentative conflict suffices. . . .

No doubt . . . cases have not always dealt with such scrupulous regard for State action where Congress has not patently terminated it. Metaphor — "occupied the field" — has at times done service for close analysis. But the rules of accommodation that have been most consistently professed as well as the dominant current of decisions make for and not against the *modus vivendi* achieved by the two agencies in the labor relations field, which the Government, as *amicus curiae*, here sponsored. Such an arrangement assures the effectuation of the policies which underlie the National Labor Relations Act and the "Little Wagner Act" of New York in a manner agreed upon by the two Boards for dealing with matters affecting interests of common concern. "Where the Government has provided for collaboration the courts should not find conflict." [13] . . .

. . . A shrewd critic has thus expressed the considerations that in the past have often lain below the surface of merely doctrinal applications: "Formally the enterprise is one of the interpretation of the Act of Congress to discover its scope. Actually it is often the enterprise of reaching a judgment whether the situation is so adequately handled by national prescription that the impediment of further state requirements is to be deemed a bane rather than a blessing." [14] In the submission by the Board before us, we have the most authoritative manifestation by national authority that State collaboration would be a blessing rather than a bane, and yet judicial construction would forbid the aid which the agency of Congress seeks in carrying out its duty. It is surely a responsible inference that the result will be to leave uncontrolled large areas of industrial conflict. Neither what Congress has said in the National Labor Relations Act, nor the structure of the Act, nor its policy, nor its actual operation, should be found to prohibit the Board from exercising its discretion so as to enlist the aid of agencies charged with like duties within the States in enforcing a common policy by a distribution of cases appropriate to respective State and National interests.

A few short years before his appointment to the Court, Frankfurter delivered the lectures that were to become his book: *The Commerce Clause under Marshall, Taney and Waite.*[15] There he said: [16]

13. Union Brokerage Co. v. Jensen, 322 U.S. 202, 209 (1944). [F.F.]

14. Powell, *Current Conflicts between the Commerce Clause and State Police Power*, 12 Minn. L. Rev. 607 (1920). [F.F.]

15. (1937).

16. *Id.* at 21–22.

The result of this sequence of cases [17] was to make the Court collaborator with Congress in the regulation of foreign and interstate commerce, and thereby to bring before the Court questions inescapably implicating legislative policy. Policy is at stake because the actualities of life do not lend themselves to that scrupulous insulation of disparate interests which, formally at least, is the presupposition of the distribution of governmental authority as between the central government and the states. The history of the commerce clause, from the pioneer efforts of Marshall to our own day, is the history of imposing artificial patterns upon the play of economic life whereby an accommodation is achieved between the interacting concerns of states and nation. The problems of the commerce clause are problems in this process of accommodation, however different the emphasis of preference of interest, and however diverse the legal devices by which different judges may make these accommodations. Because such are the problems and such the relevant considerations for their adjustment, the constitutional labors of the Supreme Court, especially with the commerce clause, are accurately described as statecraft. But it is an exercise in statesmanship hemmed in by the restrictions attending the adjudicatory process. Far-reaching political principles arise through the accidents of unrelated and intermittent cases, presenting issues confined by the exigencies of the legal record, depending for elucidation upon the learning and insight of counsel fortuitously selected for a particular case, and imprisoning the judgment, at least in part, within legal habituations and past utterances.

Felix Frankfurter could as well have written this at the end of his judicial tenure as before it began.

It was not surprising, therefore, that when the Court emasculated the Marshall Court's decision in *Brown v. Maryland*, the judgment brought forth a wrathful dissent from Frankfurter. In *Youngstown Co. v. Bowers*,[18] he railed not only at the Court's cavalier treatment of such hoary precedent but at the Court's unwise conclusion as well. Believer in federalism he might be, but Frankfurter recognized its threats to the unity of the nation: [19]

As one follows the tortuous and anguished endeavors to establish a free trade area within Western Europe, unhampered by interior barriers, against the opposition of inert and narrow conceptions of

17. Gibbons v. Ogden, 9 Wheat 1 (1824); Brown v. Maryland, 12 Wheat. 419 (1827); Willson v. Black-Bird Creek Marsh Co., 2 Pet. 245 (1829).

18. 358 U.S. 534 (1959).

19. *Id.* at 551–53, 555–60, 564–66, 574–75.

self-interest by the component nations, admiration for the far-sighted statecraft of the Framers of the Constitution is intensified. Guided by the experience of the evils generated by the parochialism of the new States, the wise men at the Philadelphia Convention took measures to make of the expansive United States a free trade area and to withdraw from the States the selfish exercise of power over foreign trade, both import and export. They accomplished this by two provisions in the Constitution: the Commerce Clause and the Import-Export Clause.

The former reached its aim, as a matter of settled judicial construction, by placing the regulation of commerce among the States in the hands of Congress, except insofar as predominantly local interests give the States concurrent power until displaced by congressional legislation. This leeway to the States was established by the decision in *Cooley v. Board of Wardens*,[20] foreshadowed by Marshall's decision in *Willson* v. *Black Bird Creek Marsh Co.*[21] This permissive area for state action has given rise as we know too well, to multitudinous litigation.

But in dealing with foreign commerce the Constitution left no such leeway. It rigorously confined the States to what might be "absolutely necessary," the only constitutional permission in terms so drastically limited, and beyond this permission of what is "absolutely necessary" state action was barred except by consent of Congress as expressive of the national interest. Thus, hardly any room was left by the Constitution for judicial construction of the command, "No State shall, without the Consent of the Congress, lay any Imposts or Duties on Imports or Exports, except what may be absolutely necessary for executing its inspection Laws. . . ." This strict limitation on the States was still further qualified by the requirement that the "net Produce of all Duties and Imposts, laid by any State on Imports or Exports, shall be for the Use of the Treasury of the United States; and all such Laws shall be subject to the Revision and Controul of the Congress."

For one hundred and thirty-two years, in a course of decision following Chief Justice Marshall's seminal discussion in *Brown* v. *Maryland*,[22] this Court has held, without a single deviation, that a State may not tax imports from foreign countries while retained by the importer in their original "package" or form prior to the use of the goods or their sale. Today the Court, I am bound most respectfully to say, disregards this historic course of constitutional adjudication

20. 12 How. 299 (1851). [F.F.]

21. 2 Pet. 245 (1829). [F.F.]

22. 12 Wheat. 419 (1827). [F.F.]

by allowing the States of Wisconsin and Ohio, and, therefore, all the States, to tax foreign imports despite the prohibition of Art. I, § 10, cl. 2, that "No State shall, without the Consent of the Congress, lay any Imposts or Duties on Imports or Exports, . . ." as that clause has been authoritatively interpreted by this Court. And it does so, moreover, without overruling the decisions which the basis and logic of this new reading of the Constitution can no longer sustain. But they remain decisions of this Court. Thus, we are left with a confusing series of conflicting cases amidst which the States must blindly move in determining the extent of their constitutional power to tax. This confusion is substituted for a principle so plain of application that the controversies in this Court over the meaning of this far-reaching constitutional provision have numbered less than a dozen in our entire history. Of course, I do not believe that we should overrule this consistent course of decisions. But to do so would at least have the merit of explicit announcement of a new legal policy, with its concomitant repercussions on the conduct of our national economic life. . . .

Primary among the forces which led to the inclusion of Art. I, § 10, cl. 2, the Import-Export Clause, in the Constitution, was the deeply felt necessity of vesting exclusive power over foreign economic relations and foreign commerce in the new National Government. The importance of control over duties, imposts, and subsidies as an instrument of foreign trade and as a protection for the encouragement and growth of domestic manufactures was recognized as a matter of course by the Framers. For the effective exercise of this control it was necessary that the Government speak with one voice when regulating commercial intercourse with foreign nations. Orderly and effective policy would be impossible if thirteen States, each with their distinctive interests, and often conflicting, one with another, were allowed to exercise their own initiative in the regulation of foreign economic affairs. And so the States were prohibited from such regulation — they were forbidden, except by leave of Congress, to lay any duties on imports or on exports. Second only to this goal in importance, was the need to secure to the National Government an important source of revenue. The Framers assumed that, for many years, duties on foreign imports would be the prime source of national funds; the revenue on whose constant flow the operations of government would depend. It therefore was essential to the fiscal well-being of the new country to ensure exclusive access to this revenue to the National Government. Subordinate to these goals in importance was the desire to prevent the seaboard States, possessed of important ports of entry, from levying taxes on goods flowing through their ports to inland States. It was important not to allow

these States to take advantage of their favorable geographical
position in order to exact a price for the use of their ports from the
consumers dwelling in less advantageously situated parts of the
country. This fear of the use of geographical position to exact a
form of tribute found an especially forceful expression in the
absolute prohibition against duties on exports by either Nation
or States.

The Import Clause was a result of the desire to safeguard these
national goals and realize these necessities. Thus, the considerations
governing its interpretation marked out for it a special path in the
stream of constitutional adjudication — a course which diverged in
many respects from the history of the Commerce Clause: that
broad grant of power designed primarily to assure national control
over commercial trade among the States. The often difficult, and
continually delicate, considerations of the economic impact of a
challenged tax, of the directness of its burden upon commerce, of
its potential or actual discrimination against interstate trade, which
have been of controlling importance to the proper evaluation of
state taxes challenged under the Commerce Clause, are not the
pertinent factors in assessing the constitutional validity of a tax
charged with being in violation of the bar of Art. I, § 10, cl. 2. In
the taxation of imports, the grant of power to the National Government is exclusive; the prohibition of the States, absolute. Thus the
objects of relevant inquiry have been carefully circumscribed. Once
it is clear, as a matter of economic fact, that a State has levied a tax
upon foreign goods, this Court has always found it necessary to
answer only one further question. The question was put by Chief
Justice Marshall in 1827 in *Brown* v. *Maryland*: Have the goods
retained their status as imports in the hands of the importer? If so,
the tax is invalid. If not, if the goods have become part of the
general property of the State, the tax is not barred by the Import
Clause. The answer to this question involves essentially a determination of the physical status of the foreign goods. But, however
variant the facts in different situations, the determinative principles
have remained constant. And in the cases now before us, just as in
every case this Court has decided under the Import Clause, the rules
of decision must flow from the careful and authoritative exposition
of Chief Justice Marshall in the governing case of *Brown* v. *Maryland*. The Chief Justice recognized that at some point in the importing
process foreign goods lose their immunity and become subject to the
taxing power of the State. Yet the goods must remain immune from
state levies long enough to give the constitutional prohibition its
intended effect. Every case decided under the Import Clause, from
that day to this, has been concerned with applying to the particular

facts before the Court the considerations and standards formulated in *Brown* v. *Maryland* for determining when the exclusive national power ends and state power begins. In words grown familiar with judicial statement, yet deserving of repetition here, the great Chief Justice stated both the problem and the guide for decision. "[T]here must be a point of time," Marshall postulated, "when the prohibition ceases, and the power of the State to tax commences; . . . It is sufficient for the present to say, generally, that when the importer has so acted upon the thing imported, that it has become incorporated and mixed up with the mass of property in the country, it has, perhaps, lost its distinctive character as an import, and has become subject to the taxing power of the State; but while remaining the property of the importer, in his warehouse, in the original form or package in which it was imported, a tax upon it is too plainly a duty on imports to escape the prohibition in the constitution." [23]

Since, in *Brown* v. *Maryland*, the object of importation had been sale, reasoned the Chief Justice, certainly the importer was entitled to realize that aim without being subject to state taxation. Although more subtle, more befogging cases might be imagined, it was "plain" that, at least while in the hands of the importer in its original form or package, the foreign good remained an import and thus free from state levies.

The counsel for the State of Maryland in *Brown* v. *Maryland* was its Attorney General, Roger B. Taney. Twenty years later, sitting as Chief Justice, Taney acknowledged that "further and more mature reflection" had made clear to him the wisdom of the principles laid down by his predecessor. "Indeed," said Mr. Chief Justice Taney, "goods imported, while they remain in the hands of the importer, in the form and shape in which they were brought into the country, can in no just sense be regarded as a part of that mass of property in the State usually taxed for the support of the State government." [24] . . .

The lucid standards developed by this Court for the interpretation of the Import Clause give clear guidance for the disposition of the present cases. We accept the finding of the Wisconsin courts that the imported lumber was stored for the dominant purpose of air drying. Having entered the process of manufacture, the goods had become subject to the taxing power of the State. However, neither their imported ores in No. 9 nor the foreign veneers in No. 44 had been subject to manufacturing. On tax day they lay in the manufacturer's storage area, in their original "form and shape," awaiting

23. *Id.* at 441–42 [F.F.]

24. The License Cases, 5 How. 504, 575 (1847). [F.F.]

their initial processing. Thus the taxes sought to be levied on those materials are clearly barred by the historic series of adjudications of this Court, which have established that goods so situated, whether awaiting sale or manufacture, are constitutionally immune from state taxation under the proscription of Art. I, § 10, cl. 2, of the Constitution.

Yet the Court does not choose to take this plainly marked path of constitutional decision. Rather it has effectively departed from established doctrine and upholds the challenged taxes. It does so on the basis of a theory which is as elusive to logic as it is opposed to authority — a theory which is not only unsupported by economic fact or reason and without basis in any of the invoked "realities," but which turns *Brown* v. *Maryland* and its progeny into *ad hoc* results unrelated to their rationale, and disregards the harmonious reasoning on which these decisions were based and the process of one hundred and thirty-two years of constitutional adjudication. . . .

Moreover, it cannot properly be said that the application here of the settled principles of the Import Clause results in "discrimination" in favor of foreign goods. Whether foreign goods are receiving a tax advantage over similar domestic goods can only be determined by an evaluation of the full range of imposts and duties which the importer has been required to pay to the National Government. Only then can we know, as a matter of economic reality, whether, in fact, there is discrimination. And if we find discrimination, it is the result of the decision of Congress and the President that the goods involved should, as a matter of national policy, receive preferential treatment. Certainly this Court should be reluctant to make inroads on a rule of law so well and lucidly settled that it may legitimately be regarded as an ingredient in the formulation which is made by the National Government when it determines, as a considered national policy, the extent to which import duties should be imposed.

Reluctant as one is to say so, it must be said that the Court proposes no reason for its decision which has not heretofore been rejected by this Court. Nor are we pointed to new compelling policies which must be invoked in order to upset a firmly established principle of our constitutional law; a principle which, perhaps more clearly than any other constitutional standard, has arrived at a lucid, coherent, and eminently workable distribution of power between the Nation and the States.

14   L'Envoi

At the end as at the beginning, it is appropriate to remind anyone who reads these pages that the excerpts are but excerpts and not the whole and that they have been set out not to establish the truth of the results that Frankfurter reached but rather to demonstrate the manner and mode by which he reached his results. These quotations are offered as evidence that Felix Frankfurter's personal and judicial faith rested on two fundamentals: the primary importance of the individual in our society and of reason as the means for resolving the problems that are created by man's existence within that society. There followed, for him, two necessary corollaries. That democracy and representative government were the best means for the accommodation of the interests of the group and the individual; that law was the means for securing this accommodation.

Certainly, in his judicial writings, Frankfurter idealized both the Court and the country. Love, it is said, frequently causes such distortions. And Frankfurter truly loved both Court and country. "But," as a Washington columnist wrote after Frankfurter's death, "the fact that Felix Frankfurter's standards were singularly stern, especially for one of such unbounded warmth of heart, was not what really mattered. What mattered, rather, was that he not only cherished an idea of America that was very special and very noble, he also possessed an astonishing ability to infect others with the same idea."

Of course, the cold printed page cannot infect the reader with this "incomparably noble idea of America" in the way that only Frankfurter could do in his person. But his words are all that can be objectively transmitted. The ideals that he nourished in those he befriended — great men and small — may prove to be more important than these words. But to exalt his personal imprint on those who knew him is not to demean the more assayable legacy, a part of which is reproduced herein.

As a member of the Supreme Court, Mr. Justice Frankfurter wrote approximately 750 opinions. Obviously no selection can be adequate, no excerpts can suffice to disclose what only all of his opinions set out in full could reveal: the depth and complexities of his concept of his task as an associate justice. To adapt his own words, written of Mr. Justice Brandeis: "To quote from Mr. Justice [Frankfurter's] opinions is not to pick plums from a pudding but to pull threads from a pattern." [1]

When Sir Howard Beale, then Australian ambassador to the United States, published his tribute to Frankfurter in 1964,[2] he referred to the Justice as "A Man for All Seasons," the title of Robert Bolt's play about Thomas More that Beale had attended in the company of Frankfurter. We are told, however, by a prestigious psychiatrist, Dr. Rollo May, that "the modern age . . . has ridiculed myth or explained it away because its own myths, born out of the death of the Middle Ages, are rationalism — a faith in technical reason — and individualism. You might say that ours has been the myth of a mythless society. But it's dying. The rationalists are through — they've taken us as far as they can." If Dr. May is right — and there are many signs that he is — then certainly Felix Frankfurter is not a man for this season. For individualism and reason are the essence of his teaching.

Frankfurter was not one to read contemporary novels. But I venture that there is a page in C. P. Snow's *Sleep of Reason* [3] that he would have appreciated. Just as he had found in Bolt's play the essence of his belief about the role of law. Snow wrote:

Reason. Why had so much of our time reneged on it? Wasn't that our characteristic folly, treachery or crime?

Reason was very weak as compared with instinct. Instinct was closer to the aboriginal sea out of which we had all climbed. Reason was a precarious structure. But, if we didn't use it to understand instinct, then there was no health in us at all.

Margaret said, she had been brought up among people who believed it was easy to be civilised and rational. She had hated it. It made life too hygienic and too thin. But still, she had come to think even that was better than glorifying unreason.

Put reason to sleep, and all the stronger forces were let loose. We had seen that happen in our own lifetimes. In the world: and close to us. We knew, we couldn't get out of knowing, that it meant a chance of hell.

The words Bolt put into the mouth of More that so appealed to Frankfurter were these: "This country's planted thick with laws from

1. Frankfurter, ed., Mr. Justice Brandeis 123 (1932).

2. Mendelson, ed., Felix Frankfurter, A Tribute 18 (1964).

3. P. 375.

coast to coast — man's laws, not God's — and if you cut them down — and you're just the man to do it — d'you really think that you could stand upright in the winds that would blow then?"[4] This is somewhat reminiscent of John Pym's language during his battle for parliamentary supremacy and constitutional change: "The Law is that which puts a difference betwixt Good and Evil, betwixt Just and Unjust; if you take away the Law, all things will fall into Confusion, every Man will become a Law to himself, which in the depraved condition of Human Nature, must needs produce great enormities; Lust will become a Law, and Envy will become a Law, Covetnous and Ambition will become Laws." Today's "Levellers" would not understand this teaching of More and Pym any more than they find Frankfurter's teachings acceptable.

Because Frankfurter was a self-avowed disciple of Mr. Justice Brandeis, it is perhaps not inappropriate to close this collection with Judge Learned Hand's notions of the lesson that Brandeis was teaching, for surely it was also a lesson — maybe *the* lesson — that Frankfurter, more patently the pedagogue than Brandeis, also sought to instill. The words were spoken by Hand when the United States was in a crisis as great as that which it faces today, the war against Hitler:[5]

He believed that there could be no true community save that built upon the personal acquaintance of each with each; by that alone could character and ability be rightly gauged; without that "neighborly affection" which would result no "faith" could be nourished, "charitable" or other. Only so could the latent richness which lurks in all of us come to flower. As the social group grows too large for mutual contact and appraisal, life quickly begins to lose its flavor and its significance. Among multitudes relations must become standardized; to standardize is to generalize, and to generalize is to ignore all those authentic features which mark, and which indeed alone create, an individual. Not only is there no compensation for our losses, but most of our positive ills have directly resulted from great size. With it has indeed come the magic of modern communication and quick transport; but out of these has come the sinister apparatus of mass suggestion and mass production. Such devices, always tending more and more to reduce us to a common model, subject us — our hard-won immunity now gone — to epidemics of hallowed catchword and formula. The herd is regaining its ancient and evil primacy; civilization is being reversed, for it has

4. Quoted in MENDELSON, note 2 *supra*, at 19.

5. HAND, THE SPIRIT OF LIBERTY 170 (Dilliard ed., 2d ed., 1952).

consisted of exactly the opposite process of individualization —
witness the history of law and morals. . . .

   If it is hard to see any answer to all this; the day has clearly gone
forever of societies small enough for their members to have personal
acquaintance with each other, and to find their station through the
appraisal of those who have any first-hand knowledge of them.
Publicity is an evil substitute, and the art of publicity is a black art;
but it has come to stay; every year adds to its potency and to the
finality of its judgments. The hand that rules the press, the radio, the
screen and the far spread magazine, rules the country; whether we
like it or not, we must learn to accept it. And yet it is the power of
reiterated suggestion and consecrated platitude that at this moment
has brought our entire civilization to imminent peril of destruction.
The individual is as helpless against it as the child is helpless against
the formulas with which he is indoctrinated. Not only is it possible
by these means to shape his tastes, his feelings, his desires and his
hopes; but it is possible to convert him into a fanatical zealot, ready
to torture and destroy and to suffer mutilation and death for an
obscene faith, baseless in fact and morally monstrous. This, the
vastest conflict with which mankind has ever been faced, whose
outcome still remains undecided, in the end turns upon whether the
individual can survive; upon whether the ultimate value shall be this
wistful, cloudy, errant You or I, or that Great Beast, Leviathan, that
phantom conjured up as an ignis fatuus in our darkness and a
scapegoat for our futility.

   We Americans have at last chosen sides; we believe that if it may
be idle to seek the Soul of Man outside Society, it is certainly idle
to seek Society outside the Soul of Man. We believe this to be
the transcendent stake; we will not turn back; in the heavens we have
seen the sign in which we shall conquer or die. But our faith will
need again and again to be refreshed; and from the life we com-
memorate today we may gain refreshment. A great people does not go
to its leaders for incantations or liturgies by which to propitiate
fate or to cajole victory; it goes to them to peer into the recesses of
its own soul, to lay bare its deepest desires; it goes to them as it goes
to its poets and its seers. And for that reason it means little in what
form this man's message may have been; only the substance of it
counts. If I have read it aright, this was that substance. "You may
build your Towers of Babel to the clouds; you may contrive
ingeniously to circumvent Nature by devices beyond even the understanding of all but a handful; you may provide endless distractions
to escape the tedium of your barren lives; you may rummage the
whole planet for your ease and comfort. It shall avail you nothing;
the more you struggle, the more deeply you will be enmeshed. Not

until you have the courage to meet yourselves face to face; to take
true account of what you find; to respect the sum of that account
for itself and not for what it may bring you; deeply to believe that
each of you is a holy vessel unique and irreplaceable; only then will
you have taken the first steps along the path of Wisdom. Be content
with nothing less; let not the heathen beguile you to their temples,
or the Sirens with their songs. Lay up your treasure in the Heaven
of your hearts, where moth and rust do not corrupt and thieves cannot
break through and steal."

Yes, Felix Frankfurter would have agreed with this lesson. And
he, unlike some of his epigones among whom I should like to be
numbered, would have been, as he always was, optimistic about its
future. He certainly would make no case against change. During a
large part of his life he was instrumental in bringing about change in
our society. He would have deplored change, however, that would
destroy individual responsibility and change that would reject law as
the instrument for bringing it about. If not the man for this season,
one may hope that he will be the man for the next one, if there is a
next one.

Index